ARNOLD'S

ENGLISH

TEXTS

General Editor JAMES SUTHERLAND
Emeritus Professor of English Literature,
University of London

NEO-CLASSICAL CRITICISM 1660-1800

Edited by
IRÈNE SIMON
Professor of English, University of Liège

EDWARD ARNOLD

© IRÈNE SIMON 1971

First published 1971
by Edward Arnold (Publishers) Ltd.,
41 Maddox Street,
London, W1R 0AN

Cloth edition ISBN: 0 7131 5590 6
Paper edition ISBN: 0 7131 5606 6

Printed in Great Britain by
The Camelot Press Ltd., London and Southampton

General Preface

THE design of this series is to present fully annotated selections from English literature which will, it is hoped, prove satisfactory both in their breadth and their depth. To achieve this, some of the volumes have been planned so as to provide a varied selection from the poetry or prose of a limited period, which is both long enough to have developed a literary movement, and short enough to allow for adequate representation of the chief writers and of the various cross-currents within the movement. Examples of such periods are the late seventeenth century and the early eighteenth century. In other volumes the principle of selection is to present a literary kind (e.g. satirical poetry, the literary ballad). Here it is possible to cover a longer period without sacrificing the unified and comprehensive treatment which is the governing idea for the whole series. Other volumes, again, are designed to present a group of writers who form some kind of "school" (e.g. the Elizabethan sonneteers, the followers of Ben Jonson), or who were closely enough linked for their work to be brought together (e.g. the poetry of Johnson and Goldsmith).

The present volume is concerned with the neo-classical period. Neo-classical criticism in England (as in France) established a consensus of literary theory and practice to which, in general, the creative writers subscribed, and in accordance with which their writing was shaped and controlled. Yet although the English critics owed much to their French predecessors and contemporaries, and coincided with them on many important issues, their interpretation of the "rules" was more liberal and less doctrinaire, and they showed a typically English willingness to compromise between what ideally should be done (e.g. in such questions as unity, regularity, decorum, and "correctness") and what the English reader or playgoer really liked (e.g. variety, fullness of life and action, originality).

In this selection of critical opinion from the later seventeenth century to the closing years of the eighteenth century, Professor Simon has arranged her material in a number of sections for the convenience of the reader. Beginning with the General Principles that governed all the criticism of the period, she proceeds to a section on the Genres, showing how, and to what extent, the various "kinds" were affected by those general principles. A section on the problems of Style (so important in the neo-classical period) is followed by one on Native Literature, where the tensions between the English and the French critics become apparent: the English, with their vested interest in Shakespeare, Spenser, and the other writers of "the last age", were driven to find means of justifying their irregularity and incorrectness, and in doing so they developed a new historical criticism. A final section deals with neo-classical views on the Business of Criticism, and with the question of Taste, which became increasingly important to the critics of the later eighteenth century.

While the main emphasis naturally falls on the central doctrines of English neo-classical criticism—seen perhaps at their clearest in Sir Joshua Reynolds—Professor Simon has also kept in view such critics as Young, Joseph Warton and Hurd, who were breaking new ground. A special feature of this volume is her long critical Introduction, which sets forth and interprets the various doctrines and theories, and their developments, with admirable lucidity.

Contents

Introduction

The restoration of Charles II may not have ushered in another Augustan age as some poets had forecast in verses celebrating the event, but it encouraged men of letters to attempt new ways of writing to suit the taste of their patrons, many of whom had been used abroad to a kind of literature very different from that which had delighted their fathers. The works of the previous age continued to please, but at the same time they were felt to lack the polish and correctness that the age demanded. Besides, writers had to make a new start for, as Dryden said, the Elizabethans had ruined their estate; but they were walking uneasily between two worlds, loath to discard the old values altogether, yet seeking their way towards new forms of art. As a consequence of the breakdown of tradition poets felt the need to justify their procedures, while their readers on the other hand submitted every work to a critical inquiry. This was indeed a sceptical age that accepted nothing upon trust, and in no field had the critical temper such free scope as in literature, where it was open to anyone to damn a play or to shower praise on a trifle. However irritating this may have been to poets, it resulted in a greater awareness among writers and readers alike of the problems of literature, and from this arose the need to define its aims and methods. While the Elizabethans had been content to create, mid-seventeenth-century poets were too self-conscious merely to follow their own bent; they inquired into the grounds of their art and attempted to account for their practice in terms of a theory of poetry. As a result there developed a critical activity such as no other age had known, and this fostered the growth of literary criticism proper.

The arts of poetry of the sixteenth century had concentrated exclusively on matters of technique, and critical remarks about the merits of some poem or poet hardly raised the question of the nature of poetry. Sidney was the first to face the problem, and in his spirited defence of poetry he defined the function of art in true humanist fashion; that is, he assigned to it a part to play in reclaiming man from the fallen state: for him poetry is an imitation of nature which contributes to the improvement of mankind by lifting the soul to the contemplation of the ideal. But Sidney was only concerned to vindicate poetry as a noble science and did not descend to particulars, so that, except for some remarks about the drama, the *Apology for Poetry* gives few directions about the kind of poetry that answers the purpose.

Jonson, in his turn, outlined an *ars poetica* in which he defined his own brand of classicism by borrowing freely and adapting from a wide variety of critics, both ancient and modern; but though his directions for style in particular clearly set a premium on the *lucidus ordo* which was to be the ideal of a later generation, he did not deal with problems of structure nor explain what his conception of poetry as imitation of nature involved; nor again, apart from brief remarks, did he submit any work of literature to criticism. By the middle of the seventeenth century, criticism began to include both a theory of poetry and detailed discussions of the qualities required of poems, or of the particular poem under consideration. Much of it was occasional, so that it usually dealt with practical problems viewed from the standpoint of a certain conception of poetry.

Restoration criticism was indeed the first reasoned attempt to lay down principles of evaluation and to define standards of literary excellence. The conception of poetry from which these criteria derived was that which Renaissance commentators of Aristotle had elaborated with Horace as their guide. Sidney and Jonson were familiar with the work of these scholars, but by mid-century the learned commentaries of Aristotle had been brought within the reach of the *honnête homme* by French critics, so that English poets and critics did not have to turn to the heavy tomes of Scaliger or Vossius or the Italians. Since the thirties French critics had been trying to curb the extravagances of the wilder spirits, particularly in the theatre, and to restrain the vagaries of wit by making it subservient to propriety and common sense. La Mesnardière's *Poétique* (1639), Father Mambrun's *De epico carmine* (1652) and d'Aubignac's *La Pratique du théâtre* (1657) defined the nature and function of poetry in accordance with the interpreters of the *Poetics*, and like these determined the scope of each kind of poem, its particular ends and the means best suited to attain these. As a result the whole field of literature was mapped out as neatly as the gardens of Versailles were to be, and the poet was given clear directions for the practice of his craft.

The general tendency of the doctrine was unmistakable: it was conservative, restrictive and prescriptive; it distrusted the freedom of genius and strove to confine the creative energy within narrower bounds; it limited the field in which the imagination could exercise itself and subjected it to the sovereign arbiter, reason; it set not only norms but models and laid down not only principles but specific rules; it discouraged experiment and recommended imitation; instead of extolling genius it taught rules, instead of looking forward to undiscovered countries it looked back to the tried methods of the past. The need to prune and to restrain was felt the more acutely as current taste gave support to absurdities of all kinds, whether on the popular stage or in the salons. Surprise, novelty, whatever was off the beaten path was sure of success: on the one hand the public's taste for variety and marvellous events had to be catered for by strange shows; on the other the most extravagant conceits were prized as the finest wit. The reformers were out to reclaim literature from the corruption of popular taste and from the eccentricities of minority groups for whom the practice of poetry was a refined *jeu d'esprit*, a complicated charade to divert an idle class. To those critics the sensationalism of the plays acted at the Hôtel de Bourgogne as well as the tinsel of the false wit enjoyed by the aristocracy were sure evidence of the irresponsibility of men of letters, who for the sake of giving immediate pleasure distorted art from its true end, which is to give instruction through pleasure. The critics' insistence on the tried values of the past was thus, partly at least, a return to the humanist tradition in poetry. At the same time it is clear that the men who subscribed to the doctrine defined by the French Academy were weary of adventure, they were looking for order and security. Through the Academy, as through his home policy, Richelieu was setting his house in order and putting an end to the lawlessness of the earlier seventeenth century; as he was marshalling all the forces of the kingdom to serve his grand political design, so the critics were teaching genius to serve under nature and reason. The extraordinary flowering of French literature in the later seventeenth century only proved that, as Pope was to say, "The winged Courser, like a gen'rous Horse,/Shows most true Mettle when you *check* his Course."

It was inevitable that in their search for principles or precedents English writers and critics in mid-century should turn to France, for they too were dissatisfied with the extravagances of wit and weary of the disorders in the body politic. In England as in France the troublesome years of strife had left the country exhausted, longing for peace and order, and in the field of literature for clearer outlines and more stately edifices than the complicated structures of the preceding age had to offer. Poets did not repudiate their literary past as the French were too prone to do, but since it no longer answered their needs they looked for direction in the achievements of their neighbours. They were ready to strike out in new ways; the doctrine elaborated in France gave support to the kind of things they were attempting, and provided a rationale for what the sensibility of the age required: order, clarity, simplicity, and decorum.

At the heart of this doctrine was the conception, supposed to be derived from Aristotle's *Poetics*, of art as mimesis and of nature as the end and test of art. The question: In what sense does poetry imitate nature? was not raised until much later in the period, and critics were content to repeat the Horatian tag—out of context—*ut pictura poesis*. Nor was the precise import of the term *nature* ever stated explicitly, so that there remained considerable scope for variation. Diverse interpretations could be found side by side or within the period, but though these could be used to support different ideals or to justify different procedures, on the whole the term defined clearly enough the new trend in literature, i.e. the repudiation of what is not acceptable to common sense and decorum. Poetry was no longer considered as a divine madness, it was regarded as an art, and as such it was thought to have specific rules which all craftsmen must know if they are to ply their trade properly. It was the business of the poet to learn those rules so as to be able to achieve his purpose; far from trusting in his own genius he should learn from those who had truly imitated nature. Such alone were the ancients: their works had stood the test of time, they had been enjoyed in all ages and under all climes, which is the best evidence that they mirror nature and appeal to what is common to all men, not to the taste of a particular time or place. It is this general human truth that poetry is to render. In order to rise above what is merely local and transitory, the poet should form his taste by reading the ancients; he should also consider what means they had used to express these general truths. To study the ancients was only a short-cut to studying nature: they were to be the guides, their works the models upon which the moderns could hardly hope to improve.

According to these critics the end of poetry is to teach and delight. The instruction and pleasure will depend on the kind of poetry, for as there are different aspects of nature to be imitated so there are different kinds of poems; each has its own end and provides its own kind of instruction and pleasure. The realm of poetry is divided into several provinces or genres, and each has its specific rules in accordance with the particular aspect of nature it purports to imitate and the particular end it pursues. Thus epic poetry arouses admiration for the heroic virtues and is therefore a school for princes; tragedy raises terror and pity and administers poetic justice; comedy corrects men's manners through ridicule, etc. Poetry may imitate higher or lower aspects of nature, so that there is a hierarchy of genres, and a hierarchy of styles to suit each of these. Not all genres were defined with equal care and some were never given much attention. Critics concentrated on the highest genres, tragedy and epic, and worked out detailed theories for each. Since the battle for the new poetics was fought in France over Corneille's *Le Cid*, the requirements for drama were given special attention from the first, and dramatic practice was submitted to strict rules.

Nature being the test of art, the fiction of the poet should strike the reader as true to his experience of life; consequently the first criterion is credibility or probability: unless the reader or spectator believes the story to be true he cannot be moved by it, nor take pleasure in it, nor derive instruction from it. Probability applies at once to the action, the characters and the diction of the poem; it is not enough for the events to be credible, the characters must be suited to the part they have to play and they must behave and speak in a way that is both in keeping with this role and acceptable to the audience. Moreover, events and characters must be credible in themselves and they must be consistent within the framework of the poem. Emphasis on inner consistency led critics to stress some requirements for both events and characters, which resulted in further limiting the scope of the poet, especially of the dramatist. Such were the unities of action, time and place, which appeared to critics to be the necessary conditions of credibility. Such also were the requirements for characters, which turned Horace's dicta about various types of men into strict rules of propriety reflecting the nice code of manners of the age. Such also were the rules for style, which raised the accidentals of contemporary usage to the level of universal nature, notwithstanding their close dependence on social etiquette. The nicety of critics in fact turned the age-old notion of decorum into a set of requirements determined by the social life of the time. As a consequence, general nature, which poets were to seek in the works of the ancients, had to be dressed in seventeenth-century clothes before it was found to be true, i.e. credible or acceptable to the *honnête homme*. Similarly, the notion of truth to nature or credibility as it applied to events was to be interpreted in terms of the public's readiness to assent to some kinds of truth; this led to endless discussions about the relative part which the probable and the marvellous play in poetry, particularly in epic poetry and in tragedy.

So much were the critics concerned to limit the use of the marvellous and to make action time and theatre time coincide, that one cannot fail to see that the theory had a naturalistic basis though it insisted all through that the nature art imitates is a stylisation of actual nature. Consequently the general truth that poetry was to render was qualified both by the social code which determined the readers' assent and by their refusal to go beyond the testimony of their senses. Similarly, critics urged poets to imitate the ancients as the best guides to general nature; the cult of the ancients was thus sanctioned by reason. Yet the recommendations to follow the ancients and to follow reason were at bottom contradictory, and the opposition was to appear later on in the century in the quarrel of the ancients and the moderns. The difference could be ignored at first, and reason could be worshipped at the same altar as the ancients, but the tendency of French criticism to equate the concepts *nature* and *reason* (cf. Boileau: "aimez donc la raison; que toujours vos écrits/Empruntent d'elle seule et leur lustre et leur prix") inevitably tended to narrow down the scope of poetry.

From these general principles could be deduced more or less strict rules for each genre. Here again the requirements were determined partly by the "nature of the thing", i.e. deduced from the nature and end of each genre, partly by the example of the ancients. Thus critics decided what were to be the constituent parts of an epic from their analysis of the *Aeneid*: because a certain organisation of the material and a certain kind of incidents had been found to please in epics of the past, such was to be the pattern for future epics. Similar rules were deduced for most genres from the practice of the ancients, though agreement was not always so easy as it was about works like the *Aeneid* which commanded general admiration. Thus some critics could argue that pastoral poetry should be modelled on Virgil, while others preferred Theocritus and inferred altogether different rules from his practice. Or critics might misunderstand the ancients' procedure, as was the case with the ode, which was long thought to be purposely without order (cf. Boileau: "Chez elle un beau désordre est un effet de l'art").

Whatever these differences, one thing was clear: there were genres with their several rules to answer their several purposes. The first thing the poet should ask himself was what kind of poem he wanted to write; from this would follow: what is the instruction the poem is to convey, and how will it delight the reader? what are the means best suited to achieve this end? Similarly, when approaching any poem the critic would first ask himself to what genre the work belonged, what instruction it intended to convey, whether the plot and characters did convey it, whether the design of the poem and the characters were such that nature was imitated all through, whether the style was suitable to the characters and to the sentiments they expressed, etc. Any critical examination would therefore consider in turn: the fable, the manners (i.e. the characters), the sentiments, the diction and the metre.

What best characterises neo-classical criticism is indeed the kind of questions it asked about literature in general and about any poem under consideration. To the twentieth-century reader these may seem to be idle questions; yet they reflect an approach to literature which has the merit of concentrating on the work of art, on its style and structure, on the quality of the constituent parts, on the poet's treatment of his material and on the adequacy of the poetic means for producing certain effects. Besides helping to define the function of poetry Aristotle's *Poetics* had provided a useful method for analysing literary works. His Renaissance commentators, and the French critics after them, elaborated his principles and distinguished a number of critical concepts which were to make discussions of literature more precise and therefore more fruitful. The main drawback of the method was that it dealt with each of the constituents severally and tended to atomise instead of giving a unified view of the poem as a whole. Still, this was compensated for by the stress on the moral or fable, which was thought to be the soul of any poem and which was therefore the first aspect of any work to be examined. This insistence on the fable shows that for these critics art was to be judged in terms of the good and the true, since the category of the beautiful was not to be granted autonomous existence until the next century. For all their moralistic approach neo-classical critics had grasped that the overall meaning of any work of art is the principle in terms of which all its aspects should be judged; as Pope said: "A perfect Judge will *read* each Work of Wit/With the same Spirit that its Author *writ*." In their view, however, the poem could not mean more than the poet intended it to mean, for their conception of the artist's procedure implied a conscious application of means to achieve a given end. They were ready to recognise that certain effects resulted from a lucky hit rather than from a deliberate choice, but this applied only to details not to the general purpose. They were still, in fact, governed by the rhetorical tradition, which had deeply influenced the sixteenth-century interpretations of Aristotle. Works of literature were therefore judged in terms of the effect they produced, and the poet was advised to adapt his means to the end he wished to achieve, i.e. to the particular instruction and pleasure he wished to give his readers. The mimetic and the rhetorical traditions blended so completely that when Father Rapin set out to expound Aristotle's *Poetics* he could resort to Cicero and Quintilian to make the key notions clear. In particular, the advice given to the poets was similar to that given to orators, so that to a large extent the arts of oratory still applied to poetry. What was new was the concern for structure, and, as a consequence, the attention given to the constituent parts of a poem, together with the insistence that poems be moulded on the same patterns as those of the ancients.

Such, then, in its main outline, was the critical doctrine which had been shaped in France while England was divided by the Civil War. English writers who had been in touch with the literary circles in Paris readily followed the same directions. When in 1656 Cowley published the first part of his *Davideis*, he prefaced it with an account of the poem along the lines which discussions of epic poetry had defined. Similarly Davenant wrote an account of his *Gondibert* (1650) in which he defined the scope and purpose of his poem as well as the means proper for attaining his end. He submitted this to his friend Hobbes, who justified Davenant's practice by grounding it in a theory of poetry akin to that which French critics were outlining. Such prefaces and theoretical accounts had become a habit with French writers, and the practice was continued in England after the Restoration. Since the theatres were reopened soon after Charles's return, discussions first centred on dramatic practice. Here indeed critics were confronted with two different traditions, that of the Elizabethans and that of the new French drama.

The debate about which was the right procedure was instituted just when Corneille, who had toed the line since his defeat in the *Querelle du Cid*, published his *Examens* and *Discours* (1660), in which he set out his own views about the drama. Though himself deeply influenced by "Aristotelian" criticism, Corneille was by no means ready to submit to all the rules laid down by the Academy, which he felt to be destructive of the best dramatic effects. To their rigid doctrine he opposed his experience as a practising dramatist, who knew how to move admiration; as he said, hinting at Scudéry and other detractors of *Le Cid*, "il est facile aux spéculatifs d'être sévères." In fact Corneille was a heretic, a survivor of an earlier age who prized the grand effects which could move audiences in despite of the nicer critics. The popularity of Corneille's dramatic criticism in England and the influence of his admirer Saint-Evremond certainly contributed to encourage writers to dissent from the orthodox creed of France. Though the French neo-classical doctrine expressed needs and tendencies which were largely shared in England, it could not be accepted wholesale. Neither in the years following the Restoration nor at any time during the period—not even when the prestige of the doctrine reached its highest mark (1674-94)— were the French theories received without qualifications. For one thing this would have entailed the complete repudiation of the native tradition, and this was clearly impossible, however much older works were found to offend against the nicer taste of a later generation. For another, the strict classicism which the French theory encouraged, and which is seen at its best in the plays of Racine, was fundamentally alien to the English temper. The public in England wanted external action, movement and variety, where the French staked all on internal action, character and unity of tone.

The differences between the French and the English were particularly clear in dramatic criticism, where neither the native tradition nor the response of the public could be ignored. That is why Dryden's *Essay of Dramatic Poesy* is such an important document: being "problematical" it weighs the pros and cons of the different forms of drama, thereby indicating clearly what recommended each to the contemporary theatre-goer; it also reveals unmistakably what the age demanded: more order, simplicity and decorum, yet not to the point of sacrificing variety to correctness; an imitation of nature that should be a stylisation of reality, yet not too far removed from it; characters in action who would move the spectators through their truth, and whose destiny would serve to edify through the working out of justice; in other words a compromise between the native tradition and the French drama.

From the first, then, English criticism adapted the neo-classical doctrine to its own needs. The fundamental principles and the general tendency of the theory remained unchanged, but on the whole English critics allowed the poet greater freedom. Though correctness was highly desirable, it was seen to border on dullness; though looseness of structure was severely condemned, too neat a design was felt to be against nature; though decorum was a prime requisite, it was not allowed to stifle the natural impulses altogether. The concept "nature" was interpreted much more liberally than it was in France; as adherence to actual truth it could be invoked to justify departures from the rules of art, or as heightening of reality to sanction flights above what is acceptable to strict common sense. What it could not be taken to mean was the particular or the singular, for that would have amounted to denying the basic axiom of the doctrine, that art mirrors universal truths.

English critics set the same formal requirements on art as did the French, but it was understood that these should never cramp the expression of nature or confine it in too narrow a mould. To justify these departures they more than once stressed their right as free-born Englishmen to dissent from the orthodox creed; or they drew attention to the difference between the French and the English temper, though they stopped half-way in what would easily have developed into an argument for the relativity of taste. For on this they were no less positive than the French: there were standards of taste irrespective of time and place; departures from these were merely expressions of bad taste. They were ready to add correctives to account for their love of variety or for the French acceptance of a nice code of manners, but they were by no means prepared to sanction departures from true wit such as Shakespeare's puns, or to accept the "incorrect" syntax of the Elizabethans.

It should be remembered, too, that the French critics who were best known in England, besides Corneille, were not the rigid legislators of Parnassus who had founded the orthodoxy, but more liberal critics like Boileau, Rapin, Le Bossu and Bouhours, who, now that the battle was fought and won, could occasionally dissent from their elders, and, as Boileau did, make fun of their poetry. If Boileau's satires did not impugn the principles of neo-classical doctrine, they showed that adherence to formal principles was not enough, that a sense of style was a prime requisite of the poet; implicitly they showed also that whatever the poet may learn, it is all of no avail "si son astre en naissant ne l'a formé poète".

Though England never had an Academy to fix standards of correctness, the critics shared a number of assumptions. These appear from the way they posed problems more than from the answers they gave; for the answers might vary according to circumstances, and critics might seem to contradict themselves or each other (for instance, stressing the power of art or of genius, the limitations of rules or the need of them), while they were merely considering the problem from a different angle. Most problems were posed in terms of an alternative, as Dryden had done in the *Essay of Dramatic Poesy*, weighing the merits of the ancients *versus* the moderns, then of the French *versus* the English.

Art—Nature : The Rules—the Graces

The basic assumption was that poetry is an art; like all arts it must have rules, which practitioners must learn from their elders. Yet knowledge of the laws of art is not enough; a poet is born as well as made. Hence the question of the relative merits of art and nature (or genius). Since the main object of these critics was at first to restrain the extravagances of wit, the stress was laid on the power of art, and at times the part played by nature was almost obscured. It usually fell to poets to vindicate the rights of nature in front of the cocksureness of critics who, having learnt the rules, thought they could measure poetry with ready-made yardsticks. Thus Dryden and Pope more than once had to assert that the poet knows better than the criticasters, indeed that the poet is the best critic. Neither meant that genius is its own lawgiver, any more than did Temple when he stated that the rules had been overrated since all they could do was to prevent a poor poet from being even worse. Gildon now stressed the freedom of genius, now the need to know the rules, according as he was fighting against little critics or trying to stem the tide of enthusiasm. On whichever term critics might put the emphasis, they agreed that both nature and art were necessary. As Pope said in the Preface to the *Iliad*, invention "furnishes art with all her materials", but art is the prudent steward that manages the riches of nature. They also agreed in repudiating enthusiasm or the divine frenzy as the source of poetry; with Temple they preferred to ascribe the workings of genius to natural rather than to supernatural causes.

The laws of art had been inferred from works which had pleased generally and pleased long; they were the principles along which the ancients had worked and which might therefore serve as guides for the modern poet. Far from being arbitrary rules laid down by the legislators of Parnassus, they were "nature methodized", i.e. they taught the way to imitate nature truly as the ancients had done. The poet was not only to grasp the essence of nature, but to present it in such a way as to make it shine; true wit, Pope said, is "nature to advantage dressed". The tried methods of the ancients would show the modern poet how to dress nature in the best robes. Thus the rules of art would help the modern poet both to recapture universal truths and to present them in the best light.

Yet, considering the detailed doctrine the French had elaborated and the minute rules they had defined for each genre, considering also the readiness of some critics to judge merely by rules, many poets and critics, all through the period, felt it necessary to distinguish between the laws, or general principles, of poetry, and the "mechanic rules", or specific requirements such as the unities in drama. The attacks on mechanic rules were mostly aimed at the unities and at some arbitrary requirements for style. These did not come from rebels against neo-classicism, but from men concerned to preserve its genuine humanistic basis from the cramping effect of narrow-minded critics who judged works by rules alone. Far from indicating that the neo-classical doctrine is beginning to crack, these attacks reveal its true nature, at least as understood by responsible critics who resisted the attempts of little wits to reduce all principles to mere recipes.

However important the rules for achieving the end of poetry, "Some beauties yet no precepts can declare." These were felt to elude rational explanation and from the start were granted a special place in neo-classical poetics. Critics were thus compelled to recognise the limitations of their theory by admitting that some mysterious power could succeed where art was powerless, and that some beauties could only be attained by transgressing the rules of art. Such a confession of failure on the part of criticism would have threatened its very existence if the part played by this mysterious power had not been severely limited—only "great wits" could dare to offend gloriously—and if the notion had not, by then, been a commonplace of criticism. The "graces beyond the reach of art" or the "je-ne-sais-quoi" could have been exploited to undermine the neo-classical doctrine; instead it served to render criticism more flexible, more true to the nature of art, and it encouraged the search for beauties, a useful counterpoise to the procedure of too much negative criticism.

Taste would tell the poet when to transgress the laws, just as it would make the critic appreciate irregular beauties. Though French neo-classical criticism allowed for the "je-ne-sais-quoi", it did so only grudgingly for fear of the graces which the *mondains* had prized so much. It was made much of by Bouhours, and the graces were treated almost as something divine in his *Entretiens d'Ariste et d'Eugène*, but this was a departure from the *grand goût* which the main neo-classicists had tried to form. In England, on the contrary, irregular beauties were recognised from the first because of the native works which so often pleased though they flouted the rules. Shakespeare critics from Rowe onwards had to face the problem, and though they often said that Shakespeare would have been even greater if he had had the good fortune to know the rules, the evident pleasure they took in his plays makes one wonder if they were not merely paying lip-service to current critical fashion. Gildon alone feared that such praise of irregular beauties might encourage little wits to write as the spirit prompted them without any regard for correctness. Yet he too had earlier inveighed against the mechanic rules and vindicated the freedom of the poet.

Fancy—Judgment

The "je-ne-sais-quoi" was a means of admitting the irrational within a rational framework. A similar problem arose in connection with the creative process, which from Davenant and Hobbes onward was ascribed to the twin work of imagination and judgment, the inventive faculty roaming through the fields to collect materials while the other decided on the fitness of the materials and accordingly selected and rejected. The excesses of the enthusiasts had discredited imagination while the eccentricities of metaphysical wit had rendered the irresponsible play of wit distasteful. Inevitably a premium was put on the ordering faculty that could restrain such extravagances, and the stress came to be laid more and more on judgment. Since poetry was to be an imitation of nature, it appeared that judgment had an essential part to play if poetry was to mirror truth. The works of fancy might delight for a while, but they were not to be trusted. Without imagination poetry would be impossible, but it was a dangerous ally in an age that had learnt to distrust the irrational and wanted solid truth. Hence the subordinate role which critics often ascribed to imagination, especially after Locke added the weight of his authority to the distinction between the assembling and the discriminating faculties and entered a caveat against the dangers of the imagination.

All discussions of literature were governed by this dichotomy, and critics repeatedly took writers to task for offending against common sense, while poets like Dryden and Pope reminded their readers that a poet must fly, not creep along the ground, and that, faced with correctly dull works, the reader "cannot *blame* indeed—but [he] may *sleep*". In spite of Pope's attempt in the *Essay on Criticism* to show that imagination (then called fancy or wit) and judgment are only the two sides of the same coin and therefore work jointly, the two "faculties" continued to be viewed as distinct and pulling in opposite directions until the critics of the Scottish school showed that in the creative process the imagination itself exercises judgment. The result of the current conception was not only to check the adventurous fancy, but to give countenance to the view that poetry was no more than a pleasant way of dressing up truths. Against this view, shared by Locke among others, the poets insisted that poetry not only dresses up but reveals truths. It was the contention of Pope in the *Essay on Criticism* that art reflects "*Unerring Nature*, still divinely bright", and that this "clear, unchanged and universal light" is the soul that informs the body of poetry. For the neo-classical critics art was indeed a conveyer of truth, contributing to the moral improvement of man; the difficulty lay in attributing to the specifically poetic faculty, imagination, an insight into truth, since imagination had been discredited. In the early part of the period "reason" was still the all-inclusive faculty which the humanists had extolled, but as it came to apply to the ratiocinative process alone, imagination had to take over part of the function ascribed to it, so that Reynolds praised imagination as the proper vehicle for apprehending truths.

Imitation of Nature—Imitation of the Ancients
Tradition—Originality : The Ancients—the Moderns

Poetry is an art of imitation, intended to give instruction and delight. It imitates nature, i.e. the universal order of things—which may be either the general, the generic, the average or the typical, but never the particular— and thereby reflects truths which are valid in all times and places. Art rises above the local and transitory and appeals to what is common to all men. For the neo-classicists nature means primarily human nature, which is everywhere the same. Whatever differences the age and clime might produce, art was to mirror man, not the idiosyncrasies of particular men. These were regarded as oddities, the proper subject for the grotesque, but unworthy of great art. The thoughts and feelings expressed should be such as other men might share, not those that are peculiar to a man as distinct from other men. The pleasure afforded by art was, in fact, the pleasure of recognition rather than of novelty, though something new was necessary for the shock of recognition to be produced. The works which have stood the test of time embody such truths or they could not have been appreciated by men living in such different ages and countries. Since they imitate nature so truly these works are the best models, they are safe guides to nature. Rather than look into his heart and write the poet was to learn from the ancients how best to follow nature; like Virgil he would find, as Pope said, that nature and Homer were still the same.

Yet the poet was not to be a mere copier, he was not to do *what* the masters had done, but *as* they had done. Only if he was an original could he claim to be a poet. What was valued, however, was originality within a tradition, not the uncouth voice of rude genius. This was a civilised age, one in which poetry like the other arts addressed itself to men living in society and in

which the cry of the individual, however poignant, must not be heard.
What the poet was to express were general truths, not individual feelings;
these, however deep, were of no concern to others in so far as they were
peculiar to him as an individual. Similarly, ideas or feelings should be expressed in a way that was recognisable as a poetic mode, fitting into a
tradition, employing the same means as poets of the past and adapting them
to the contemporary context. Every poem should be an addition to the
treasures accumulated through the ages, a reinterpretation of themes for-
ever new in a manner at once modelled on the past and speaking to the
present. The original genius was one who, having absorbed the lessons of
the past, could speak in his own voice and to his own time as one of the
ancients might have done. He who would hear the true voice of Pope
should turn to the *Epistle to Augustus*, and for the true voice of Johnson to the
Vanity of Human Wishes. Horace did not teach Pope what was wrong with
his age, nor did Juvenal teach Johnson that all is vanity and vexation of spirit.
Each spoke the truth as he saw it by donning the clothes of the ancient whose
temper was closest to his, and uttered his feelings the more forcefully as he
could lean on the precedent of the ancient poet. Gay could lift his description
of the streets of London above the level of mere local truth and turn his
pictures into delightful *objets d'art* by playfully adapting the viewpoint
and language of the georgic poet, and thereby enhancing both the beauty
of his pieces and the contrast with the bucolic scenes of tradition. In the
same way Pope's criticism of Hanoverian England in the *Dunciad* was
given more weight by being cast in the mould of the *Aeneid*, and the pleasure
it gave resulted both from the treatment of the contemporary scene and
from the variation on a well-known theme and pattern. The poem was no
less serious for being intended to elicit the disinterested pleasure proper to
the work of art which resulted from the aptness of the parody.

Looking at nature—whether external or human nature—through the
eyes of the ancients made it not more stale but more significant. For men of
that age, to think and feel like others before them was a guarantee of truth, a
proof that they were faithful to the wisdom of the ages and in true humanist
fashion handing it down to later generations by adding their small contribution to the heritage. Only within the tradition could they be truly themselves; all assertion of self that repudiated the past was mere upstart pride.
In art this would mean building without foundations and thus condemning
one's productions to sure destruction. By ignoring what could be learnt
from the experience of others, poets would simply revert to the state of
uncouth genius or of infantilism and bring upon themselves the ridicule of
the educated public. This was the lesson that Reynolds taught in all his
Discourses, advising his students to imitate the masters, not in order to

reproduce the same works but in order to learn from them how to achieve similar beauties. It was a difficult lesson to teach, for he had to warn the budding artist both against over-confidence in his own talent and against excessive reliance on the example of the masters. The course he laid down for students to follow was one that would ensure the freedom of the artist once he had mastered his craft. Given genius, the training and disciplining through attention to the works of the masters would enable the artist to express himself with greater confidence. Unless he did have genius, the schooling would be of no use, for it would only produce another copier.

In an age when such emphasis was laid on imitation, it was inevitable that the distinction between imitation and copy should not always have been clear. Hence the host of minor writers who could produce decent enough verses, but had nothing much to say. Hence also the host of critics who could pick out the beauties and defects of poems but failed to distinguish between mere copiers and true originals. Nowhere indeed was the notion of originality clearly defined; its import, like that of nature, must be inferred from the practice of the major poets and from critical judgments passed on actual works rather than from any theoretical pronouncements. Neo-classical criticism no doubt discouraged experiment and engaged writers to follow safe routes. It was emphatically conservative; out of respect for tradition it tended to underrate genius and genuinely believed that no modern could emulate the ancients. The moderns were puny creatures compared with the ancients; in fields where knowledge accumulates, such as science (or natural philosophy as it was then called), they might boast of having gone further than the ancients, but in the humanities and particularly in the arts all their productions came short of the great works of the past: the *Iliad* and the *Aeneid* had been enjoyed, and were still enjoyed, by all; whereas modern works could only hope to please for a while and in any case were doomed to decay since they were written in languages that had not the permanence of Latin and Greek. "Our Sons their Fathers *failing Language* see/And such as *Chaucer* is shall *Dryden* be," Pope complained, forgetting that only in the schools had Latin and Greek stood still.

The neo-classicists' reverence for the ancients, and their insistence that the poet tread in their path, no doubt revealed their lack of confidence in genius, and may have discouraged writers from trusting in their own powers. In the mid-eighteenth century the prestige of the ancients, though still undisputed, began to be felt as a restrictive influence that might deter an original genius from being truly himself. Young's *Conjectures on Original Composition* (1759) was a timely reminder that imitation is not mere repetition or copy. All neo-classicists would have agreed when he stated:

He that admires not ancient authors betrays a secret he would conceal, and tells the world that he does not understand them. Let us be as far from neglecting, as from copying, their admirable compositions: sacred be their rights, and inviolable their fame. Let our understanding feed on theirs; they afford the noblest nourishment; but let them nourish, not annihilate, our own. Let us build our compositions with the spirit, and in the taste, of the ancients; but not with their materials.

But his main concern was to exhort writers to greater confidence in themselves; he therefore went on to stress the divine nature of genius, the fact that it "comes out of Nature's hand, as Pallas out of Jove's head, at full growth and mature". In other words, that it needs no learning; for this is mere "borrowed knowledge", whereas genius is "knowledge innate". The next step was to believe that "genius can set us right in composition without the rules of the learned", and to teach reverence for "the divinely-inspired enthusiast". Starting from the neo-classicists' premises, Young thus completely subverted their doctrine by erecting the self as sole guide and arbiter, not the tradition. His *Conjectures on Original Composition*, though expressing his admiration for the ancients, marks the beginning of the age of the bards, when enthusiasm was to be valued more and more.

In the quarrel between "the ancients" and "the moderns" at the end of the seventeenth and the beginning of the eighteenth century both sides were agreed that in the arts nothing could compare with the works of antiquity. The "ancients" maintained, moreover, that nature was decaying and could no longer produce such wits as Aristotle or Homer; they were ready to grant that learning had progressed, but this was only thanks to the great wits of the past on whose shoulders the modern dwarfs were standing. To this the "moderns" retorted that nature had not exhausted its store and that wits as great as those of antiquity could appear in any age, and they instanced modern scientists whose contribution to learning owed little to the ancients. What was at stake was the belief in progress; while the "moderns" cited advance in learning as evidence of progress, their opponents justified their belief in decay through the evidence of the arts. Though this made little difference to their conception of poetry, it is clear that the "moderns'" attitude encouraged confidence in the writer's own powers and in the long run might foster greater independence towards the models. That the "moderns" did not share the—often blind—admiration of the "ancients" for the masterpieces of the past appeared in their editorial work, for they often took the liberty to correct and "improve" the masters' work; as a consequence, the critic, i.e. the editor, became to the "ancients" the epitome of the upstart wit who had no respect for great works and substituted the caprices of his puny wit for the wisdom of the masters. The intensity of the attacks on the "moderns" and on the best representative of textual criticism, Bentley, was no doubt due to personal animus, and the upholders of the ancients clearly failed to distinguish between the genuine learning that aimed at the restoration of authentic texts and the pretentiousness that led editors to believe they knew better than their authors (Bentley's work as editor of Horace is not to be put on the same level as his pedagogic corrections of Milton). All the same, in their onslaught on the "moderns" men like Swift and Pope aimed mainly at the upstart pride, the self-satisfaction and self-assertion which the belief in progress seemed to imply. They were, in fact, defending tradition from the inroads of independent genius; for they wished to safeguard the republic of letters against the intrusion of the city wits and other dunces, whose growing number threatened to submerge the land.

This belief in the decay of nature did not prevent neo-classical critics from branding former ages as barbarous or "gothic": culture had decayed since the great days of Athens and Rome; luckily, since the Renaissance the arts had been reclaimed from corruption and an attempt had been made to restore right taste. England had lagged behind, but at last she too had come to pay allegiance to the true masters. This had led to greater correctness in language and in standards of taste; but it was the business of criticism to defend good taste against the corrupting influence of the uneducated public or of false critics and bad poets. Critics thought of themselves as the guardians of values both moral and literary; their standards were those of an aristocracy of taste which was bound one day to be outnumbered through the growth of the reading public.

Ancient and French Models—the Native Tradition
Unity—Variety

The neo-classicists' condemnation of native literature did not, however, amount to a wholesale repudiation of it. To Dryden, who in the "Defence of the Epilogue to the Second Part of *The Conquest of Granada*" had expressed the severest strictures against them, the Elizabethans were still "the giants before the flood"; they might lack polish, use false grammar, have a coarse taste and abound in false wit, but their works offered a rich store of characters and had plenty of life. He might tailor *Troilus and Cressida* to make it more correct, but he loved Shakespeare. Rymer was the only one who found nothing to praise in Shakespeare, as a consequence of which posterity has ignored his own virtues as a critic and approved Macaulay's view that he was the worst critic the age produced. Dryden paid a most moving tribute to Chaucer, and, like Pope, modernised some of his tales. The tribute he paid to Milton in writing *The State of Innocence* may be of doubtful value, but his high regard for the poet is all the more significant in view of his own religious and political bias. Nor did the educated public wait for *The Spectator* to discover Milton, as has often been said; when Addison wrote his weekly papers on *Paradise Lost*, the poem had already run through several editions. Pope not only valued Milton but counted on his readers being familiar with *Paradise Lost*, since many of his effects in *The Dunciad* as well as in *An Essay on Man* depend on the reader's recognition of the parallel with Milton's poem. The new literature of France satisfied the taste for orderliness and for neat structures, but it did not satisfy fully because it seemed to reduce nature to a pattern. The English public wanted more life, it wanted variety and movement. Correctness was devoutly to be wished, provided it did not cramp life. Nor were the niceties of polite behaviour the same as correctness; the stiffness and formality of much French drama struck English critics as a deviation from nature, because, as Dryden pointed out in the preface to *All for Love*, the French mistook mere local habits for general nature. From the start, the native tradition was there to counterbalance the weight of the French example and to bring in the necessary correctives to the doctrines of the formalist critics from whom English neo-classicists borrowed freely. Nothing is more illuminating than to compare Dryden's *Grounds of Criticism in Poetry* (1679) with his preface to *All for Love* (1678): the former, in which he follows his French sources closely, lays down rigid principles; while the other, in which he justifies his own practice, shows the need to break some of the rules if nature is to be truly imitated. It was not only practising poets who had recourse to experience to test the value of principles; critics like Dennis, who more than any was out to define standards, also measured theory against practice and judged accordingly. As a result some of the rules were found to be useless or worse than useless.

The unities so dear to French critics were found to contribute to greater compactness, but also to be too restrictive. Unity of action alone appeared to be essential, but the interpretation given to it shows that English neo-classicists were not prepared to sacrifice variety. Dryden among others argued that a sub-plot did not destroy the unity of action provided it somehow contributed to further the main action, or even provided there was some link between the characters involved in one plot and those involved in the other. So used were public and writers alike to the multiple plots of the Elizabethans that they could not countenance the bare outline of French tragedies; these seemed to them to lack interest because the matter was too uniform. Similarly, they argued that the unity of tone was not destroyed by elements alien to it, since, as Dryden said, contraries set off each other. All these arguments reveal clearly the English taste for diversity; they also reveal the critics' failure to grasp both the ideal that the French critics were striving after and the nature of the multiple unity of Elizabethan drama. Dryden's argument, for instance, is at bottom a justification of duality, not of unity—whether multiple or not. This accounts for the survival, with the sanction of some critics, of tragi-comedy, that is, of a mixed genre.

As to the unities of time and of place, they were never accepted by English critics, and only occasionally did dramatists strive to respect them. There was a definite tendency to limit both the diversity of places and the time-span of the action, but no critic expected "Qu'en un jour, qu'en un lieu, un seul fait accompli/Tienne jusqu'à la fin le théâtre rempli." While the unity defined by Racine in his preface to *Bérénice* has the austerity of the Jansenists' rule, the unity which English critics recommended was unity within variety, regularity within diversity, order yet fullness of life. If the matter was too uniform, or ordered too regularly, the work would give no pleasure and would therefore fail to reach its end, since instruction could not be conveyed except through pleasure. This taste for diversity is characteristic of English neo-classical criticism; it shows that it has its basis in the facts of experience more than in any rigid doctrine: no argument, however sound its foundation in reason, could oppose the test of experience. Rymer's advocacy of the use of a chorus in tragedy derived from the assumption that the ancients had used one to good purpose; this was sound theory, given the assumptions of neo-classical criticism, yet Dennis had no difficulty in showing that experience would soon prove the theory wrong. Similarly, Dryden argued persuasively in favour of rhyme in tragedy, but experience taught him that the couplet is an unsuitable medium for English dramatic poetry. In every respect, indeed, it may be said that English neo-classical criticism differs from French in that it steers a middle course between what in theory seems desirable and what in practice is found to work. It has been compared with the course followed in religion by the Latitude-men, who were in favour of comprehension within the Church.

Plot—Character

Renaissance critics, misunderstanding Aristotle's term *mythos*, had wondered which was the more important, character or plot? The strict rules of French drama had led to the concentration of the action on the crisis, as a consequence of which the interest centred not on external action but on the soul in conflict. French drama staked all on passions and sentiments. This could not satisfy the English public, and the critics agreed that the plots of the

French plays were too bare; nor did they appreciate the psychological depth of French drama, they complained that these plays had too few characters. What English taste demanded was more outward movement and a greater variety of characters. Critics praised English comedy in particular for the many humours it staged and English plays in general for their greater inventiveness; that is, for the diversity of the materials. Here again, English neo-classicism was less austere than French. In fact, what the critics approved was very different from the classical conception of drama, which is best exemplified by the plays of Racine; instead of concentration and depth they encouraged diversity and breadth; whereas the French excluded, the English wished to include. The same tendency appears in other fields, for instance in epic and in satire, where a greater variety of materials and of tone was found delightful because it gave a lively impression of nature.

The Probable—the Marvellous

The first requirement for plot and characters in drama was that they be probable. The concept implies both inner and outward consistency: events should follow from each other and persons should behave in keeping with their character; at the same time events must be such as would be credible in ordinary life, and characters must conform to the norms of life. Since the criterion involved recourse to experience, the standards of credibility were inevitably determined by the ethos of the time. Critics condemned the use of marvellous events, or at least limited it very strictly, and the question was raised whether pagan or Christian agents were the more suitable. Characters too had to behave and express themselves according to type, and the age had rigid notions about the behaviour and speech proper to each type of men. The French were more finical about social decorum, but the English too thought in terms of types. Thus a king's behaviour should be kingly; hence, to make a king a murderer would offend against propriety. A soldier should be honest and even blunt; so, Rymer argued, Shakespeare had offended against propriety in making Iago a liar. If it was argued that some soldiers did lie, then the critic would answer that poetry is not to imitate accidentals but general truths, not the exceptional but the universal.

For all the stress on nature and credibility, the early years of the neo-classical period witnessed the development of heroic tragedy, which openly flouted probability in its search for grand effects. Far from imitating nature, heroic tragedy painted larger than life, delighted in surprising events and in characters of super-human size, and aimed at moving admiration for the novelty and loftiness of its materials. Though short-lived, the genre had its supporters, and Dryden claimed that the poet was not bound to creep close to actual nature, but must fly; that tragedy might move admiration like the epic and that its effects need not be limited to pity and terror. In fact, he was using some of the arguments Corneille had put forward to defend his own practice. The heroic tragedy was a freak, and it was killed by ridicule. The taste for grand effects and spectacle was later catered for by the opera or by operatic shows, which most neo-classical critics dismissed as below contempt. Dryden did try, however, to give it letters patent and to include it among the recognised genres; but though other serious writers wrote libretti, this kind of work appealed too exclusively to the senses—especially after the introduction of Italian plays—ever to be regarded as a just imitation of nature. Again and again it fell under the fire of responsible critics because of the many improbabilities it made use of. The widespread criticism of opera is characteristic of the neo-classicists' refusal to go beyond nature, of their reluctance to suspend disbelief, and of the naturalistic tendency of their assumptions. Probability was also required in epic poetry, but the marvellous could play a larger part there since the end of the genre was to raise admiration. The characters, too, were to be of heroic stature, that is, above the ordinary. Machines, or supernatural agents, would hardly have commanded belief on the stage—though they were used more and more for spectacular effects in operatic shows—but they were quite in order in the epic. In France critics raised the question of the use of Christian agents: some, like Boileau, felt that this was to blaspheme against religion ("De la foi d'un chrétien les mystères terribles/D'ornements égayés ne sont point susceptibles"); others thought that only such agents could command belief. Though the question does not seem to have troubled English critics to the same extent, yet there was hesitation as to what kind of supernatural agents could serve the purpose, and Dryden, for instance, put forward the view that guardian angels might be made to intervene in the lives of men without shocking either reason or religion. Pope, as we know, made use of the most delightful—and appropriate—machines in *The Rape of the Lock*, but even then Dennis demurred, because he did not see how the sylphs further the action, and this was the purpose that machines were supposed to serve. In mock-epic, such as *The Rape of the Lock*, however, machines did not have to be accepted with more than a suspension of disbelief.

Poetic Justice

In one respect the neo-classicists were ever ready to suspend their disbelief and to disregard the facts of experience; that is, in the administration of justice. Since the end of poetry was to teach, the imitation of nature must present the order of things as it ought to be, not the sorry spectacle of things as they actually are; at least this should be so in the view taken of men's destiny. Their behaviour and sentiments must be probable, but the consequences of their actions must conform with the notion of a just God ruling over men's lives. Given the moral purpose of art, and the fairly narrow conception of the way art teaches, this was perhaps inevitable. It was not only the sentimentalists like Richard Steele and the reforming clergymen like Jeremy Collier who required that rewards and punishments be meted out at the end of a play to satisfy the public's moral sense. Johnson, for all his sound common sense, could not bear the spectacle of utter waste at the end of *King Lear* and demanded that Cordelia be spared. The moralistic approach not only gave support to the ancients' conception of comedy as effecting the correction of follies; it gave rise to a new genre, the sentimental comedy, which moved to benevolence instead of correcting through laughter. In tragedy poetic justice was to be administered equally, so that the ways of Providence should be vindicated. Some critics, for instance Addison, demurred at this sentimental twist given to tragedy; others, like Pope, made fun of a narrow conception of justice which flouted the truth of experience. But the tide of sentiment was too strong to be resisted; even Dennis, who had defended the Restoration comedy of manners and opposed Steele's new brand of comedy, considered poetic justice as a requirement of tragedy.

The end of tragedy was to raise terror and pity in order to purge these passions. What purgation meant was far from clear, but the most frequent interpretation was that, by seeing what consequences attend ill-regulated passions, men would be cured of their vices. Tragedy thus served to warn, while epic served to exhort to virtue by presenting patterns of heroic behaviour. At first there was some confusion between the ends pursued by the two genres, and heroic tragedy was thought to aim, like the epic, at arousing admiration. Hence the extraordinary action, the superhuman characters and the never-never-land in which they seemed to move. Tragedy proper was to be a school of virtue, too, but this could only be effected by the administration of poetic justice.

Formal Requirements: Design—Style

The neo-classical critic's first questions when approaching a poem would be: what truth is it intended to convey? is the end it pursues one proper to the genre? Next he would inquire whether the fable or moral was properly embodied in the design of the poem, that is, whether the plot was such as to bring out this truth. But the plot consisted of the actions of characters, and these must be suited to the part they had to play. Hence, examination of design involved characters and the sentiments they expressed as well as the overall structure. Since the objections against earlier poetry bore mainly on the unrelatedness of parts to the whole, particularly on the gratuitous sallies of wit, a premium was put on design and clear ordering of all elements towards a given purpose. Such had also been the tendency of the French formalist critics in their attempt to curb the extravagances of wit and the lawlessness of the popular theatre. Both d'Aubignac's *La Pratique du théâtre* and Le Bossu's *Traité du poème épique* concentrated on what kind of materials to use and how to organise them. French dramatic theory recommended the use of a simple plot and of few episodes, and made of the unities indispensable aids to probability. English critics, on the other hand, preferred double plots. The requirements for epic poetry were derived from the description of the *Aeneid*, and therefore included, besides the use of a proposition and invocation, the necessity to adorn the tale with certain episodes such as games and a visit to the underworld. In this, English and French critics agreed, though neither country produced an epic worth reading today.

Besides these structural requirements neo-classical criticism also laid down rules for style. In principle these were fairly simple—tragedy and epic poetry should be written in a lofty style, the minor genres in the middle and satire in the low style; but criticism of individual works paid considerable attention to various aspects of style. Indeed it soon appeared that a writer might follow all the formal rules and yet fail dismally if his style was not adequate. There was of course no opposition between the requirements for design and those for style, nor between critics who paid greater attention to the one than to the other. The point is that the emphasis first fell on design, as a reaction against previous excesses, so that some critics of the earlier part of the period—like Rymer—discuss this exclusively, whereas Pope need only quote two lines from Blackmore's epic to damn him as a poet.

In style as in overall design the tendency was towards clarity, order and correctness. The reaction against metaphysical wit and against the absurd language of the enthusiasts resulted in a special emphasis being put on naturalness, which often meant distrust of metaphorical language. Philosophers, divines and scientists alike denounced the danger of confusion through misuse of words. For the purpose of exposition and of critical examination metaphors were misleading because some readers might take the vehicle of the thought literally. Hence the wish expressed by the Royal Society that the scientists should aim at mathematical plainness, that is, should use words as mathematical symbols, free of sensuous or emotional connotations and therefore unlikely to influence opinion through aspects immaterial to the question under examination. At the same time the influence of conversation and of the press on prose style made for a simpler sentence structure and for greater directness in expression. These factors, combined with the rationalistic bias of neo-classical theory, favoured plainness, denotation and direct statement. In an age that regarded art as a reflection of nature, i.e. of truth, poetry could not be encouraged to cheat by using words metaphorically. Similes were in order because they helped the understanding without cheating it; or they were decorations which served to render truth more attractive. The neo-classical critics' approach to poetry did not allow for meanings other than the plain and the allegorical, so that they ignored what the poet intimates by other means.

Poets, however, soon felt that to distrust figurative language was to strike at the very root of poetry. Dryden more than once contended that poetry beautifies and therefore must have recourse to such embellishments as figures of style, or that poetry is not bound to adhere too closely to actual nature and therefore may employ figures to elevate or to warm the heart. Gradually, as the fanatics' jargon began to be forgotten, it was taken for granted not only that figurative language is acceptable in poetry but that it constitutes its main beauty. Epic poetry required that the style be both perspicuous and sublime; metaphors were the best means of raising the language, and Aristotle had sanctioned their use. Beauties-and-defects criticism mostly concentrated on the poet's use of figures; though these were generally treated as mere decoration, some poets and critics saw that metaphor is the proper language of poetry. In his Preface to the *Iliad* Pope praised Homer for using daring figures and metaphors and for finding out "living words". Yet, whatever his own practice, he does not seem to have recognised the true role of metaphors in poetry: his main concern when dealing with them was whether they were adequate and proportionable to the sense. Usually, metaphors and similes were praised for being "speaking pictures"; as such they were particularly apt in descriptions, where their use was amply justified by the current interpretation of Horace's *ut pictura poesis.*

Correctness, like perspicuity, was a requirement for style in general; it meant both correct usage according to the norms of the day and correct level of style with regard to the particular genre. Language was a central concern from the time of the Restoration, when the need was felt to define standards of correct usage, to the days of Lindley Murray. Moreover, the hierarchy of genres implied a hierarchy of styles and different standards of correctness according to each. The higher the style the more it admitted of decoration, i.e. of figures of speech. Many critical examinations—especially of the beauties-and-defects kind—dwell at length on the stylistic aspects of the poem in order to show whether the figures are appropriate to the genre. Pope's *Peri Bathous* lists many examples of figures which engender confusion or bombast or which deflate the thought. Since tragedy and the epic were the highest genres, the diction proper to them received most attention; the poetic diction of the eighteenth century which was to be repudiated by the romantics was, in fact, the diction required for the epic. Here decorousness was essential, and entailed not only the use of general and generalising terms rather than words referring to concrete objects, but of words or phrases calling up echoes from the literary tradition; moreover since the whole aimed at sublimity lofty images were necessary, and these had to be culled from what was recognised as "high". Conversely, the effects achieved in mock-epic poetry or in satire depended on the reader realising that the words and images were "low". The neo-classicists' conception of style thus reflects the age's sense of a social hierarchy, as does their conception of manners, i.e. of the behaviour and sentiments proper to each kind of character. The narrowing down of the traditional concept of decorum is indeed the best evidence of the close relation between the critical doctrine and the social philosophy of the age.

Rhyme—Blank Verse

In prosody as in style correctness was the ideal. This implied primarily syllabic regularity and due placing of pauses in the couplet; but as time went on further refinements were thought necessary, such as avoiding a hiatus, varying the rhymes, etc. The technicalities of verse were given much attention, and the result was the high level of competence of many men who, though no poets, could write verse easily. The use of the couplet had become general from the middle of the seventeenth century, and after the Restoration writers wondered whether blank verse or rhyme was the better medium for drama, the controversy being carried on mainly by Dryden and Howard. For a few years plays were written in couplets, but Dryden himself, who had argued for rhyme, soon grew tired of it and gave up the practice. The interest of the controversy lies mainly in the kind of arguments put forward by each side: for Howard blank verse is the best medium because it is closest to actual speech; for Dryden on the contrary rhyme, though making the language of the stage different from that of everyday life, is an added beauty which, far from distorting nature, heightens it.

What was at stake in the quarrel was the critics' conception of nature, and the arguments used by each reveal the imprecision of the fundamental assumption of neo-classical criticism, imitation of nature. The controversy over rhyme in drama illustrates the age's dilemma: truth to nature, or decorum; while Pope's formula, "True wit is nature to advantage dressed", expresses the desirable tension between the two terms. In an age that set so much store on art the danger was that writers might take so much care of the dress that they forgot the body to be dressed.

Taste

The neo-classical theory of poetry, which was designed to safeguard the humanistic values, could thus give support to a conception of poetry according to which art was no more than ornament so that the poet's craft was all that mattered. This was a long way from Aristotle's defence of poetry as a vehicle of truth against Plato's argument that it is the shadow of a shadow. Yet the neo-classicists' emphasis on the formal aspects of poetry was a consequence of their wish to establish universal standards of excellence. They wished to ascertain right taste or to improve taste, for they believed that there is good taste and bad taste as surely as there is truth or falsehood. They believed, too, that since art reflects truth the norms of aesthetic judgment are as universal as the norms of truth. Human nature being the same in all ages and places, it is to be expected that what has pleased will continue to please. Aesthetic norms can therefore be discovered by considering what gives pleasure to all men, or at least to all educated men, for this consensus of opinion is evidence that such taste has its foundation in objective data. These must be sought either in the objects that give pleasure, that is, in their formal qualities, or in the subjects who enjoy them, that is, in the constitution of the human mind. In either case they will be free from the pressure of fashion. Since the works of the ancients had been enjoyed universally, the criterion of excellence was first sought in their formal qualities. Later in the period, the philosophical critics like Kames, Beattie, Gerard, and Alison sought them in the nature of the aesthetic response. By viewing the problem from the standpoint of the subject these critics, like Burke, opened the way to a different approach to poetry, but their own standards were those of the earlier neo-classicists, and they were as much concerned as their predecessors to ascertain right taste by defining universal principles of aesthetic judgment.

As a reaction against the caprices of fashion and the mere assertion of individual preferences the neo-classicists sought to restore criteria of excellence which were accepted universally. They assumed that the principles of taste are universal even though tastes may vary. They made allowances for differences due to time or place, and usually invoked these to account for the shortcomings of earlier poets, for instance Shakespeare, or to excuse their own faults, as Dryden often did. But they believed that true taste, like truth, is uniform in all men. The main emphasis of neo-classical criticism is therefore on universality: art mirrors general nature, it expresses universal truths and appeals to all men; the foundation of aesthetic pleasure is universal since it lies either in the qualities of the object perceived or in the constitution of the human mind as such; the consensus of educated opinion is a guarantee of universality. It little mattered to these critics that the educated readers were only a small part of human kind. When, in the later eighteenth century, the historical sense began to develop, critics like Richard Hurd stressed changes in taste which rendered the notion of universality questionable. At the same time the exploration of the sources of aesthetic pleasure put in evidence aspects of emotional response which would entail a new emphasis on individual variations. In any case the growing emotional-ism was threatening the basis of aesthetic judgment as defined by neo-classical criticism, while interest in external nature was giving a special twist to the conception of art as imitation of nature. Though cracks began to appear in the neo-classical framework, it held together as long as the premiss was not challenged, the postulate that there are universal principles of taste and that though tastes may vary they can be rectified by education, that is, through familiarity with the masterpieces of the past. These remained the lodestar, for Shaftesbury as much as for Pope and for Hume as much as for Johnson. So long as imitation of nature, in one sense or another, was thought to be the object of art, the works of the ancients would be the guides, and poets would find Nature and Homer still the same. Only when the mimetic theory gave way to an expressive theory would the poet have first to look into his heart and write; he would then address not the generality of men but, as Wordsworth did, tell in a lover's ear alone what once to *him* befell.

*

The extracts given below illustrate the principles of neo-classical criticism and some of the problems raised by critics in that period. A list of the editions used (see references at the end of each extract) will be found on pp. 215–18. The spelling, punctuation, and accidentals have been modernised.

I GENERAL PRINCIPLES

Poetry as an Art

Poetry is an art; its object is to imitate nature. There are rules for obtaining this end, and these rules are known: they are those which Aristotle inferred from the practice of the ancients.

JOHN DRYDEN, A Defence of *An Essay of Dramatic Poesy* (1668)

I never heard of any other foundation of dramatic poesy than the imitation of nature; neither was there ever pretended any other by the ancients or moderns, or me, who endeavour to follow them in that rule. This I have plainly said in my definition of a play:[1] that it is a just and lively image of human nature, &c. Thus the foundation, as it is generally stated, will stand sure, if this definition of a play be true; if it be not, he[2] ought to have made his exception against it, by proving that a play is not an imitation of nature, but somewhat else which he is pleased to think about.

But 'tis very plain that he has mistaken the foundation for that which is built upon it, though not immediately; for the direct and immediate consequence is this: if nature be to be imitated, then there is a rule for imitating nature rightly; otherwise there may be an end, and no means conducing to it. Hitherto I have proceeded by demonstration; but as our divines, when they have proved a Deity because there is order, and have inferred that this Deity ought to be worshipped, differ afterwards in the manner of the worship; so having laid down that nature is to be imitated, and that proposition proving the next, that then there are means which conduce to the imitating of nature, I dare proceed no further positively; but have only laid down some opinions of the ancients and moderns, and of my own, as

[1] The definition given by Lisideius in *An Essay of Dramatic Poesy*. (See extract, p. 67 below.)
[2] Sir Robert Howard, who in the Preface to *The Great Favourite* (1668) defended blank verse in tragedy as nearest to nature.

means which they used, and which I thought probable for the attaining of that end. [I, 122.]

JOHN DRYDEN, A Parallel of Poetry and Painting. Preface to the
                        Translation of C. A. du Fresnoy, *De Arte
                        Graphica* (1695)

I have already shewn that one main end of poetry and painting is to please, and have said something of the kinds of both, and of their subjects, in which they bear a great resemblance to each other. I must now consider them as they are great and noble arts; and as they are arts, they must have rules, which may direct them to their common end. . . . This is notoriously true in these two arts; for the way to please being to imitate nature, both the poets and the painters in ancient times, and in the best ages, have studied her; and from the practice of both these arts, the rules have been drawn by which we are instructed how to please, and to compass that end which they obtained by following their example. For nature is still the same in all ages, and can never be contrary to herself. . . .

Having thus shewn that imitation pleases, and why it pleases in both these arts, it follows that some rules of imitation are necessary to obtain the end; for without rules there can be no art, any more than there can be a house without a door to conduct you into it. [II, 191, 194.]

JOHN DENNIS, *The Grounds of Criticism in Poetry* (1704)

That an art so divine in its institution is sunk and profaned and miserably debased, is a thing that is confessed by all. But since poetry is fallen from the excellence which it once attained to, it must be fallen either by the want of parts, or want of industry, or by the errors of its professors. But that it cannot be for want of parts, we have shewn clearly in the *Advancement of Modern Poetry*;[3] nor can it be supposed to be for want of industry, since so many of its professors have no other dependence. It remains then that it must have fallen by their errors and for want of being guided right. Since therefore 'tis for want of knowing by what rules they ought to proceed, that poetry is fallen so low, it follows then that it is the laying down of those rules alone that can re-establish it. In short,

[3] 1701.

poetry is either an art, or whimsy and fanaticism.[4] If it is an art, it follows that it must propose an end to itself, and afterwards lay down proper means for the attaining that end; for this is undeniable, that there are proper means for the attaining of every end, and those proper means in poetry we call the rules. Again, if the end of poetry be to instruct and reform the world, that is, to bring mankind from irregularity, extravagance, and confusion, to rule and order, how this should be done by a thing that is in itself irregular and extravagant, is difficult to be conceived. Besides, the work of every reasonable creature must derive its beauty from regularity; for reason is rule and order, and nothing can be irregular either in our conceptions or our actions any further than it swerves from rule, that is, from reason. As man is the more perfect, the more he resembles his Creator, the works of man must needs be more perfect, the more they resemble his Maker's. Now the works of God, though infinitely various, are extremely regular. [I, 335.]

JOHN DENNIS, *The Causes of the Decay and Defects of Dramatick Poetry* (1725?)

If [Poetry] is an art it must have a system of rules, as every art has, and that system must be known. For there can no more be an art that has a system of rules which are not known, than there can be a country which hath a body of laws that are not promulgated. But there is for poetry no system of known rules but those which are in Aristotle and his interpreters, and therefore if they are not the rightful rules poetry is not an art. [II, 283.]

RICHARD HURD, Dissertation on the Idea of Universal Poetry (1766)

This notion of the end of poetry, if kept steadily in view, will unfold to us all the mysteries of the poetic art. There needs but to evolve the philosopher's idea, and to apply it, as occasion serves. The art of poetry will be, universally, *The Art of Pleasing*; and all its rules, but so many means which experience finds most conducive to that end:

Sic animis natum inventumque poema juvandis.[5]

[4] frenzy (in a derogatory sense).
[5] Horace, *Ars Poetica*, 377. ("Thus poetry, which was invented to charm men's minds.")

Aristotle has delivered and explained these rules, so far as they respect one species of poetry, the dramatic, or, more properly speaking, the tragic; and when such a writer as he shall do as much by the other species, then, and not till then, a complete *Art of Poetry* will be formed. [pp. 4–5.]

ROBERT LOWTH, *Lectures on the Sacred Poetry of the Hebrews* (1787)[6]

Moreover, as in all other branches of science, so in poetry, art or theory consists in a certain knowledge derived from the careful observation of nature, and confirmed by practice and experience; for men of learning having remarked in things what was graceful, what was fit, what was conducive to the attainment of certain ends, they digested such discoveries as had been casually made, and reduced them to an established order or method. Whence it is evident, that art deduces its origin from the works of genius, not that genius has been formed or directed by art; and that it is properly applied in illustrating the works of even those writers who were either ignorant of its rules, or inattentive to them. Since then it is the purpose of sacred poetry to form the human mind to the constant habit of true virtue and poetry, and to excite the more ardent affections of the soul in order to direct them to their proper end, whoever has a clear insight into the instruments, the machinery as it were, by which this end is effected, will certainly contribute not a little to the improvement of the critical art. [pp. 45–6.]

The End of Poetry

The end of poetry is to teach and delight; pleasure is the immediate, instruction the ultimate end.

THOMAS RYMER, *Tragedies of the Last Age* (1677)
Some would blame me for insisting and examining only what is apt to please, without a word of what might profit.

[6] The lectures were first published in Latin as *De sacra poesi Hebraeorum praelectiones* (1753).

1. I believe the end of all poetry is to please.

2. Some sorts of poetry please without profiting.

3. I am confident whoever writes a tragedy cannot please but must also profit; 'tis the physic of the mind that he makes palatable.

And besides the purging of the passions, something must stick by observing that constant order, that harmony and beauty of Providence, that necessary relation and chain, whereby the cause and the effects, the virtues and rewards, the vices and their punishments are proportioned and linked together, how deep and dark soever are laid the springs, and however intricate and involved are their operations. [p. 75.]

SIR WILLIAM TEMPLE, Of Poetry (1690)

The dramatic poesy has been composed of all these;[1] but the chief end seems to have been instruction, and under the disguise of fables, or the pleasure of story, to shew the beauties and the rewards of virtue, the deformities and misfortunes or punishment of vice; by examples of both to encourage one, and deter men from the other; to reform ill customs, correct ill manners, and moderate all violent passions. These are the general subjects of both parts, though comedy give us but the images of common life, and tragedy those of the greater and more extraordinary passions and actions among men. [p. 187.]

JOHN DRYDEN, A Parallel of Poetry and Painting. Preface to the Translation of C. A. du Fresnoy, De Arte Graphica (1695)

I will now proceed, as I promised, to the author of this book.[2] He tells you almost in the first lines of it, that "the chief end of painting is to please the eyes; and 'tis one great end of poetry to please the mind." Thus far the parallel of the arts holds true: with this difference, that the principal end of painting is to please, and the chief design of poetry is to instruct. In this the latter seems to have the advantage of the former. But if we consider the artists themselves on

[1] i.e. the various subjects of poetry, which, Temple says, have generally been: praise, instruction, story, love, grief and reproach.

[2] C. A. du Fresnoy, De Arte Graphica (1668).

both sides, certainly their aims are the very same: they would both make sure of pleasing, and that in preference to instruction. [II, 186.]

JOHN DENNIS, *The Grounds of Criticism in Poetry* (1704)
We have said above, that as poetry is an art, it must have a certain end, and that there must be means that are proper for the attaining that end, which means are otherwise called the rules. But that we may make this appear the more plainly, let us declare what poetry is. Poetry then is an art by which a poet excites passion (and for that very cause entertains sense) in order to satisfy and improve, to delight and reform the mind, and so to make mankind happier and better: from which it appears that poetry has two ends, a subordinate, and a final one; the subordinate one is pleasure, and the final one is instruction. [I, 336.]

JOHN DENNIS, *A Defence of Sir Fopling Flutter* (1722)
Every poem is qualified to instruct and to please most powerfully by that very quality which makes the forte and characteristic of it, and which distinguishes it from all other kinds of poems. As tragedy is qualified to instruct and to please by terror and compassion, which two passions ought always to be predominant in it, and to distinguish it from all other poems; epic poetry pleases and instructs chiefly by admiration, which reigns throughout it, and distinguishes it from poems of every other kind. Thus comedy instructs and pleases most powerfully by the ridicule, because that is the quality which distinguishes it from every other poem. [II, 249.]

LEONARD WELSTED, A Dissertation Concerning the Perfection of the English Language, the State of Poetry, etc. (1724)
Does not poetry instruct too, while it pleases? Does it not instruct much more powerfully, through its superior charm of pleasing? When a man of good understanding reads books of humanity, he meets with very little in them that he did not know before; he is not, strictly, the wiser for the reading of them; all his profit, which is all his pleasure, is, that he sees his own natural sentiments supported sometimes by different reasonings, and the truths he approved in his private judgment, authorized by the judgment of others; he sees

them placed, perhaps, in more clear, in more various, or in more beautiful lights. Does not poetry oblige him as much? Does it not give him the same profit and pleasure, and that in a livelier and more indirect way? Besides that, it impresses more strongly on the memory whatever it inculcates, by the natural help of numbers: moral writers recommend virtue, but poetry adorns it; the moralist gains his reader to approve of it; the poet, to be in love with it: the one simply proposes truth and virtue to us, the other shews them in a flood of light, and enforces them, as it were, with the power of enchantment. Is it not, lastly, the privilege of poetry that it mostly gives us truer ideas, and always more elegant ones, of the thing in question than any other sort of writing? Is there anything that so much polishes men's manners, or gives so fine an edge to their wit? Is it not this which gives the strongest tincture of good nature to the heart? And does it not keep men in good humour with themselves, and guard them from that gloominess which care and disappointment are apt to spread over the soul? [pp. xliv–xlv.]

JOSEPH TRAPP, *Lectures on Poetry* (1742)[3]
From hence I am naturally led to enquire into the use and end of poetry, which is generally reckoned twofold, *viz.* to *instruct* and to *please.* So that we come now to the last branch of our definition, wherein we asserted that poetry was designed *for the pleasure and improvement of mankind,* according to that well-known saying of Horace

Aut prodesse volunt, aut delectare poetae.
A poet should instruct, or please, or both.
(Roscommon)[4]

It is agreed, then, by all, that this is the twofold end of poetry; but which the principal, is still a doubt. It may bear a dispute, indeed, which is in fact the principal; but which ought to be so, surely can be none: for in this, as in all other arts, the advantage ought to be considered before the pleasure. Some, indeed, of our modern writers think otherwise, and boldly pronounce pleasure to be the

[3] The lectures were first published in Latin as *Praelectiones poeticae* (1711, 1715, 1719).
[4] *Ars Poetica*, 333, translated by Wentworth Dillon, Earl of Roscommon (1680).

chief end of poetry. It can't be denied but this opinion is perfectly consonant to their writings; in which they not only principally consult their readers' pleasure, but in opposition to their advantage. Witness those lewd poems with which this divine art is polluted. But if we would consult reason, we should allow that even in verse what improves us ought to be more regarded than what delights us. I own, the severest wits that lay down the most rigid precepts of virtue ought to have a view to pleasure in their compositions; for it is the distinguishing mark of the poet from the philosopher, that though virtue is the aim of both, yet the one presses it closer, indeed, but in a less engaging manner. In the dry method of a teacher he defines his subject, he explains his terms, and then gives you rules; the other clothes his precepts in examples, and imperceptibly insinuates them under the beautiful disguise of narration. I own, likewise, that readers are generally more sensible of the pleasure they receive than the profit, even when it is less proposed by the writers; for it is that makes the strongest impression upon the imagination; nay, and I grant that this is what writers themselves ought to study. Yet notwithstanding all this, profit may be the chief end of poetry, and ought to be so; but for that very reason pleasure should be joined to it, and accompany it, as a handmaid, to minister to its occasions. When children are allured with the sweetened draught, or gilded pill, they, as the physician intended, consider nothing but the beauty of the one, or the taste of the other; but it is well known, this was not the chief intent of the physician in his prescription.

This rule relates principally to the more perfect and sublimer kinds of poetry, and especially the epic and dramatic. For we don't pretend that epigram, elegy, songs, and the like conduce much to the improvement of virtue. It is enough if these writings keep within the bounds of chastity, and give no offence to good manners. Poets sometimes write, not so much to move others' passions as to indulge their own. And as pleasure is the chief, or, perhaps, the only effect of this sort of levities, so it may very innocently be proposed by authors as the chief end of them. Though even from these lesser flights one advantage arises, that they improve the wit, and polish the style, both of the writer and the reader; a circumstance that may be observed in favour of all kinds of poetry. [pp. 24–25.]

ROBERT LOWTH, *Lectures on the Sacred Poetry of the Hebrews* (1787)

Poetry is commonly understood to have two objects in view, namely, advantage and pleasure, or rather an union of both. I wish those who have furnished us with this definition, had rather proposed utility as its ultimate object, and pleasure as the means by which that end may be effectually accomplished. The philosopher and the poet indeed seem principally to differ in the means by which they pursue the same end. Each sustains the character of a preceptor, which the one is thought best to support if he teach with accuracy, with subtlety, and with perspicuity; the other, with splendour, harmony and elegance. The one makes his appeal to reason only, independent of the passions; the other addresses the reason in such a manner as even to engage the passions on his side. The one proceeds to virtue and truth by the nearest and most compendious ways; the other leads to the same point through certain deflexions and deviations, by a winding, but pleasanter path. It is the part of the former so to describe and explain these objects, that we must necessarily become acquainted with them; it is the part of the latter so to dress and adorn them, that of our own accord we must love and embrace them. [pp. 6–8.]

Genius—Art

Poetic genius is a gift of nature, but it needs the help of art and learning.

SIR WILLIAM DAVENANT, Preface to *Gondibert* (1650)

And wit is the laborious and the lucky resultances of thought, having towards its excellence, as we say of the strokes of painting, as well a happiness as care. It is a web consisting of the subtlest threads, and like that of the spider is considerately woven out of our selves; for a spider may be said to consider, not only respecting his solemness and tacit posture (like a grave scout in ambush for his enemy), but because all things done are either from consideration or chance, and the works of chance are accomplishments of an instant, having commonly a dissimilitude, but hers are the works of time, and have their contextures alike. [II, 20.]

THOMAS HOBBES, Answer to Davenant's Preface to *Gondibert* (1650)

But why a Christian should think it an ornament to his poem, either to profane the true God or invoke a false one, I can imagine no cause but a reasonless imitation of custom, of a foolish custom, by which a man enabled to speak wisely from the principles of nature and his own meditation, loves rather to be thought to speak by inspiration, like a bagpipe. [II, 59.]

JOHN DRYDEN, The Grounds of Criticism in Tragedy. Prefixed to *Troilus and Cressida* (1679)

To describe [the passions] naturally, and to move them artfully, is one of the greatest commendations which can be given to a poet: to write pathetically, says Longinus,[1] cannot proceed but from a lofty genius. A poet must be born with this quality; yet, unless he helps himself by an acquired knowledge of the passions, what they are in their own nature, and by what springs they are to be moved, he will be subject either to raise them where they ought not to be raised, or not to raise them by the just degrees of nature, or to amplify them beyond the natural bounds, or not to observe the crisis and turns of them in their cooling and decay: all which errors proceed from want of judgment in the poet, and from being unskilled in the principles of moral philosophy. Nothing is more frequent in a fanciful writer than to foil himself by not managing his strength; therefore, as in a wrestler, there is first required some measure of force, a well-knit body, and active limbs, without which all instruction would be vain; yet these being granted, if he want the skill which is necessary to a wrestler, he shall make but small advantage of his natural robustuousness: so, in a poet, his inborn vehemence and force of spirit will only run him out of breath the sooner, if it be not supported by the help of art. The roar of passion, indeed, may please an audience, three parts of which are ignorant enough to think all is

[1] *On the Sublime*, viii.

moving which is noise, and it may stretch the lungs of an ambitious actor, who will die upon the spot for a thundering clap; but it will move no other passion than indignation and contempt from judicious men. [I, 253–4.]

JOHN DRYDEN, A Parallel of Poetry and Painting. Preface to the Translation of C. A. du Fresnoy, *De Arte Graphica* (1695)

Invention is the first part, and absolutely necessary to them both;[2] yet no rule ever was or ever can be given how to compass it. A happy genius is the gift of nature: it depends on the influence of the stars, say the astrologers, on the organs of the body, say the naturalists; 'tis the particular gift of Heaven, say the divines, both Christians and heathens. How to improve it, many books can teach us; how to obtain it, none; that nothing can be done without it, all agree. [II, 194–5.]

CHARLES GILDON, *Miscellaneous Letters and Essays* (1694)

But 'tis agreed by the universal and unanimous consent of almost all nations and authors, that poetry not only contains all other arts and sciences, but has this prerogative peculiar to itself, that no rules, no masters with the best instructions, can teach it, unless those who apply themselves to this divine science are destined to the sacred function by nature and a genius. Whence arose that maxim, allowed of by all men of sense, *Poeta nascitur non fit*, that a poet is born not made. And from hence it follows in my opinion that a poet derives the honour of that name from his nature and genius, not from his art; *this* every scholar has, *that* none but the darlings of heaven and nature. *This* may be acquired by a studious pedant, *that* must be born, and grow up with the auspicious babe, for *Poeta nascitur non fit*. [p. 14.]

SIR WILLIAM TEMPLE, Of Poetry (1690)

The names given to poets, both in Greek and Latin,[3] express the same opinion of them in those nations; the Greek signifying makers or creators, such as raise admirable frames and fabrics out of nothing,

[2] i.e. poetry and painting.   [3] i.e. ποιητής; vates.

which strike with wonder and with pleasure the eyes and imaginations of those who behold them; the Latin makes the same word common to poets and to prophets. Now as creation is the first attribute and highest operation of divine power, so is prophecy the greatest emanation of divine spirit in the world. As the names in those two learned languages, so the causes of poetry are, by the writers of them, said to be divine, and to proceed from a celestial fire, or divine inspiration; and by the vulgar opinions, recited or related to in many passages of those authors, the effects of poetry were likewise thought divine and supernatural, and power of charms and enchantments were ascribed to it.

> Carmina vel coelo possunt deducere lunam,
> Carminibus Circe socios mutavit Ulyssis,
> Frigidus in pratis cantando rumpitur anguis.[4]

But I can easily admire poetry, and yet without adoring it; I can allow it to arise from the greatest excellency of natural temper, or the greatest race of native genius, without exceeding the reach of what is human or giving it any approaches of divinity, which is, I doubt, debased or dishonoured by ascribing to it anything that is in the compass of our action, or even comprehension, unless it be raised by an immediate influence from itself. I cannot allow poetry to be more divine in its effects than in its causes, nor any operation produced by it to be more than purely natural, or to deserve any other sort of wonder than those of music, or of natural magic, however any of them have appeared to minds little versed in the speculations of nature, of occult qualities, and the force of numbers or of sounds. Whoever talks of drawing down the moon from heaven by force of verses or of charms, either believes not himself, or too easily believes what others told him, or perhaps follows an opinion begun by the practice of some poet upon the facility of some people, who knowing the time when an eclipse would happen, told them he would by his charms call down the moon at such an hour, and was by them thought to have performed it. [pp. 174-5.]

[4] Virgil, *Eclogues*, viii. 69-71. ("Charms may even draw the moon down from heaven; through her charms Circe transformed the companions of Ulysses; hearing the voice of the magician, the cold serpent dies in the meadow.")

ALEXANDER POPE, *An Essay on Criticism* (1711)
>   In *poets* as true *genius* is but rare,
>   True *taste* as seldom is the *critic*'s share;
>   Both must alike from Heaven derive their light,
> 14   These *born* to judge, as well as those to write. . . .
>
>   True ease in writing comes from art, not chance,
> 363   As those move easiest who have learn'd to dance.

ANTHONY ASHLEY COOPER, THIRD EARL OF SHAFTESBURY,
Advice to an Author (1710)

'Tis strange to see how differently the vanity of mankind runs in different times and seasons. 'Tis at present the boast of almost every enterpriser in the muses' art, that by his genius alone, and a natural rapidity of style and thought, he is able to carry all before him; that he plays with his business, does things in passing, at a venture, and in the quickest period of time. In the days at Attic elegance, as works were then truly of another form and turn, so workmen were of another humour, and had their vanity of a quite contrary kind. They became rather affected in endeavouring to discover the pains they had taken to be correct. They were glad to insinuate how laboriously, and with what expense of time, they had brought the smallest work of theirs (as perhaps a single ode or satire, an oration or panegyric) to its perfection. When they had so polished their piece, and rendered it so natural and easy, that it *seemed* only a lucky flight, a hit of thought, or flowing vein of humour, they were then chiefly concerned lest it should *in reality* pass for such, and their artifice remain undiscovered. They were willing it should be known how serious their play was, and how elaborate their freedom and facility. [I, 233–4.]

JOSEPH ADDISON, *The Spectator*, no. 160 (3 September 1711)

Among great geniuses, those few draw the admiration of all the world upon them, and stand up as the prodigies of mankind, who by the mere strength of natural parts, and without any assistance of art and learning, have produced works that were the delight of their own times and the wonder of posterity. There appears something nobly wild and extravagant in these great natural geniuses that is infinitely more beautiful than all the turn and polishing of what the French call a *bel esprit*, by which they would express a genius refined by conversation, reflection, and the reading of the most polite authors. The greatest genius which runs through the arts and sciences, takes a kind of tincture from them, and falls unavoidably into imitation.

Many of these great natural geniuses that were never disciplined and broken by rules of art are to be found among the ancients, and in particular among those of the more Eastern parts of the world. Homer has innumerable flights that Virgil was not able to reach, and in the Old Testament we find several passages more elevated and sublime than any in Homer. At the same time that we allow a greater and more daring genius to the ancients, we must own that the greatest of them very much failed in, or, if you will, that they were much above the nicety and correctness of the moderns. In their similitudes and allusions, provided there was a likeness, they did not much trouble themselves about the decency of the comparison. Thus Solomon resembles the nose of his beloved to the tower of Lebanon which looks towards Damascus;[5] as the coming of a thief in the night is a similitude of the same kind in the New Testament.[6] It would be endless to make collections of this nature: Homer illustrates one of his heroes encompassed with the enemy, by an ass in a field of corn that has his sides belaboured by all the boys of the village without stirring a foot for it;[7] and another of them tossing to and fro in his bed, and burning with resentment, to a piece of flesh broiled on the coals.[8] This particular failure in the ancients opens a large field of raillery to the little wits, who can laugh at an indecency but not relish the sublime in these sorts of writings. The present Emperor of Persia, conformable to this Eastern way of thinking, amidst a great many pompous titles, denominates himself the *Sun of Glory* and the *Nutmeg of Delight*. In short, to cut off all cavilling against the ancients, and particularly those of the warmer climates, who had most heat and life in their imaginations, we are to consider that the rule of observing what the French call the *bienséance* in an allusion has been found out of latter

[5] The Song of Sol. vii. 4.
[6] I Thess. v. 2; 2 Pet. iii. 10.
[7] *Iliad*, ii. 558-65.   [8] *Odyssey*, xx. 25-30.

years and in the colder regions of the world, where we would make some amends for our want of force and spirit by a scrupulous nicety and exactness in our compositions. Our countryman Shakespeare was a remarkable instance of this first kind of great geniuses.

I cannot quit this head without observing that Pindar was a great genius of the first class, who was hurried on by a natural fire and impetuosity to vast conceptions of things, and noble sallies of imagination. At the same time, can anything be more ridiculous than for men of a sober and moderate fancy to imitate this poet's way of writing in those monstrous compositions which go among us under the name of Pindarics? When I see people copying works, which, as Horace has represented them,[9] are singular in their kind and inimitable; when I see men following irregularities by rule, and by the little tricks of art straining after the most unbounded flights of nature, I cannot but apply to them that passage in Terence:

> incerta haec si tu postules
> Ratione certa facere, nihilo plus agas,
> Quam si des operam, ut cum ratione insanias.[10]

In short a modern Pindaric writer compared with Pindar, is like a sister among the Camisards[11] compared with Virgil's sybil:[12] there is the distortion, grimace, and outward figure, but nothing of that divine impulse which raises the mind above itself, and makes the sounds more than human.

There is another kind of great geniuses which I shall place in a second class, not as I think them inferior to the first, but only for distinction's sake as they are of a different kind. This second class of great geniuses are those that have formed themselves by rules, and

[9] *Odes*, iv. 2. 1–4.

[10] *Eunuchus*, 61–3. ("You may as well pretend to be mad and in your senses at the same time, as to think of reducing these uncertainties into certainties by reason.")

[11] The Camisards were French Calvinists from the Cévennes. Many of them had fled to England to escape persecution; they claimed to be divinely inspired, to hear voices and see visions. These enthusiasts, usually referred to as the French Prophets, flourished from 1706 to 1708.

[12] *Aeneid*, vi. 42–4.

submitted the greatness of their natural talents to the corrections and restraints of art. Such among the Greeks were Plato and Aristotle, among the Romans Virgil and Tully,[13] among the English Milton and Sir Francis Bacon.

The genius in both these classes of authors may be equally great, but shews itself after a different manner. In the first it is like a rich soil in a happy climate, that produces a whole wilderness of noble plants rising in a thousand beautiful landscapes without any certain order and regularity. In the other it is the same rich soil under the same happy climate, that has been laid out in walks and parterres, and cut into shape and beauty by the skill of the gardener.

The great danger in these latter kind of geniuses is, lest they cramp their own abilities too much by imitation, and form themselves altogether upon models, without giving full play to their own natural parts. An imitation of the best authors is not to compare with a good original; and I believe we may observe that very few writers make an extraordinary figure in the world who have not something in their way of thinking or expressing themselves that is peculiar to them and entirely their own. [II, 126–30.]

JAMES BEATTIE, Of Imagination (1783)

Nor let the man of genius imagine that nature has done everything for him, and that he has nothing to do for himself. In one or two instances, uncultivated genius may have risen to distinction; but who will say that equal genius, with culture, is not more likely to be distinguished? We have heard of dramatic writers who, trusting to their natural powers, whereof, it seems, they had a higher idea than anybody else ever had, thought learning below their ambition, because Shakespeare was not learned: a conceit which, far from being a proof of genius, was only an indication of folly, and an apology for idleness. Shakespeare, it is true, had little school-learning; but we must not thence infer that he was either ignorant or idle. In observing the characters of men, and the appearances of the inanimate and irrational world, as well as in the study of his native tongue, of which he was a complete master, he must have been indefatigable; and he seems to have possessed, in a most

13 Cicero.

uncommon degree, the talent of selecting, from the books that came in his way, such knowledge as might be of use to him in his poetical capacity. [p. 154.]

Wit—Judgment

The inventive faculty—called wit or fancy—must be regulated by judgment, but imagination itself selects and orders its materials.

THOMAS HOBBES, *Leviathan* (1651)

This *natural wit* consists principally in two things: celerity of imagining, that is, swift succession of one thought to another; and steady direction to some approved end. On the contrary a slow imagination makes that defect, or fault of the mind, which is commonly called *dullness*, *stupidity*, and sometimes by other names that signify slowness of motion, or difficulty to be moved. . . .

And whereas in this succession of men's thoughts there is nothing to observe in the things they think on, but either in what they be like one another, or in what they be unlike, or what they serve for, or how they serve to such a purpose; those that observe their similitudes, in case they be such as are but rarely observed by others, are said to have a *good wit*; by which, in this occasion, is meant a *good fancy*. But they that observe their differences and dissimilitudes, which is called distinguishing, and discerning, and judging between thing and thing, in case such discerning be not easy, are said to have a *good judgment*; and particularly in matter of conversation and business, wherein times, places, and persons are to be discerned, this virtue is called *discretion*. The former, that is, fancy, without the help of judgment, is not commended as a virtue; but the latter, which is judgment and discretion, is commended for itself, without the help of fancy. Besides the discretion of times, places, and persons necessary to a good fancy, there is required also an often application of his thoughts to their end; that is to say, to some use to be made of them. This done, he that has this virtue will be easily fitted with similitudes that will please, not only by illustrations of his discourse and adorning it with new and apt metaphors, but also by the rarity of their invention. But without steadiness, and direction to some end, a great fancy is one kind of madness. . . .

In a good poem, whether it be epic or dramatic, as also in sonnets, epigrams, and other pieces, both judgment and fancy are required; but the fancy must be more eminent, because they please for the extravagancy, but ought not to displease by indiscretion. . . .

And in any discourse whatsoever, if the defect of discretion be apparent, how extravagant soever the fancy be, the whole discourse will be taken for a sign of want of wit; and so will it never when the discretion is manifest, though the fancy be never so ordinary. . . .

So that where wit is wanting, it is not fancy that is wanting, but discretion. Judgment therefore without fancy is wit, but fancy without judgment not. [pp. 43–4.]

THOMAS HOBBES, Preface to *Homer's Odyssey* (1675)
A fourth [virtue of a heroic poem] is in the elevation of fancy, which is generally taken for the greatest praise of heroic poetry; and is so, when governed by discretion. For men more generally affect and admire fancy than they do either judgment, or reason, or memory, or any other intellectual virtue; and, for the pleasantness of it, give to it alone the name of wit, accounting reason and judgment but for a dull entertainment. For in fancy consists the sublimity of a poet, which is that poetical fury which the readers for the most part call for. It flies abroad swiftly to fetch in both matter and words; but if there be not discretion at home to distinguish which are fit to be used and which not, which decent[1] and which undecent[2] for persons, times and places, their delight and grace is lost. But if they be discreetly used, they are greater ornaments of a poem by much than any other. [II, 70.]

JOHN DRYDEN, To Roger, Earl of Orrery, Prefixed to *The Rival Ladies* (1664)

My Lord,
This worthless present was designed you long before it was a play; when it was only a confused mass of thoughts, tumbling over

[1] proper, suitable.   [2] improper.

one another in the dark; when the fancy was yet in its first work, moving the sleeping images of things towards the light, there to be distinguished, and then either chosen or rejected by the judgment; it was yours, my Lord, before I could call it mine. And I confess, in that first tumult of my thoughts there appeared a disorderly kind of beauty in some of them, which gave me hope something worthy my Lord of Orrery might be drawn from them. But I was then in that eagerness of imagination which, by overpleasing fanciful men, flatters them into the danger of writing; so that, when I had moulded it into that shape it now bears, I looked with such disgust upon it, that the censures of our severest critics are charitable to what I thought (and still think) of it myself. [I, 2.]

THOMAS RYMER, *Tragedies of the Last Age* (1677)
Say others, poetry and reason, how come these to be catercousins? Poetry is the child of fancy, and is never to be schooled and disciplined by reason; poetry, say they, is blind inspiration, is pure enthusiasm,[3] is rapture and rage all over.

But fancy, I think, in poetry, is like faith in religion; it makes far discoveries, and soars above reason, but never clashes, or runs against it. Fancy leaps, and frisks, and away she's gone; whilst reason rattles the chains, and follows after. Reason must consent and ratify whatever by fancy is attempted in its absence; or else 'tis all null and void in law. However, in the contrivance and economy of a play, reason is always principally to be consulted. Those who object against reason, are the fanatics[4] in poetry, and are never to be saved by their good works. [p. 20.]

JOHN DRYDEN, The Grounds of Criticism in Tragedy. Prefixed to
Troilus and Cressida (1679)
No man should pretend to write who cannot temper his fancy with his judgment: nothing is more dangerous to a raw horseman than a hotmouthed jade without a curb. [I, 255.]

---

[3] Supernatural inspiration; at the time in the derogatory sense of fancied inspiration, religious extravagance.
[4] Unreasoning enthusiasts (see preceding note), who disparaged good works.

WENTWORTH DILLON, EARL OF ROSCOMMON, *An Essay on Translated Verse* (1684)

Beware what spirit rages in your breast;
For ten inspired ten thousand are possessed.
Thus make the proper use of each extreme,
And write with fury, but correct with phlegm. [II, 306.]

SIR WILLIAM TEMPLE, Of Poetry (1690)

But though invention be the mother of poetry, yet this child is, like all others, born naked, and must be nourished with care, clothed with exactness and elegance, educated with industry, instructed with art, improved by application, corrected with severity, and accomplished with labour and with time, before it arrives at any great perfection or growth: 'tis certain that no composition requires so many several ingredients, or of more different sorts than this, nor that, to excel in any qualities, there are necessary so many gifts of nature and so many improvements of learning and of art. For there must be an universal genius, of great compass as well as great elevation; there must be a sprightly imagination or fancy, fertile in a thousand productions, ranging over infinite ground, piercing into every corner, and by the light of that true poetical fire discovering a thousand little bodies or images in the world, and similitudes among them unseen to common eyes, and which could not be discovered without the rays of that sun.

Besides the heat of invention and liveliness of wit, there must be the coldness of good sense and soundness of judgment to distinguish between things and conceptions which, at first sight or upon short glances, seem alike; to choose among infinite productions of wit and fancy which are worth preserving and cultivating, and which are better stifled in the birth, or thrown away when they are born, as not worth bringing up. Without the forces of wit, all poetry is flat and languishing; without the succours of judgment, 'tis wild and extravagant. The true wit of poesy is that such contraries must meet to compose it: a genius, both penetrating and solid; in expression both delicacy and force; and the frame or fabric of a true poem must have something both sublime and just, amazing and agreeable. There must be a great agitation of mind to invent, a great calm to

judge and correct; there must be, upon the same tree, and at the
same time, both flower and fruit. To work up this metal into
exquisite figure, there must be employed the fire, the hammer, the
chisel, and the file. There must be a general knowledge both of
nature and of arts, and, to go the lowest that can be, there are
required genius, judgment, and application; for, without this last,
all the rest will not serve turn, and none ever was a great poet that
applied himself much to anything else. [pp. 179–80.]

ALEXANDER POPE, *An Essay on Criticism* (1711)

80   Some, to whom Heav'n in wit[5] has been profuse,
      Want as much more, to turn it to its use;
      For *wit* and *judgment* often are at strife,
      Tho' meant each other's aid, like *man* and *wife*.
      'Tis more to *guide* than *spur* the muse's steed;
85   Restrain his fury, than provoke his speed;
      The winged courser, like a gen'rous horse,
      Shows most true mettle when you *check* his course.

CHARLES GILDON, *The Complete Art of Poetry* (1718)
For fancy and judgment must join in every great poet, as courage
and judgment in every great general; for where either is wanting,
the other is useless, or of small value. Fancy is what we generally
call nature, or a genius; judgment is what we mean by art, the union
of which in one man makes a complete poet. [p. 125.]

ALEXANDER GERARD, *An Essay on Taste* (1759)
The first and leading quality of genius is invention, which consists
in a great extent and comprehensiveness of imagination, in a readiness of associating the remotest ideas that are any way related. In a
man of genius, the uniting principles are so vigorous and quick,
that, whenever any idea is present to the mind, they bring into view
at once all others that have the least connexion with it. As the
magnet selects, from a quantity of matter, the ferruginous particles

---

[5] Pope is playing on the ambiguity of the term *wit* in order to show that
imagination and judgment are the two sides of the creative faculty.

which happen to be scattered through it, without making an impression on other substances; so imagination, by a similar sympathy, equally inexplicable, draws out from the whole compass of nature such ideas as we have occasion for, without attending to any others; and yet presents them with as great propriety, as if all possible conceptions had been explicitly exposed to our view, and subjected to our choice.

At first, these materials may lie in a rude and undigested chaos; but when we attentively review them, the same associating power which formerly made us sensible of their connexion leads us to perceive the different degrees of that connexion; by its magical force ranges them into different species, according to these degrees; disposes the most strongly related into the same member; and sets all the members in that position which it points out as the most natural. Thus, from a confused heap of materials, collected by fancy, genius, after repeated reviews and transpositions, designs a regular and well-proportioned whole. [pp. 168–9.]

SIR JOSHUA REYNOLDS, Discourse 13 (1786)
All theories which attempt to direct or to control the art[6] upon any principles falsely called rational, which we form to ourselves upon a supposition of what ought in reason to be the end or means of art, independent of the known first effect produced by objects on the imagination, must be false and delusive. For though it may appear bold to say it, the imagination is here the residence of truth. If the imagination be affected, the conclusion is fairly drawn; if it be not affected, the reasoning is erroneous, because the end is not obtained; the effect itself being the test, and the only test, of the truth and efficacy of the means.

There is in the commerce of life, as in art, a sagacity which is far from being contradictory to right reason, and is superior to any occasional exercise of that faculty, which supersedes it, and does not wait for the slow progress of deduction, but goes at once, by what appears a kind of intuition, to the conclusion. A man endowed with this faculty feels and acknowledges the truth, though it is not always in his power, perhaps, to give a reason for it; because he

[6] i.e. the art of painting; but Reynolds' views are equally applicable to poetry.

cannot recollect and bring before him all the materials that gave birth to his opinion; for very many and very intricate considerations may unite to form the principle, even of small and minute parts, involved in, or dependent on a great system of things; though these in process of time are forgotten, the right impression still remains fixed in his mind.

This impression is the result of the accumulated experience of our whole life, and has been collected, we do not always know how, or when. But this mass of collective observation, however acquired, ought to prevail over that reason which, however powerfully exerted on any particular occasion, will probably comprehend but a partial view of the subject; and our conduct in life, as well as in the arts, is, or ought to be, generally governed by this habitual reason: it is our happiness that we are enabled to draw on such funds. If we were obliged to enter into a theoretical deliberation on every occasion before we act, life would be at a stand, and art would be impracticable.

It appears to me, therefore, that our first thoughts, that is, the effect which anything produces on our minds on its first appearance, is never to be forgotten; and it demands for that reason, because it is the first, to be laid up with care. If this be not done, the artist may happen to impose on himself by partial reasoning; by a cold consideration of those animated thoughts which proceed, not perhaps from caprice or rashness (as he may afterwards conceit[7]), but from the fullness of his mind, enriched with the copious stores of all the various inventions which he had ever seen, or had ever passed in his mind. These ideas are infused into his design, without any conscious effort; but if he be not on his guard, he may reconsider and correct them, till the whole matter is reduced to a commonplace invention.

This is sometimes the effect of what I mean to caution you against; that is to say, an unfounded distrust of the imagination and feeling, in favour of narrow, partial, confined, argumentative theories, and of principles that seem to apply to the design in hand; without considering those general impressions on the fancy in which real principles of sound reason, and of much more weight and importance, are involved, and, as it were, lie hid, under the appearance of a sort of vulgar sentiment.

[7] imagine.

Reason, without doubt, must ultimately determine everything; at this minute it is required to inform us when that very reason is to give way to feeling.

Though I have often spoken of that mean conception of our art which confines it to a mere imitation, I must add that it may be narrowed to such a mere matter of experiment, as to exclude from it the application of science, which alone gives dignity and compass to any art. But to find proper foundations for science is neither to narrow or to vulgarize it; and this is sufficiently exemplified in the success of experimental philosophy. It is the false system of reasoning, grounded on a partial view of things, against which I would most earnestly guard you. And I do it the rather, because those narrow theories, so coincident with the poorest and most miserable practices, and which are adopted to give it countenance, have not had their origin in the poorest minds, but in the mistakes, or possibly in the mistaken interpretations, of great and commanding authorities. We are not, therefore, in this case misled by feeling, but by false speculation. [pp. 230–32.]

True Wit

Wit or fine writing does not consist in brilliant or uncommon thoughts, but in a lively expression of truth.

SIR WILLIAM DAVENANT, Preface to *Gondibert* (1650)
That which is not, yet is accompted wit, I will but slightly remember, which seems very incident to imperfect youth and sickly age. Young men, as if they were not quite delivered from childhood, whose first exercise is language, imagine it consists in the music of words, and believe they are made wise by refining their speech above the vulgar dialect, which is a mistake almost as great as that of the people who think orators (which is a title that crowns at riper years those that have practised the dexterity of tongue) the ablest men, who are indeed so much more unapt for governing as they are more fit for sedition; and it may be said of them as of the

witches of Norway, who can sell a storm for a dollar, which for ten thousand they cannot allay. From the esteem of speaking they proceed to the admiration of what are commonly called *conceits*, things that sound like the knacks or toys of ordinary epigrammatists, and from thence, after more conversation and variety of objects, grow up to some force of fancy. Yet even then, like young hawks, they stray and fly far off, using their liberty as if they would never return to the lure, and often go at check[1] ere they can make a steady view and know their game. [II, 21-2.]

JOSEPH GLANVILL, *An Essay Concerning Preaching* (1678)

I do not by this reprehend all wit whatsover in preaching, nor anything that is truly such: for true wit is a perfection in our faculties, chiefly in the understanding and imagination. Wit in the understanding is a sagacity to find out the nature, relations, and consequences of things; wit in the imagination is a quickness in the fancy to give things proper images; now the more of these is in sermons, the more of judgment and spirit, and life: and without wit of these kinds preaching is dull and unedifying. The preacher should endeavour to speak sharp and quick thoughts, and to set them out in lively colours; this is proper, grave, and manly wit, but the other, that which consists in inversions of sentences, and playing with words, and the like, is vile and contemptible fooling.

I have this to advertise[2] more under this head, that even the wit that is true, that may be used, and ought to be endeavoured, should not be hunted after out of the road. A man in a journey will not run over hedges to gather flowers; and the preacher is much to blame that forsakes the direct course of his matter to fetch in notions and elegancies; such as are grave, and pertinent, and lie in his way he may use, but to set his fancy a-ranging, and beating abroad after them, is folly and affectation. [pp. 71-3.]

ALEXANDER POPE, *An Essay on Criticism* (1711)

Some to *conceit* alone their taste confine,
290 And glitt'ring thoughts struck out at ev'ry line;
Pleased with a work where nothing's just or fit;
One *glaring chaos* and *wild heap of wit*:

[1] forsake the proper game.   [2] to warn.

Poets like painters, thus, unskill'd to trace
The *naked nature* and the *living grace*,
295 With *gold* and *jewels* cover ev'ry part,
And hide with *ornaments* their *want of art*.
True wit is *Nature* to advantage drest,
What oft was *thought*, but ne'er so well *exprest*,
Something, whose truth convinc'd at sight we find,
300 That gives us back the image of our mind:
As shades more sweetly recommend the light,
So modest plainness sets off sprightly wit:
For *works* may have more *wit* than does 'em good,
As *bodies* perish through excess of *blood*.
305   Others for *language* all their care express,
And value *books*, as women *men*, for *dress*:
Their praise is still: "The style is excellent":
The *sense*, they humbly take upon content.
Words are like *leaves*; and where they most abound,
310 Much *fruit* of *sense* beneath is rarely found.
False eloquence, like the *prismatic glass*,
Its gawdy colours spreads on *ev'ry place*;
The face of Nature we no more survey,
All glares *alike*, without *distinction* gay;
315 But true *expression*, like th' unchanging *sun*,
Clears, and *improves* whate'er it shines upon,
It *gilds* all objects, but it *alters* none.
Expression is the *dress* of *thought*, and still
Appears more *decent* as more *suitable*;
320 A vile conceit in pompous words exprest,
Is like a clown in regal purple drest;
For diff'rent *styles* with diff'rent *subjects* sort,
As several garbs with country, town, and court.

JOSEPH ADDISON, *The Spectator*, no. 62 (11 May 1711)
It may be expected, since I am upon this subject, that I should take
notice of Mr. Dryden's definition of wit; which, with all the deference that is due to the judgment of so great a man, is not so properly a
definition of wit as of good writing in general. Wit, as he defines it,

is "a propriety of words and thoughts adapted to the subject."[3] If this be a true definition of wit, I am apt to think that Euclid was the greatest wit that ever set pen to paper: it is certain there never was a greater propriety of words and thoughts adapted to the subject than what that author has made use of in his *Elements*. I shall only appeal to my reader if this definition agrees with any notion he has of wit: if it be a true one, I am sure Mr. Dryden was not only a better poet, but a greater wit than Mr. Cowley, and Virgil a much more facetious man than either Ovid or Martial.

Bouhours, whom I look upon to be the most penetrating of all the French critics, has taken pains to shew that it is impossible for any thought to be beautiful which is not just and has not its foundation in the nature of things; that the basis of all wit is truth; and that no thought can be valuable of which good sense is not the groundwork.[4] Boileau has endeavoured to inculcate the same notion in several parts of his writings, both in prose and verse.[5] This is that natural way of writing, that beautiful simplicity which we so much admire in the compositions of the ancients; and which nobody deviates from but those who want strength of genius to make a thought shine in its own natural beauties. Poets who want this strength of genius to give that majestic simplicity to nature which we so much admire in the works of the ancients, are forced to hunt after foreign ornaments, and not to let any piece of wit of what kind soever escape them. I look upon these writers as Goths in poetry, who,

[3] "A propriety of thoughts and words, or, in other terms, thoughts and words elegantly adapted to the subject." ("Apology for Heroic Poetry and Poetic Licence", prefixed to *The State of Innocence*, 1677).

[4] Dominique Bouhours, in *La Manière de bien penser dans les ouvrages de l'esprit*, Dialogue I (1687).

[5] Particularly in the Preface to the 1701 edition of his *Works*, to which Addison refers in the next extract, from *Spectator* no. 253: "Qu'est-ce qu'une pensée neuve, brillante, extraordinaire? Ce n'est point, comme se le persuadent les ignorants, une pensée que personne n'a jamais eue ni dû avoir: c'est au contraire une pensée qui a dû venir à tout le monde, et que quelqu'un s'avise le premier d'exprimer. Un bon mot n'est un bon mot qu'en ce qu'il dit une chose que chacun pensait, et qu'il la dit d'une manière vive, fine, et nouvelle." Compare with the extract from Johnson's "Life of Cowley", pp. 64ff. below.

like those in architecture, not being able to come up to the beautiful simplicity of the old Greeks and Romans, have endeavoured to supply its place with all the extravagances of an irregular fancy. [I, 267–8.]

JOSEPH ADDISON, *The Spectator* no. 253 (20 December 1711)
I am sorry to find that an author who is very justly esteemed among the best judges, has admitted some strokes of this nature[6] into a very fine poem, I mean *The Art of Criticism*, which was published some months since, and is a masterpiece in its kind.[7] The observations follow one another like those in Horace's *Art of Poetry*, without that methodical regularity which would have been requisite in a prose author. They are some of them uncommon, but such as the reader must assent to when he sees them explained with that elegance and perspicuity in which they are delivered. As for those which are the most known, and the most received, they are placed in so beautiful a light, and illustrated with such apt allusions, that they have in them all the graces of novelty, and make the reader who was before acquainted with them, still more convinced of their truth and solidity. And here give me leave to mention what Monsieur Boileau has so very well enlarged upon in the Preface to his *Works*, that wit and fine writing doth not consist so much in advancing things that are new, as in giving things that are known an agreeable turn.[8] It is impossible for us who live in the later ages of the world to make observations in criticism, morality, or in any art or science, which have not been touched upon by others. We have little else left us but to represent the common sense of mankind in more strong, more beautiful or more uncommon lights. If a reader examines Horace's *Art of Poetry*, he will find but very few precepts in it which he may not meet with in Aristotle, and which were not commonly known by all the poets of the Augustan Age. His way of expressing and applying them, not his invention of them, is what we are chiefly to admire. [II, 482–4.]

SAMUEL JOHNSON, Life of Cowley (1779)
Cowley, like other poets who have written with narrow views

[6] i.e. attacks against other writers.   [7] Pope's *Essay on Criticism*.
[8] Preface to the 1701 edition of his *Works*. See p. 63, n. 5.

and, instead of tracing intellectual pleasure to its natural sources in the mind of man, paid their court to temporary prejudices, has been at one time too much praised and too much neglected at another.

Wit, like all other things subject by their nature to the choice of man, has its changes and fashions, and at different times takes different forms. About the beginning of the seventeenth century appeared a race of writers that may be termed the metaphysical poets, of whom in a criticism on the works of Cowley it is not improper to give some account.

The metaphysical poets were men of learning, and to shew their learning was their whole endeavour: but, unluckily resolving to shew it in rhyme, instead of writing poetry they only wrote verses, and very often such verses as stood the trial of the finger better than of the ear: for the modulation was so imperfect that they were only found to be verses by counting the syllables.

If the father of criticism has rightly denominated poetry $\tau \acute{\epsilon} \chi \nu \eta$ $\mu \iota \mu \eta \tau \iota \kappa \acute{\eta}$, *an imitative art*,[9] these writers will without great wrong lose their right to the name of poets, for they cannot be said to have imitated any thing: they neither copied nature nor life; neither painted the forms of matter nor represented the operations of intellect.

Those, however, who deny them to be poets allow them to be wits. Dryden confesses of himself and his contemporaries that they fall below Donne in wit, but maintains that they surpass him in poetry.

If wit be well described by Pope as being "that which has been often thought, but was never before so well expressed",[10] they certainly never attained nor ever sought it, for they endeavoured to be singular in their thoughts, and were careless of their diction. But Pope's account of wit is undoubtedly erroneous; he depresses it below its natural dignity, and reduces it from strength of thought to happiness of language.

If by a more noble and more adequate conception that be considered as wit which is at once natural and new, that which though not obvious is, upon its first production, acknowledged to be just;

[9] The phrase does not appear in the *Poetics*, but in Chapter viii Aristotle defines poetry as a form of $\mu \acute{\iota} \mu \eta \sigma \iota \varsigma$.

[10] See the extract from *An Essay on Criticism* quoted p. 62 (ll. 297–8).

C

if it be that, which he that never found it, wonders how he missed; to wit of this kind the metaphysical poets have seldom risen. Their thoughts are often new, but seldom natural: they are not obvious, but neither are they just: and the reader, far from wondering that he missed them, wonders more frequently by what perverseness of industry they were ever found.

But wit, abstracted from its effects upon the hearer, may be more rigorously and philosophically considered as a kind of *discordia concors*; a combination of dissimilar images, or discovery of occult resemblances in things apparently unlike. Of wit, thus defined, they have more than enough. The most heterogeneous ideas are yoked by violence together; nature and art are ransacked for illustrations, comparisons, and allusions; their learning instructs, and their subtlety surprises; but the reader commonly thinks his improvement dearly bought, and, though he sometimes admires, is seldom pleased.

From this account of their compositions it will be readily inferred that they were not successful in representing or moving the affections.[11] As they were wholly employed on something unexpected and surprising, they had no regard to that uniformity of sentiment which enables us to conceive and to excite the pains and the pleasure of other minds: they never enquired what on any occasion they should have said or done, but wrote rather as beholders than partakers of human nature; as beings looking upon good and evil, impassive and at leisure; as Epicurean deities making remarks on the actions of men and the vicissitudes of life, without interest and without emotion. Their courtship was void of fondness and their lamentation of sorrow. Their wish was only to say what they hoped had never been said before. [I, 18–20.]

[11] the feelings.

Imitation of Nature

Nature is the end and test of art. Poetry imitates general or ideal nature; it mirrors universal truths, not the individual but the species. The poet should not copy nature too closely, he must select what is suitable to his design and avoid what is imperfect or merely particular.

JOHN DRYDEN, *An Essay of Dramatic Poesy* (1668)
[Lisideius] had no sooner said this, but all desired the favour of him to give the defintion of a play; and they were the more importunate, because neither Aristotle, nor Horace, nor any other who writ of that subject, had ever done it.

Lisideius, after some modest denials, at last confessed he had a rude notion of it; indeed rather a description than a definition, but which served to guide him in his private thoughts, when he was to make a judgment of what others writ: that he conceived a play ought to be *A just and lively image of human nature, representing its passions and humours, and the changes of fortune to which it is subject, for the delight and instruction of mankind.* [I, 25.]

JOHN DRYDEN, A Defence of *An Essay of Dramatic Poesy* (1668)
But I will be bolder, and do not doubt to make it good, though a paradox, that one great reason why prose is not to be used in serious plays is because it is too near the nature of converse:[1] there may be too great a likeness; as the most skilful painters affirm that there may be too near a resemblance in a picture: to take every lineament and feature is not to make an excellent piece, but to take so much only as will make a beautiful resemblance of the whole: and, with an ingenious flattery of nature, to heighten the beauties of some parts, and hide the deformities of the rest. [I, 114.]

JOHN DRYDEN, A Parallel of Poetry and Painting. Preface to the Translation of C. A. du Fresnoy, *De Arte Graphica* (1695)
The business of [Bellori's] preface[2] is to prove that a learned painter

[1] conversation.

[2] G. P. Bellori's Preface to his *Vite de pittori* (1672), from which Dryden has quoted a long extract.

should form to himself an idea of perfect nature. This image he is to set before his mind in all his undertakings, and to draw from thence, as from a storehouse, the beauties which are to enter into his work; thereby correcting nature from what actually she is in individuals, to what she ought to be, and what she was created. Now, as this idea of perfection is of little use in portraits (or the resemblance of particular persons), so neither is it in the characters of comedy and tragedy, which are never to be made perfect, but always to be drawn with some specks of frailty and deficience; such as they have been described to us in history, if they were real characters, or such as the poet began to shew them at their first appearance, if they were only fictitious (or imaginary). The perfection of such stage-characters consists chiefly in their likeness to the deficient faulty nature, which is their original. Only as it is observed more at large hereafter, in such cases there will always be found a better likeness and a worse, and the better is constantly to be chosen: I mean in tragedy, which represents the figures of the highest form amongst mankind. Thus in portraits, the painter will not take that side of the face which has some notorious blemish in it; but either draw it in profile (as Apelles did Antigonus, who had lost one of his eyes), or else shadow the more imperfect side. For an ingenious flattery is to be allowed to the professors of both arts, so long as the likeness is not destroyed. 'Tis true that all manner of imperfections must not be taken away from the characters; and the reason is, that there may be left some grounds of pity for their misfortunes. We can never be grieved for their miseries who are thoroughly wicked, and have thereby justly called their calamities on themselves. Such men are the natural objects of our hatred, not of our commiseration. If on the other side their characters were wholly perfect (such as, for example, the character of a saint or martyr in a play), his or her misfortunes would produce impious thoughts in the beholders; they would accuse the heavens of injustice, and think of leaving a religion where piety was so ill requited. I say the greater part would be tempted to do so, I say not that they ought; and the consequence is too dangerous for the practice. In this I have accused myself for my own *St Catherine*;[3] but let truth prevail. Sophocles has taken the just medium in his Oedipus. He is somewhat arrogant at his first

[3] *Tyrannic Love* (1670).

entrance, and is too inquisitive through the whole tragedy; yet these imperfections being balanced by great virtues, they hinder not our compassion for his miseries; neither yet can they destroy that horror which the nature of his crimes has excited in us. Such in painting are the warts and moles which, adding a likeness to the face, are not therefore to be omitted. But these produce no loathing in us. But how far to proceed, and where to stop, is left to the judgment of the poet and the painter. In comedy there is somewhat more of the worse likeness to be taken, because that is often to produce laughter, which is occasioned by the sight of some deformity; but for this I refer the reader to Aristotle.[4] 'Tis a sharp manner of instruction for the vulgar, who are never well amended till they are more than sufficiently exposed.

That I may return to the beginning of this remark concerning perfect ideas, I have only this to say, that the parallel is often true in epic poetry. The heroes of the poets are to be drawn according to this rule. There is scarce a frailty to be left in the best of them; any more than is to be found in a divine nature. And if Aeneas sometimes weeps, it is not in bemoaning his own miseries, but those which his people undergo. If this be an imperfection, the Son of God, when he was incarnate, shed tears of compassion over Jerusalem. And Lentulus[5] describes him often weeping, but never laughing; so that Virgil is justified even from the Holy Scriptures. I have but one word more, which for once I will anticipate from the author of this book. Though it must be an idea of perfection from which both the epic poet and the history painter draws, yet all perfections are not suitable to all subjects; but every one must be designed according to that perfect beauty which is proper to him. An Apollo must be distinguished from a Jupiter, a Pallas from a Venus; and so in poetry, an Aeneas from any other hero; for piety is his chief perfection. [II, 183–5.]

THOMAS RYMER, *Tragedies of the Last Age* (1677)
In framing a character for tragedy, a poet is not to leave his reason, and blindly abandon himself to follow fancy; for then his fancy might be monstrous, might be singular and please nobody's maggot

4 *Poetics*, v.
5 Supposed author of the apocryphal Epistle to the Roman Senate.

but his own; but reason is to be his guide, reason is common to all people, and can never carry him from what is natural.

Many are apt to mistake use for nature, but a poet is not to be an historiographer, but a philosopher, he is not to take nature at the second hand, soiled and deformed as it passes in the customs of the unthinking vulgar. [p. 62.]

ALEXANDER POPE, *An Essay on Criticism* (1711)

> First follow NATURE, and your judgment frame
> By her just standard, which is still the same:
> 70 *Unerring Nature*, still divinely bright,
> One *clear*, *unchang'd*, and *universal* light,
> Life, force, and beauty, must to all impart,
> At once the *source*, and *end*, and *test* of *art*.
> *Art* from that fund each *just supply* provides,
> 75 Works *without show*, and *without pomp* presides:
> In some fair body thus th' informing soul
> With spirits feeds, with vigour fills the whole,
> Each motion guides, and ev'ry nerve sustains;
> *Itself unseen*, but in th' *effects*, remains.

ANTHONY ASHLEY COOPER, THIRD EARL OF SHAFTESBURY,
An Essay on the Freedom of Wit and Humour
(1709)

A painter, if he has any genius, understands the truth and unity of design; and knows he is even then unnatural, when he follows nature too close, and strictly copies life. For his art allows him not to bring all nature into his piece, but a part only. However, his piece, if it be beautiful, and carries truth, must be a whole by itself, complete, independent, and withal as great and comprehensive as he can make it. So that particulars, on this occasion, must yield to the general design; and all things be subservient to that which is principal, in order to form a certain easiness of sight: a simple, clear, and united view, which would be broken and disturbed by the expression of anything peculiar, or distinct.

Now the variety of nature is such as to distinguish everything she forms by a peculiar original character; which, if strictly observed, will make the subject appear unlike to anything extant in the world besides. But this effect the good poet and painter seek industriously to prevent. They hate minuteness, and are afraid of singularity, which would make their images, or characters, appear capricious and fantastical. The mere face-painter, indeed, has little in common with the poet; but, like the mere historian, copies what he sees, and minutely traces every feature and odd mark. 'Tis otherwise with the men of invention and design. 'Tis from the many objects of nature, and not from a particular one, that those geniuses form the idea of their work. Thus the best artists are said to have been indefatigable in studying the best statues, as esteeming them a better rule than the perfected human bodies could afford. And thus some considerable wits have recommended the best poems, as preferable to the best of histories, and better teaching the truth of characters and nature of mankind.

Nor can this criticism be thought high-strained. Though few confine themselves to these rules, few are insensible of them. Whatever quarter we may give to our vicious poets, or other composers of irregular and short-lived works, we know very well that the standing pieces of good artists must be formed after a more uniform way. Every just work of theirs comes under those natural rules of proportion and truth. The creature of their brain must be like one of Nature's formation. It must have a body and parts proportionable, or the very vulgar will not fail to criticize the work, when it has neither head nor tail. For so common sense (according to just philosophy) judges of those works which want the justness of a whole, and shew their author, however curious and exact in particulars, to be in the main a very bungler. [I, 142–6.]

SAMUEL JOHNSON, *Rasselas* (1759)
"Being now resolved to be a poet, I[6] saw everything with a new purpose; my sphere of attention was suddenly magnified; no kind of knowledge was to be overlooked. I ranged mountains and deserts for images and resemblances, and pictured upon my mind every tree of the forest and flower of the valley. I observed with equal

[6] Imlac.

care the crags of the rock and the pinnacles of the palace. Sometimes I wandered along the mazes of the rivulet, and sometimes watched the changes of the summer clouds. To a poet nothing can be useless. Whatever is beautiful, and whatever is dreadful, must be familiar to his imagination: he must be conversant with all that is awfully vast or elegantly little. The plants of the garden, the animals of the wood, the minerals of the earth, and meteors of the sky, must all concur to store his mind with inexhaustible variety: for every idea is useful for the enforcement or decoration of moral or religious truth; and he who knows most, will have most power of diversifying his scenes, and of gratifying his reader with remote allusions and unexpected instruction.

"All the appearances of nature I was therefore careful to study; and every country which I have surveyed has contributed something to my poetical powers."

"In so wide a survey", said the prince, "you must surely have left much unobserved. I have lived, till now, within the circuit of these mountains, and yet cannot walk abroad without the sight of something which I had never beheld before, or never heeded."

"The business of a poet," said Imlac, "is to examine, not the individual, but the species; to remark general properties and large appearances. He does not number the streaks of the tulip, or describe the different shades in the verdure of the forest: he is to exhibit in his portraits of nature such prominent and striking features as recall the original to every mind; and must neglect the minuter discriminations, which one may have remarked, and another have neglected, for those characteristics which are alike obvious to vigilance and carelessness.

"But the knowledge of nature is only half the task of a poet: he must be acquainted likewise with all the modes of life. His character requires that he estimate the happiness and misery of every condition, observe the power of all the passions in all their combinations, and trace the changes of the human mind as they are modified by various institutions and accidental influences of climate or custom, from the sprightliness of infancy to the despondence of decrepitude. He must divest himself of the prejudices of his age and country; he must consider right and wrong in their abstracted and invariable state; he must disregard present laws and opinions, and rise to general and transcendental truths, which will always be the same. He must therefore content himself with the slow progress of his name, contemn the applause of his own time, and commit his claims to the justice of posterity. He must write as the interpreter of nature, and the legislator of mankind, and consider himself as presiding over the thoughts and manners of future generations, as a being superior to time and place." [pp. 62–3.]

SAMUEL JOHNSON, Preface to *The Plays of William Shakespeare*
(1765)
Nothing can please many, and please long, but just representations of general nature. Particular manners can be known to few, and therefore few only can judge how nearly they are copied. The irregular combinations of fanciful invention may delight a while, by that novelty of which the common satiety of life sends us all in quest; but the pleasures of sudden wonder are soon exhausted, and the mind can only repose on the stability of truth.

Shakespeare is above all writers, at least above all modern writers, the poet of nature; the poet that holds up to his readers a faithful mirror of manners and of life. His characters are not modified by the customs of particular places, unpractised by the rest of the world; by the peculiarities of studies or professions, which can operate but upon small numbers; or by the accidents of transient fashions or temporary opinions: they are the genuine progeny of common humanity, such as the world will always supply, and observation will always find. His persons act and speak by the influence of those general passions and principles by which all minds are agitated, and the whole system of life is continued in motion. In the writings of other poets a character is too often an individual; in those of Shakespeare it is commonly a species. [p. 106.]

SAMUEL JOHNSON, Life of Cowley (1779)
The fault of Cowley, and perhaps of all the writers of the meta-physical race, is that of pursuing his thoughts to their last ramifica-tions, by which he loses the grandeur of generality, for of the greatest things the parts are little; what is little can be but pretty, and by claiming dignity becomes ridiculous. Thus all the power of description is destroyed by a scrupulous enumeration; and the force

of metaphors is lost when the mind by the mention of particulars is turned more upon the original than the secondary sense, more upon that from which the illustration is drawn than that to which it is applied. [I, 45.]

SIR JOSHUA REYNOLDS, Discourse 3 (1776)

The wish of the genuine painter must be more extensive: instead of endeavouring to amuse[7] mankind with the minute neatness of his imitations, he must endeavour to improve them by the grandeur of his ideas; instead of seeking praise by deceiving the superficial sense of the spectator, he must strive for fame by captivating the imagination.

The principle now laid down, that the perfection of this art does not consist in mere imitation, is far from being new or singular. It is, indeed, supported by the general opinion of the enlightened part of mankind. The poets, orators, and rhetoricians of antiquity, are continually enforcing this position, that all the arts receive their perfection from an ideal beauty, superior to what is to be found in individual nature. They are ever referring to the practice of the painters and sculptors of their times, particularly Phidias (the favourite artist of antiquity), to illustrate their assertions. As if they could not sufficiently express their admiration of his genius by what they knew, they have recourse to poetical enthusiasm: they call it inspiration, a gift from heaven. The artist is supposed to have ascended the celestial regions, to furnish his mind with this perfect idea of beauty. "He", says Proclus, "who takes for his model such forms as nature produces, and confines himself to an exact imitation of them, will never attain to what is perfectly beautiful. For the works of nature are full of disproportion, and fall very short of the true standard of beauty. So that Phidias, when he formed his Jupiter, did not copy any object ever presented to his sight, but contemplated only that image which he had conceived in his mind from Homer's description."[8] And thus Cicero, speaking of the same Phidias: "Neither did this artist," says he, "when he carved the image of Jupiter or Minerva, set before him any one human figure

[7] to engage the attention of.

[8] Proclus, *In Platonis Timaeum*, ed. Diehl, Leipzig, 1903, p. 265, 18. (Cf. *Timaeus*, 28a–b.)

as a pattern which he was to copy; but having a more perfect idea of beauty fixed in his mind, this he steadily contemplated, and to the imitation of this, all his skill and labour were directed."[9]

The moderns are not less convinced than the ancients of this superior power existing in the art; nor less sensible of its effects. Every language has adopted terms expressive of this excellence. The *gusto grande* of the Italians, the *beau idéal* of the French, and the *great style*, *genius*, and *taste* among the English, are but different appellations of the same thing. It is the intellectual dignity, they say, that ennobles the painter's art; that lays the line between him and the mere mechanic; and produces those great effects in an instant which eloquence and poetry, by slow and repeated efforts, are scarcely able to attain. . . .

This great ideal perfection and beauty are not to be sought in the heavens, but upon the earth. They are about us, and upon every side of us. But the power of discovering what is deformed in nature, or, in other words, what is particular and uncommon, can be acquired only by experience; and the whole beauty and grandeur of the art consists, in my opinion, in being able to get above all singular forms, local customs, particularities, and details of every kind.

All the objects which are exhibited to our view by nature, upon close examination will be found to have their blemishes and defects. The most beautiful forms have something about them like weakness, minuteness, or imperfection. But it is not every eye that perceives these blemishes. It must be an eye long used to the contemplation and comparison of these forms; and which, by a long habit of observing what any set of objects of the same kind have in common, has acquired the power of discerning what each wants in particular. This long laborious comparison should be the first study of the painter who aims at the great style. By this means, he acquires a just idea of beautiful forms; he corrects nature by herself, her imperfect state by her more perfect. His eye being enabled to distinguish the accidental deficiencies, excrescences, and deformities of things, from their general figures, he makes out an abstract idea of their forms more perfect than any one original; and what may seem a paradox, he learns to design naturally by drawing his figures unlike to any object. This idea of the perfect state of nature, which

9 Cicero, *Orator*, ii. 9.

the artist calls the ideal beauty, is the great leading principle by which works of genius are conducted. . . .

Thus it is from a reiterated experience, and a close comparison of the objects in nature, that an artist becomes possessed of the idea of that central form, if I may so express it, from which every deviation is deformity. [pp. 42–3, 44–5.]

Imitation of the Ancients

The ancients have imitated nature rightly and discovered the best means for pleasing generally. To follow them is therefore to follow nature.

JOHN DRYDEN, *An Essay of Dramatic Poesy* (1668)
Certainly, to imitate the ancients well, much labour and long study is required; which pains, I have already shown, our poets would want encouragement to take, if they had ability to go through with it. Those ancients have been faithful imitators and wise observers of that nature which is so torn and ill represented in our plays; they have handed down to us a perfect resemblance of her; which we, like ill copiers, neglecting to look on, have rendered monstrous and disfigured. [I, 27.]

JOHN DRYDEN, Heroic Poetry and Poetic Licence. Prefixed to
The State of Innocence (1677)
Virgil and Horace, the severest writers of the severest age, have made frequent use of the hardest metaphors, and of the strongest hyperboles: and in this case the best authority is the best argument. For generally to have pleased, and through all ages, must bear the force of universal tradition. And if you would appeal from thence to right reason, you will gain no more by it in effect than, first, to set up your reason against those authors; and, secondly, against all

those who have admired them. You must prove why that ought not to have pleased which has pleased the most learned and the most judicious; and to be thought knowing, you must first put the fool upon all mankind. If you can enter more deeply than they have done into the causes and resorts[1] of that which moves pleasure in a reader, the field is open, you may be heard: but those springs of human nature are not so easily discovered by every superficial judge. It requires philosophy as well as poetry to sound the depth of all the passions; what they are in themselves, and how they are to be provoked; and in this science the best poets have excelled. Aristotle raised the fabric of his *Poetry* from observation of those things in which Euripides, Sophocles, and Aeschylus pleased: he considered how they raised the passions, and thence has drawn rules for our imitation. From hence have sprung the tropes and figures for which they wanted a name who first practised them, and succeeded in them. Thus I grant you that the knowledge of nature was the original rule; and that all poets ought to study her, as well as Aristotle and Horace, her interpreters. But then this also undeniably follows, that those things which delight all ages must have been an imitation of nature; which is all I contend. Therefore is rhetoric made an art; therefore the names of so many tropes and figures were invented: because it was observed they had such and such effect upon the audience. Therefore catachreses and hyperboles have found their place amongst them; not that they were to be avoided, but to be used judiciously, and placed in poetry as heightenings and shadows are in painting, to make the figure bolder, and cause it to stand off to sight. [I, 200–201.]

JONATHAN SWIFT, *The Battle of the Books* (1704)
"Not to disparage myself," said [the spider],[2] "by the comparison with such a rascal, what art thou but a vagabond without house or home, without stock or inheritance, born to no possession of your own, but a pair of wings and a dronepipe? Your livelihood is an universal plunder upon nature; a freebooter over fields and gardens; and, for the sake of stealing, will rob a nettle as easily as a violet.

[1] springs.
[2] The spider defends the moderns, the bee represents those who follow the ancients.

Whereas I am a domestic animal, furnished with a native stock within myself. This large castle (to show my improvements in the mathematics)[3] is all built with my own hands, and the materials extracted altogether out of my own person."

"I am glad," answered the bee, "to hear you grant at least that I am come honestly by my wings and my voice; for them, it seems, I am obliged to Heaven alone for my flights and my music; and Providence would never have bestowed on me two such gifts, without designing them for the noblest ends. I visit indeed all the flowers and blossoms of the field and the garden; but whatever I collect thence enriches myself, without the least injury to their beauty, their smell, or their taste. Now, for you and your skill in architecture and other mathematics, I have little to say; in that building of yours there might, for aught I know, have been labour and method enough; but, by woeful experience for us both, 'tis too plain, the materials are naught, and I hope you will henceforth take warning, and consider duration and matter as well as method and art. You boast, indeed, of being obliged to no other creature, but of drawing and spinning out all from yourself; that is to say, if we may judge of the liquor in the vessel by what issues out, you possess a good plentiful store of dirt and poison in your breast; and, though I would by no means lessen or disparage your genuine stock of either, yet I doubt you are somewhat obliged, for an increase of both, to a little foreign assistance. Your inherent portion of dirt does not fail of acquisitions, by sweepings exhaled from below; and one insect furnishes you with a share of poison to destroy another. So that, in short, the question comes all to this: whether[4] is the nobler being of the two, that which, by a lazy contemplation of four inches round, by an overweening pride, feeding and engendering on itself, turns all into excrement and venom, producing nothing at all but flybane[5] and a cobweb; or that which, by an universal range, with long search, much study, true judgment, and distinction of things, brings home honey and wax." [p. 149–50.]

---

[3] Improvements in mathematics were often urged as evidence of the excellence of the moderns.

[4] which.   [5] poison for flies.

ALEXANDER POPE, *An Essay on Criticism* (1711)

    Be *Homer*'s works your *study* and *delight*,
125 Read them by day, and meditate by night,
    Thence form your judgment, thence your maxims bring,
    And trace the muses *upward* to their *spring*;
    Still with *it self compar'd* his *text* peruse;
    And let your *comment* be the *Mantuan muse*.[6]
130   When first young Maro[6] in his boundless mind
    A work t'outlast immortal Rome designed,
    Perhaps he seemed *above* the critic's law,
    And but from *Nature's fountains* scorn'd to draw;
    But when t'examine ev'ry part he came,
135 *Nature* and *Homer* were, he found, the *same*:
    Convinc'd, amaz'd, he checks the bold design,
    And rules as strict his labour'd work confine,
    As if the Stagyrite[7] o'erlook'd each line.
    Learn hence for ancient *rules* a just esteem;
140 To copy *Nature* is to copy *them*.

ALEXANDER POPE, Preface to *Works* (1717)

All that is left us is to recommend our productions by the imitation of the ancients: and it will be found true that in every age the highest character for sense and learning has been obtained by those who have been most indebted to them. For to say truth, whatever is very good sense must have been common sense in all times; and what we call learning, is but the knowledge of the sense of our predecessors. Therefore they who say our thoughts are not our own because they resemble the ancients', may as well say our faces are not our own because they are like our fathers'; and indeed it is very unreasonable that people should expect us to be scholars, and yet be angry to find us so. [I, 7.]

THOMAS PARNELL, *An Essay on the Different Stiles of Poetry* (1713)

We are much beholden to antiquity for those excellent compositions by which writers at present form their minds; but it is not so much required of us to adhere merely to their fables, as to observe their

<hr>

[6] Virgil.   [7] Aristotle.

manner. For if we preclude our own invention, poetry will consist only in expression, or simile, or the application of old stories; and the utmost character to which a genius can arrive will depend on imitation, or a borrowing from others, which we must agree together not to call stealing, because we take only from the ancients. There have been poets amongst ourselves, such as Spenser and Milton, who have successfully ventured further. These instances may let us see that invention is not bounded by what has been done before, they may open our imaginations, and be one method of preserving us from writing without schemes. [sig. A4–A4v.]

EDWARD YOUNG, *Conjectures on Original Composition* (1749)
Yet let not assertors of classic excellence imagine that I deny the tribute it so well deserves. He that admires not ancient authors betrays a secret he would conceal, and tells the world that he does not understand them. Let us be as far from neglecting, as from copying, their admirable compositions: sacred be their rights, and inviolable their fame. Let our understandings feed on theirs; they afford the noblest nourishment: but let them nourish, not annihilate, our own. When we read, let our imagination kindle at their charms; when we write, let our judgment shut them out of our thoughts; treat even Homer himself as his royal admirer[8] was treated by the Cynic:[9] bid him stand aside, not shade our composition from the beams of our own genius; for nothing original can rise, nothing immortal can ripen, in any other sun.

Must we then, you say, not imitate ancient authors? Imitate them, by all means; but imitate aright. He that imitates the divine *Iliad* does not imitate Homer; but he who takes the same method which Homer took for arriving at a capacity of accomplishing a work so great. Tread in his steps to the sole fountain of immortality; drink where he drank, at the true Helicon, that is, at the breast of Nature. Imitate; but imitate not the composition, but the man. For may not this paradox pass into a maxim? *viz.* "The less we copy the renowned ancients, we shall resemble them the more." [pp. 19–21.]

[8] Alexander the Great.
[9] Diogenes, whose remark to Alexander follows.

JOSEPH WARTON, *An Essay on the Writings and Genius of Pope*
(1756)

I should be sensibly touched at the injurious imputation of so ungenerous, and indeed impotent a design, as that of attempting to diminish, or sully the reputation of so valuable a writer as Pope, by the most distant hint or accusation of his being a plagiary; a writer to whom the English poesy, and the English language, is everlastingly indebted. But we may say of his imitations, what his poetical father Dryden said of another,[10] who deserved not such a panegyric so justly as our author: "He invades authors like a monarch, and what would be theft in other poets, is only victory in him."[11] For indeed he never works on the same subject with another without heightening the piece with more masterly strokes, and a more artful pencil. And, as was observed of Augustus, what he finds merely coarse brick, he leaves magnificent marble.[12] Those who flattered themselves that they should diminish the reputation of Boileau by printing, in the manner of a commentary at the bottom of each page of his works, the many lines he has borrowed from Horace and Juvenal,[13] were grossly deceived. The verses of the ancients, which this poet has turned into French with so much address, and which he has happily made so homogeneous, and of a piece with the rest of the work, that everything seems to have been conceived in a continuous train of thought by the very same person, confer as much honour on M. Despréaux[14] as the verses which are purely his own. The original turn which he gives to his translations, the boldness of his expressions, so little forced and unnatural that they seem to be born, as it were, with his thoughts,

[10] Ben Jonson.

[11] *An Essay of Dramatic Poesy*, I, 69.

[12] Suetonius, *Augustus*, xxix. This was to be applied by Johnson to Dryden. "What was said of Rome, adorned by Augustus, may be applied by an easy metaphor to English poetry embellished by Dryden, 'lateritiam invenit, marmorem reliquit', he found it brick, and he left it marble" ("Life of Dryden", I, 469).

[13] *Œuvres*. Amsterdam, 1701. The notes were not intended to diminish the reputation of Boileau, but were so interpreted by his enemies, especially by the critic of the *Journal de Trévoux* (1704).

[14] i.e. Boileau.

display almost as much invention as the first production of a thought entirely new. This induced La Bruyère to say,[15] "que Despréaux paraissait créer les pensées d'autrui". Both he and Pope might have answered to their accusers, in the words with which Virgil is said to have replied to those who accused him of borrowing all that was valuable in his *Aeneid* from Homer: "Cur non illi quoque eadem furta tentarent? Verum intellecturos, facilius esse Herculi clavum, quam Homero versum surripere."[16] [I, 97–9.]

SAMUEL JOHNSON, *Rasselas* (1759)
I was desirous to add my name to this illustrious fraternity. I read all the poets of Persia and Arabia, and was able to repeat by memory the volumes that are suspended in the mosque of Mecca. But I soon found that no man was ever great by imitation. My desire of excellence impelled me to transfer my attention to nature and to life. Nature was to be my subject, and men to be my auditors: I could never describe what I had not seen; I could not hope to move those with delight or terror, whose interests and opinions I did not understand. [p. 61.]

SIR JOSHUA REYNOLDS, Discourse I (1769)
The principal advantage of an Academy is that, besides furnishing able men to direct the student, it will be a repository for the great examples of the art. These are the materials on which genius is to work, and without which the strongest intellect may be fruitlessly or deviously employed. By studying these authentic models, that idea of excellence which is the result of the accumulated experience of past ages may be at once acquired; and the tardy and obstructed progress of our predecessors may teach us a shorter and easier way. The student receives, at one glance, the principles which many artists have spent their whole lives in ascertaining; and, satisfied with their effect, is spared the painful investigation by which they

[15] "[Boileau] passe Juvénal, atteint Horace, semble créer les pensées d'autrui et se rendre propre tout ce qu'il manie." *Discours à l'Académie* (1693).
[16] Reported by Aelius Donatus (4th c. A.D.) in his *Life* of Virgil. ("Why did they not try to steal as I did? Because they saw it was easier to snatch a beam from Hercules than a verse from Homer.")

came to be known and fixed. How many men of great natural abilities have been lost to this nation for want of these advantages! They never had an opportunity of seeing those masterly efforts of genius, which at once kindle the whole soul, and force it into sudden and irresistible approbation.

Raffaelle, it is true, had not the advantage of studying in an Academy; but all Rome, and the works of Michel Angelo in parti-cular, were to him an Academy. On the sight of the Capella Sistina, he immediately, from a dry, Gothic,[17] and even insipid manner, which attends to the minute accidental discriminations of particular and individual objects, assumed that grand style of painting which improves partial representation by the general and invariable ideas of nature. [pp. 15–16.]

SIR JOSHUA REYNOLDS, Discourse 2 (1769)
On whom, then, can [the student] rely, or who shall show him the path that leads to excellence? The answer is obvious: those great masters who have travelled the same road with success are the most likely to conduct others. The works of those who have stood the test of ages have a claim to that respect and veneration to which no modern can pretend. The duration and stability of their fame is sufficient to evince that it has not been suspended upon the slender thread of fashion and caprice, but bound to the human heart by every tie of sympathetic approbation. [p. 28.]

SIR JOSHUA REYNOLDS, Discourse 6 (1774)
It is vain for painters or poets to endeavour to invent without materials on which the mind may work, and from which invention must originate. Nothing can come from nothing.

Homer is supposed to be possessed of all the learning of his time; and we are certain that Michel Angelo and Raffaelle were equally possessed of all the knowledge in the art which had been discovered in the works of their predecessors.

A man enriched by an assemblage of all the treasures of ancient and modern art will be more elevated and fruitful in resources, in proportion to the number of ideas which have been carefully collected and thoroughly digested. There can be no doubt but that

[17] rude, uncivilised.

he who has the most materials has the greatest means of invention; and if he has not the power of using them, it must proceed from a feebleness of intellect; or from the confused manner in which those collections have been laid up in his mind.

The addition of other men's judgment is so far from weakening our own, as is the opinion of many, that it will fashion and consolidate those ideas of excellence which lay in embryo, feeble, ill-shaped, and confused, but which are finished and put in order by the authority and practice of those whose works may be said to have been consecrated by having stood the test of ages. . . .

The great use of studying our predecessors is to open the mind, to shorten our labour, and to give us the result of the selection made by those great minds of what is grand or beautiful in nature: her rich stores are all spread out before us; but it is an art, and no easy art, to know how or what to choose, and how to attain and secure the object of our choice. Thus the highest beauty of form must be taken from nature; but it is an art of long deduction and great experience to know how to find it. We must not content ourselves with merely admiring and relishing; we must enter into the principles on which the work is wrought: these do not swim on the superficies, and consequently are not open to superficial observers. [pp. 99–100, 101.]

The Ancients—the Moderns

In the arts the ancients are superior to the moderns, but it is an open question whether in the sciences the moderns owe more to the ancients or to their own powers.

JOHN DRYDEN, *An Essay of Dramatic Poesy* (1668)
I have observed in your speech[1] that the former part of it is convincing as to what the moderns have profited by the rules of the ancients; but in the latter you are careful to conceal how much

[1] Eugenius is answering Crites.

they have excelled them. We own all the helps we have from them, and want neither veneration nor gratitude while we acknowledge that to overcome them we must make use of the advantages we have received from them: but to these assistances we have joined our own industry; for (had we sat down with a dull imitation of them) we might then have lost somewhat of the old perfection, but never acquired any that was new. We draw not therefore after their lines, but those of nature; and having the life before us, besides the experience of all they knew, it is no wonder if we hit some airs and features which they have missed. I deny not what you urge of arts and sciences, that they have flourished in some ages more than others; but your instance in philosophy[2] makes for me: for if natural causes be more known now than in the time of Aristotle, because more studied, it follows that poesy and other arts may, with the same pains, arrive still nearer to perfection; and, that granted, it will rest for you to prove that they wrought more perfect images of human life than we; which, seeing in your discourse you have avoided to make good, it shall now be my task to show you some part of their defects, and some few excellencies of the moderns. [I, 32.]

SIR WILLIAM TEMPLE, An Essay upon the Ancient and Modern Learning (1690)
I have long thought that the different abilities of men which we call wisdom or prudence for the conduct of public affairs or private life, grow directly out of that little grain of intellect or good sense which they bring with them into the world; and that the defect of it in men comes from some want in their conception or birth.

> Dixitque semel nascentibus auctor,
> Quicquid scire licet.[3]

And though this may be improved or impaired in some degree by accidents of education, of study, and of conversation and business, yet it cannot go beyond the reach of its native force, no more than life can beyond the period to which it was destined by the strength or weakness of the seminal virtue.

If these speculations should be true, then I know not what

[2] science.

[3] Lucan, *Pharsalia*, ix. 575. ("for the Creator told us once for all at our birth whatever we are permitted to know."),

advantages we can pretend to modern knowledge by any we receive from the ancients; nay, 'tis possible men may lose rather than gain by them; may lessen the force and growth of their own genius by constraining and forming it upon that of others; may have less knowledge of their own, for contenting themselves with that of those before them. So a man that only translates shall never be a poet, nor a painter that only copies, nor a swimmer that swims always with bladders. So people that trust wholly to others' charity, and without industry of their own, will be always poor. Besides who can tell whether learning may not even weaken invention in a man that has great advantages from nature and birth; whether the weight and number of so many other men's thoughts and notions may not suppress his own, or hinder the motion and agitation of them, from which all invention arises, as heaping on wood, or too many sticks, or too close together, suppresses, and sometimes quite extinguishes, a little spark that would otherwise have grown up to a noble flame. The strength of mind, as well as of body, grows more from the warmth of exercise than of clothes; nay, too much of this foreign heat rather makes men faint, and their constitutions tender or weaker than they would be without them. Let it come about how it will, if we are dwarfs, we are still so though we stand upon a giant's shoulders; and even so placed, yet we see less than he, if we are naturally shorter-sighted, or if we do not look as much about us, or if we are dazzled with the height, which often happens from weakness either of heart or brain. . . .

But the consideration of poetry ought to be a subject by itself. For the books we have in prose, do any of the modern we converse with appear of such a spirit and force, as if they would live longer than the ancient have done? If our wit and eloquence, our knowledge or inventions, would deserve it, yet our languages would not; there is no hope of their lasting long, nor of anything in them; they change every hundred years so as to be hardly known for the same, or anything of the former styles to be endured by the later; so as[4] they can no more last like the ancients, than excellent carvings in wood like those in marble or brass.[5] [pp. 50–51, 63.]

[4] so that.

[5] Temple's essay drew attention to the ancients and moderns controversy then raging in France after the publication of Charles Perrault's *Le Siècle de*

WILLIAM WOTTON, *Reflections upon Ancient and Modern Learning* (1694)

It will, however, be some satisfaction to those who are concerned for the glory of the age in which they live, if, in the first place, it can be proved that as there are some parts of real and useful knowledge, wherein not only great strictness of reasoning, but force and extent of thought is required thoroughly to comprehend what is already invented, much more to make any considerable improvements, so that there can be no dispute of the strength of such men's understandings, who are able to make such improvements; so in those very things, such, and so great discoveries have been made, as will oblige impartial judges to acknowledge that there is no probability that the world decays in vigour and strength, if (according to Sir William Temple's hypothesis) we take our estimate from the measure of those men's parts, who have made these advancements in these later years; especially, if it should be found that the ancients took a great deal of pains upon these very subjects, and had able masters to instruct them at their first setting out. And secondly, if it should be proved that there are other curious and useful parts of knowledge, wherein the ancients had equal opportunities of advancing and pursuing their enquiries, with as much facility as the moderns, which were either slightly passed over, or wholly neglected, if we set the labours of some few men aside. And lastly, if it should be proved that by some great and happy inventions, wholly unknown to former ages, new and spacious fields of knowledge

Louis le Grand (1687) and of the first dialogue of his *Parallèle des Anciens et des Modernes* (1688), in which he asserted the superiority of the moderns. In his *Digression sur les Anciens et les Modernes* (1688) Fontenelle also claimed that the moderns surpassed the ancients not only in learning but in the arts. La Fontaine (*Epître à Huet*, 1687), La Bruyère (*Caractères*, Discours sur Théophraste, 1688) and Boileau (*Réflexions sur Longin*, 1692–4) defended the ancients. Boileau's *Lettre à Perrault* (1700), in which he recognised the qualities of some moderns, put an end to the controversy. Temple's essay was prompted by Fontenelle's *Digression*, which led him to examine "how far either reason or experience can be allowed to plead or determine" in favour of the moderns. The case for the moderns was stated in *Reflections upon Ancient and Modern Learning*, 1694, by William Wotton (see next extract), who yet admitted that in the arts the ancients had outdone the moderns.

have been discovered, and, pursuant to those discoveries, have been viewed, and searched into, with all the care and exactness which such noble theories required. If these three things should be done, both questions would be at once resolved, and Sir William Temple would see that the moderns had done something more than copy from their teachers, and that there is no absolute necessity of making all those melancholy reflections upon the "sufficiency and ignorance of the present age", which he, moved with a just resentment and indignation, has thought fit to bestow upon them. . . .

Yet though due allowance ought to be made for these prepossessions, one has reason to believe that this reverence for the ancient orators and poets is more than prejudice. (By orators, I understand all those writers in prose who took pains to beautify and adorn their style.) Their works give us a very solid pleasure when we read them. The best in their kind among the moderns have been those who have read the ancients with greatest care, and endeavoured to imitate them with the greatest accuracy. The masters of writing in all these several ways, to this day, appeal to the ancients as their guides; and still fetch rules from them for the art of writing. Homer, and Aristotle, and Virgil, and Horace, and Ovid, and Terence, are now studied as teachers, not barely out of curiosity, by modern poets. So likewise are Demosthenes, Aristotle, Tully, Quintilian, and Longinus, by those who would write finely in prose. So that there is reason to think that in these arts the ancients may have outdone the moderns; though neither have they been neglected in these later ages, in which we have seen extraordinary productions, which the ancients themselves, had they been alive, would not have been ashamed of. . . .

Sir William Temple will certainly agree with me in this conclusion, that former ages made greater orators, and nobler poets, than these later ages have done; though perhaps he may disagree with me about the way by which I came to my conclusion; since hence it will follow, that the present age, with the same advantages, under the same circumstances,[6] might produce a Demosthenes, a

[6] The supporters of the moderns contended that the flowering of genius among the ancients was largely due to the favourable circumstances in which they had worked.

Cicero, a Horace, or a Virgil; which, for anything hitherto said to the contrary, seems to be very probable. . . .

This seems to me to be the present state of learning, as it may be compared with what it was in former ages. Whether knowledge will improve in the next age, proportionably, as it has done in this, is a question not easily decided. It depends upon a great many circumstances, which singly will be ineffectual, and which no man can now be assured will ever meet. There seems reason, indeed, to fear that it may decay, both because ancient learning is too much studied in modern books, and taken upon trust by modern writers, who are not enough acquainted with antiquity to correct their own mistakes; and because natural and mathematical knowledge, wherein chiefly the moderns are to be studied as originals, begin to be neglected by the generality of those who should set up for scholars. For the humour of the age, as to those things, is visibly altered from what it was twenty or thirty years ago. So that though the Royal Society has weathered the rude attacks of such sort of adversaries as Stubbe,[7] who endeavoured to have it thought that studying of natural philosophy and mathematics was a ready method to introduce scepticism at least, if not atheism, into the world: yet the sly insinuations of the men of wit, that no great things have ever, or are ever like to be, performed by the men of Gresham,[8] and that every man whom they call a virtuoso, must needs be a Sir Nicholas Gim-crack,[9] have so far taken off the edge of those who have opulent fortunes, and a love of learning, that physiological studies begin to be contracted amongst physicians and mechanics. The truth is, one must spend a good deal of time and pains, of industry and attention, before he will be able thoroughly to relish them; and those who do not, rarely know their worth, and consequently do very seldom pass a right judgment upon them. [pp. 9–10, 23–4, 39, 356–7.]

[7] Henry Stubbe (1632–76) wrote several pamphlets against the Royal Society, arguing that it was destructive of religion.

[8] i.e. the members of the Royal Society and more generally the natural philosophers or scientists (from the association of the Royal Society with Gresham College).

[9] The virtuoso ridiculed in Shadwell's play *The Virtuoso* (1676).

JOHN DENNIS, *The Advancement and Reformation of Modern Poetry*
(1701)

Your Lordship knows very well that some French critics, as for instance Boileau, discerning the actual pre-eminence of the ancients, have fondly believed that they were superior to us by nature; and that others, as Perrault, very justly disdaining to own such a natural superiority, have very unjustly denied their actual pre-eminence.[10] The first part of the following treatise was intended to shew that the ancient poets had that actual pre-eminence, but that they derived it from joining their religion with their poetry; upon which, I believe, they were thrown at first by chance. The design of the second part is to shew that the moderns, by incorporating poetry with the religion revealed to us in Sacred Writ, may come to equal the ancients. But two things must always be supposed: the one, that the poets have force and skill equal to the subjects they treat of, and a sacred subject requires ten times more of both than a profane one; the other is, that this is not to be extended to those sorts of poetry in which the moderns cannot possibly make use of their religion with the same advantage that the Grecians and Romans employed theirs, as epic, pastoral, and amorous poetry. . . .

For some of the moderns who have been great admirers of their contemporaries, which is a modest expression for themselves, will by no means allow that the ancients have excelled us. From which opinion, presumption has followed, and from presumption security, and from security idleness.

But despair, on the other side, has done a great deal more harm than presumption has done on that. For some who have been of opinion that the ancients have surpassed us, have believed that they have done so because they were in themselves superior to us; from which it has happened that they have been servilely contented with following their old masters, and most of the best of the modern poetry has been but a copy of the ancient.

These different opinions have occasioned disputes, and these disputes have produced quarrels, which have been maintained with a great deal of heat on both sides. The favourers of the moderns have treated their adversaries as dejected little-souled persons, who have a

[10] See n. 5 to extract from Temple's "Essay upon the Ancient and Modern Learning", pp. 86–7 above.

base opinion of themselves and of human nature, which last they have much ado to forgive them, because they are included in the censure.

For how can it be, say they, but a scandalous despondence that obliges us to prefer other men to ourselves, when reason gives us the preference? For this, they say, is past all dispute, that they who excel others in the same kinds of writing, must have some advantages over them. And that advantage must be either from without, or from within, or from the subjects they treat of. Now we can make it appear, say the favourers of the moderns, that the ancient poets had no external or internal advantage over us; and that the advantage of the subject is rather on our side. And this is what the favourers of the moderns allege for themselves. The partisans of the ancients have, on the other side, treated the favourers of the moderns as persons that are absolutely ignorant and without taste.

That the ancients have excelled us in the greatness of poetry, they pretend to prove from the authority of all who have universally been acknowledged to be the best judges. For, say they, the consent of these, where the question is concerning a thing that is rather to be felt than to be demonstrated, is of the last importance. We defy, say they, any of the favourers of the moderns to name so much as one modern critic who has any reputation in the world, who does not acknowledge that the ancients surpass us in the greatness of poetry. For the few, say they, who have asserted the pre-eminence of the moderns, have immediately rendered themselves ridiculous to all men who have any understanding in these affairs, and at length to all the rest, excepting a little handful of men, whose arrogance and obstinacy, and extravagant vanity, has been a comedy to the rest.

So that the consent of the best critics, continue they, implies the consent of all, and the consent of mankind for so many several ages, concerning a thing that is rather to be felt than to be demonstrated, is, if not a convincing proof, at least a very strong presumption. But what has been the event of this dispute on both sides? Why, the probability of the arguments, instead of working conviction, has only exasperated the spirits of the parties; and the favourers of the moderns have treated the lovers of the ancients as so many slavish pedants; and these, on the other side, the favourers of the moderns, as so many ignorant fools.

Amidst this diversity of opinions, and these contentious ferments, I thought I should do an important service to a most noble art, if I could contribute anything to the reconciling the common friends to poetry, that they might endeavour the advancement of the common cause with greater force united.

In order, then, to the calming the fury of the contending parties, I shall endeavour to extort important concessions from both, and oblige, on the one side, the favourers of the moderns to acknowledge that the ancients are not so weak as to make the moderns presume; and engage, at the same time, the partisans of the ancients to own that the ancients are not in themselves so strong as to make the moderns despair. [I, 206–7, 208–9.]

EDWARD YOUNG, *Conjectures on Original Composition* (1749)
Quite clear of the dispute concerning ancient and modern learning, we speak not of performance, but powers. The modern powers are equal to those before them; modern performance in general is deplorably short. How great are the names just mentioned![11] Yet who will dare affirm that as great may not rise up in some future, or even in the present age? Reasons there are why talents may not *appear*, none why they may not *exist*, as much in one period as another. An evocation of vegetable fruits depends on rain, air and sun; an evocation of the fruits of genius no less depends on externals. What a marvellous crop bore it in Greece and Rome! And what a marvellous sunshine did it there enjoy! What encouragement from the nature of their governments, and the spirit of their people! Virgil and Horace owed their divine talents to Heaven; their immortal works, to men; thank Maecenas and Augustus for them. Had it not been for these, the genius of those poets had lain buried in their ashes. [pp. 46–7.]

[11] Herodotus, Thucydides, Demosthenes, Livy, and Cicero.

The Rules

The rules of poetry have been deduced from the practice of the ancients, whose works have stood the test of time. They teach the poet how best to attain his end. Yet genius may sometimes dispense with rules to achieve greater beauties, and it is a mistake for critics to lay down too many rules, some of which have no foundation in nature.

THOMAS RYMER, Preface to the Translation of Rapin, *Reflections on Aristotle's Treatise of Poesie* (1674)

It is indeed suspected that [Aristotle] dealt not always fairly with the philosophers, misreciting sometimes, and misinterpreting their opinions. But I find him not taxed of that injustice to the poets, in whose favour he is so ingenious, that, to the disadvantage of his own profession, he declares that tragedy more conduces to the instruction of mankind than even philosophy itself.[1] And however cried down in the schools and vilified by some modern philosophers, since men have had a taste for good sense, and could discern the beauties of correct writing, he is preferred in the politest courts of Europe, and by the poets held in great veneration. Not that these can servilely yield to his authority, who, of all men living, affect liberty. The truth is, what Aristotle writes on this subject are not the dictates of his own magisterial will, or dry deductions of his metaphysics; but the poets were his masters, and what was their practice he reduced to principles. Nor would the modern poets blindly resign to this practice of the ancients, were not the reasons convincing and clear

[1] Aristotle only said that "poetry is something more philosophic and of graver import than history, since its statements are of the nature rather of universals, whereas those of history are singulars" (*Poetics*, ix). Renaissance commentators, and Sidney after them, interpreting the *Poetics* in the light of Horace's *Ars Poetica*, usually stated that poetry instructs better than philosophy since it not only shows men what is good but moves them to right action.

as any demonstration in mathematics. 'Tis only needful that we understand them, for our consent to the truth of them.[2] [pp. 2–3.]

JOHN DRYDEN, The Grounds of Criticism in Tragedy. Prefixed to *Troilus and Cressida* (1679)

Because many men are shocked at the name of rules, as if they were a kind of magisterial prescription upon poets, I will conclude with the words of Rapin, in his reflections on Aristotle's work of poetry: "If the rules be well considered, we shall find them to be made only to reduce nature into method, to trace her step by step, and not to suffer the least mark of her to escape us: 'tis only by these that probability in fiction is maintained, which is the soul of poetry. They are founded upon good sense, and sound reason, rather than on authority; for though Aristotle and Horace are produced, yet no man must argue that what they write is true because they writ it; but 'tis evident, by the ridiculous mistakes and gross absurdities which have been made by those poets who have taken their fancy only for their guide, that if this fancy be not regulated, 'tis a mere caprice, and utterly incapable to produce a reasonable and judicious poem."[3] [I, 260–1.]

SIR WILLIAM TEMPLE, Of Poetry (1690)

I do not here intend to make a further critique upon poetry, which were too great a labour; nor to give rules for it, which were as great a presumption; besides, there has been so much paper blotted upon these subjects, in this curious and censuring age, that 'tis all grown tedious or repetition. The modern French wits (or pretenders) have been very severe in their censures and exact in their rules, I think to very little purpose; for I know not why they might not have contented themselves with those given by Aristotle and

[2] The view that the rules were consonant with nature and reason was held by all French neo-classicists; Rapin stated that "these rules well considered, one shall find them made only to reduce Nature into method" (*Reflections on Aristotle's Treatise of Poesie*, I. xii). This became a commonplace in English criticism; see the extracts from Dryden and Pope, below; cf. also Dennis: "The rules of Aristotle are nothing but nature and good sense reduced to a method" (*The Impartial Critic, ed. cit.*, I, 39).

[3] From Rymer's translation of Rapin's *Réflexions* (I. xii) with slight verbal changes.

Horace, and have translated them rather than commented upon them, for all they have done has been no more; so as[4] they seem by their writings of this kind rather to have valued themselves than improved anybody else. The truth is, there is something in the genius of poetry too libertine to be confined to so many rules; and whoever goes about to subject it to such constraints loses both its spirit and grace, which are ever native, and never learned, even of the best masters. 'Tis as if, to make excellent honey, you should cut off the wings of your bees, confine them to their hive or their stands, and lay flowers before them, such as you think the sweetest, and like to yield the finest extraction; you had as good pull out their stings and make arrant drones of them. They must range through fields, as well as gardens, choose such flowers as they please, and by properties and scents they only know and distinguish: they must work up their cells with admirable art, extract their honey with infinite labour, and sever it from the wax with such distinction and choice as belongs to none but themselves to perform or to judge.[5]

It would be too much mortification to these great arbitrary rulers among the French writers, or our own, to observe the worthy productions that have been formed by their rules, the honour they have received in the world, or the pleasure they have given mankind; but to comfort them, I do not know there was any great poet in Greece, after the rules of that art laid down by Aristotle; nor in Rome, after those by Horace, which yet none of our moderns pretend to have outdone. . . . After all, the utmost that can be achieved, or I think pretended, by any rules in this art, is but to hinder some men from being very ill poets, but not to make any man a very good one.[6] [pp. 181-3.]

JOHN DENNIS, *Remarks on Prince Arthur* (1696)
The manners indeed are to be constant, not because Aristotle has

[4] so that.

[5] See the argument of the bee in Swift's *Battle of the Books* (extract pp. 77-8.)

[6] For other criticism of the rules see the extracts from Farquhar and from Welsted, pp. 96-7, 101-3 below. For the distinction between mechanic rules and fundamental laws, see Johnson's *Rambler* essay, pp. 103-5 below. For "grace beyond the reach of art", see Pope and Addison, pp. 100-1, 97-9 below.

said it, for to affirm that would be absurd, but because Nature will have it so. For the rules of Aristotle, as we have said above, are but directions for the observation of Nature, as the best of the written laws are but the pure dictates of reason and repetitions of the laws of Nature. For either this must be granted, or Aristotle must be confessed to have contradicted the design which he had in prescribing those rules; which design was to teach men to please more than they could do without these rules, it being undeniable that the writer who follows Nature closest, is certain to please most. For poetry is nothing but an imitation of Nature, which Aristotle, who knew her well, has very well taught us to imitate. And he who keeps up strictly to his rules is as certain to succeed as he who lives up exactly to reason is certain of being happy. But it is as impossible for any man who has not a great genius, strictly to observe the rules, as it is for anyone who has not supernatural assistance to live up to the dictates of reason. [I, 96.]

GEORGE FARQUHAR, *A Discourse upon Comedy* (1702)
We must consider then, in the first place, that our business lies not with a French or a Spanish audience; that our design is not to hold forth to ancient Greece, nor to moralize upon the vices and defaults of the Roman commonwealth. No, no. An English play is intended for the use and instruction of an English audience, a people not only separated from the rest of the world by situation, but different also from other nations as well in the complexion and temperament of the natural body, as in the constitution of our body politic. As we are a mixture of many nations, so we have the most unaccountable medley of humours among us of any people upon earth; these humours produce variety of follies, some of them unknown to former ages; these new distempers must have new remedies, which are nothing but new counsels and instructions.[7]

Now, sir, if our *utile*, which is the end, be different from the ancients', pray let our *dulce*, which is the means, be so too; for you know that to different towns there are different ways; or if you would have it more scholastically, *ad diversos fines non idem conducit*

---

[7] Farquhar's contention is that the rules were inferred from works intended for a different public, and that the way to please is not the same in all ages and places.

medium;[8] or mathematically, one and the same line cannot terminate in two centres. But waving this manner of concluding by induction, I shall gain my point a nearer way, and draw it immediately from the first principle I set down: *That we have the most unaccountable medley of humours among us of any nation upon earth.* And this is demonstrable from common experience: we shall find a Wildair[9] in one corner, and a Morose[10] in another; nay, the space of an hour or two shall create such vicissitudes of temper in the same person that he can hardly be taken for the same man. We shall have a fellow bestir his stumps from chocolate to coffee-house with all the joy and gaiety imaginable, though he want a shilling to pay for a hack;[11] whilst another, drawn about in a coach and six, is eaten up with the spleen, and shall loll in state, with as much melancholy, vexation, and discontent, as if he were making the tour of Tyburn.[12] Then what sort of a *dulce*, (which I take for the pleasantry of the tale, or the plot of the play) must a man make use of to engage the attention of so many different humours and inclinations: will a single plot satisfy everybody? Will the turns and surprises that may result naturally from the ancient limits of time be sufficient to rip open the spleen of some, and physic the melancholy of others, screw up the attention of a rover and fix him to the stage, in spite of his volatile temper, and the temptation of a mask?[13] To make the moral instructive, you must make the story diverting; the splenetic wit, the beau courtier, the heavy citizen, the fine lady, and her fine footman, come all to be instructed, and therefore must all be diverted; and he that can do this best, and with most applause, writes the best comedy, let him do it by what rules he pleases, so they be not offensive to religion and good manners. [pp. 72–3.]

JOSEPH ADDISON, *The Spectator*, no. 592 (10 September 1714)
I have a great esteem for a true critic, such as Aristotle and Longinus among the Greeks, Horace and Quintilian among the Romans,

[8] "different ends require different means".

[9] A character in Farquhar's *Constant Couple* (1699) and in *Sir Harry Wildair* (1701).

[10] A character in Ben Jonson's *Epicœne* (1609).   [11] hackney coach.

[12] *viz.* the trip to Tyburn, where criminals were hanged.

[13] a lady masked.

D

Boileau and Dacier among the French. But it is our misfortune, that some who set up for professed critics among us are so stupid, that they do not know how to put ten words together with elegance or common propriety, and withal so illiterate, that they have no taste of the learned languages, and therefore criticize upon old authors only at second-hand. They judge of them by what others have written, and not by any notions they have of the authors themselves. The words unity, action, sentiment, and diction, pronounced with an air of authority, give them a figure among unlearned readers, who are apt to believe they are very deep, because they are unintelligible. The ancient critics are full of the praises of their contemporaries; they discover beauties which escaped the observation of the vulgar, and very often find out reasons for palliating and excusing such little slips and oversights as were committed in the writings of eminent authors. On the contrary, most of the smatterers in criticism who appear among us make it their business to vilify and depreciate every new production that gains applause, to descry imaginary blemishes, and to prove by far-fetched arguments that what pass for beauties in any celebrated piece are faults and errors. In short, the writings of these critics compared with those of the ancients are like the works of the sophists compared with those of the old philosophers.

Envy and cavil are the natural fruits of laziness and ignorance; which was probably the reason that in the heathen mythology Momus[14] is said to be the son of Nox and Somnus, of darkness and sleep. Idle men, who have not been at the pains to accomplish or distinguish themselves, are very apt to detract from others; as ignorant men are very subject to decry those beauties in a celebrated work which they have not eyes to discover. Many of our sons of Momus, who dignify themselves by the name of critics, are the genuine descendants of these two illustrious ancestors. They are often led into those numerous absurdities, in which they daily instruct the people, by not considering that, *first*, there is sometimes a greater judgment shewn in deviating from the rules of art, than in adhering to them; and *secondly*, that there is more beauty in the works of a great genius who is ignorant of all the rules of art, than in the works of a little genius[14] who not only knows, but scrupulously observes them.

[14] In Greek mythology the personification of criticism and fault-finding.

First, we may often take notice of men who are perfectly acquainted with all the rules of good writing, and notwithstanding choose to depart from them on extraordinary occasions. I could give instances out of all the tragic writers of antiquity who have shewn their judgment in this particular, and purposely receded from an established rule of the drama, when it has made way for a much higher beauty than the observation of such a rule would have been. Those who have surveyed the noblest pieces of architecture and statuary both ancient and modern, know very well that there are frequent deviations from art in the works of the greatest masters, which have produced a much nobler effect than a more accurate and exact way of proceeding could have done. This often arises from what the Italians call the *gusto grande* in these arts, which is what we call the sublime in writing.

In the next place, our critics do not seem sensible that there is more beauty in the works of a great genius who is ignorant of the rules of art, than in those of a little genius who knows and observes them. It is of these men of genius that Terence speaks in opposition to the little artificial cavillers of his time:

> Quorum æmulari exoptat negligentiam
> Potius, quam istorum obscuram diligentiam.[15]

A critic may have the same consolation in the ill success of his play, as Dr. South tells us a physician has at the death of a patient, that he was killed *secundum artem*.[16] Our inimitable Shakespeare is a stumbling-block to the whole tribe of these rigid critics. Who would not rather read one of his plays, where there is not a single rule of the stage observed, than any production of a modern critic, where there is not one of them violated? Shakespeare was indeed born with all the seeds of poetry, and may be compared to the stone in Pyrrhus's ring, which, as Pliny tells us,[17] had the figure of Apollo and the nine muses in the veins of it, produced by the spontaneous hand of Nature, without any help from art. [V, 26–8.]

[15] *Andria*, Prologue, 20–21. ("whose freedom he prefers to imitate rather than the dull correctness of his critics.")

[16] Robert South (1634–1716) in "A Sermon preached at Westminster Abbey", 1685 (*Twelve Sermons*, 6th ed., 1727, I, 316).

[17] *Natural History*, xxxvii. 3.

ALEXANDER POPE, *An Essay on Criticism* (1711)

Those RULES of old *discover'd*, not *devis'd*,
Are *Nature* still, but *Nature methodiz'd*;
90 *Nature*, like *Liberty*, is but restrain'd
By the same laws which first *herself* ordain'd. . . .

Some beauties yet, no precepts can declare,
For there's a *happiness* as well as *care*.
Music resembles *poetry*, in each
Are *nameless graces*, which no methods teach,
145 And which a *master-hand* alone can reach.
If, where the *rules* not far enough extend,
(Since rules were made but to promote their end)
Some lucky licence answers to the full
Th' intent propos'd, *that licence* is a *rule*.
150 Thus *Pegasus*, a nearer way to take,
May boldly deviate from the common track.
Great wits sometimes may *gloriously offend*,
And *rise* to *faults* true critics *dare not mend*;
From *vulgar bounds* with *brave disorder* part,
155 And *snatch a grace* beyond the reach of art,
Which, without passing thro' the *judgment*, gains
The *heart*, and all its end *at once* attains. . . .[18]

I know there are, to whose presumptuous thoughts
170 Those *freer beauties*, ev'n in *them*,[19] seem faults:
Some figures *monstrous* and *mis-shap'd* appear,
Consider'd *singly*, or beheld too *near*,
Which, but *proportion'd* to their *light*, or *place*,
Due distance *reconciles* to form and grace.
175 A prudent chief not always must display
His pow'rs in *equal ranks*, and *fair array*,
But with th' *occasion* and the *place* comply,

[18] A traditional notion in Renaissance criticism. Cf. Boileau:

Quelquefois, dans sa course, un esprit vigoureux
Trop resserré dans l'art, sort des règles prescrites,
Et de l'art même apprend à franchir leurs limites.
(*Art Poétique*, IV, 78–80)

[19] *viz.* great wits.

Conceal his force, nay seem sometimes to *fly*.
Those oft are *stratagems* which *errors* seem,
180 Nor is it *Homer nods*, but *we* that *dream*. . . .

A perfect judge will *read* each work of wit
With the same spirit that its author *writ*,
235 Survey the *whole*, nor seek slight faults to find,
Where *Nature moves*, and *rapture warms* the mind;
Nor lose, for that malignant dull delight,
The *gen'rous pleasure* to be charm'd with wit.
But in such lays as neither *ebb*, nor *flow*,
240 *Correctly cold*, and *regularly low*,
That shunning faults, one quiet *tenor* keep;
We cannot *blame* indeed—but we may *sleep*. . . .

Whoever thinks a faultless piece to see,
Thinks what ne'er was, nor is, nor e'er'shall be.
255 In ev'ry work regard the *writer's end*,
Since none can compass more than they *intend*;
And if the *means* be just, the *conduct* true,
Applause, in spite of trivial faults, is due.
As men of breeding, sometimes men of wit,
260 T'avoid *great errors*, must the *less* commit,
Neglect the rules each *verbal critic* lays,
For *not* to know some trifles, is a praise.
Most critics, fond of some subservient art,
Still make the *whole* depend upon a *part*,
265 They talk of *principles*, but *notions* prize,[20]
And all to one lov'd folly sacrifice.

LEONARD WELSTED, A Dissertation Concerning the Perfection of
the English Language, the State of Poetry, etc. (1724)
All that the ancients, or the moderns copying after them, have
written on this scheme is no more than a set of very obvious
thoughts and observations, which every man of good sense naturally knows without being taught, and which never made a good
poet, or mended a bad one; nor have they, I may venture to affirm,

[20] Cf. Johnson's distinction between rules established by custom and
principles grounded in nature, in *Rambler* essay, pp. 103–5, below.

been of any other service to mankind, than to furnish out multitudes of pretenders in poetry, that otherwise had never teased the public with their spiritless performances. Those observations or rules were primarily formed upon, and designed to serve only as comments to, the works of certain great authors who composed those works without any such help; the mighty originals, from whence they were drawn, were produced without them; and unluckily for all rules, it has commonly happened since, that those writers have succeeded the worst who have pretended to have been most assisted by them. What is here said of the rules of poetry is equally true of those of rhetoric, and some other arts. The *Art of Poetry* of Horace is, no question, a masterly piece, if one considers the style, method, and poetry of it, and yet I cannot but think, there are scattered through the odes, the satires, and epistles of that author, more elegant hints concerning poetry, and that go further into the truth of it, than are to be met with in his professed dissertation on that subject. As to the numerous treatises, essays, arts, etc., both in verse and prose, that have been written by the moderns on this groundwork, they do but hackney the same thoughts over again, making them still more trite. Most of these pieces are nothing but a pert insipid heap of commonplace; nor do any, or all of them put together, contribute in any considerable degree, if they contribute at all, towards the raising or finishing a good genius. The truth is, they touch only the externals or form of the thing, without entering into the spirit of it; they play about the surface of poetry, but never dive into its depths; the secret, the soul of good writing, is not to be come at through such mechanic laws; the main graces and the cardinal beauties of this charming art lie too retired within the bosom of Nature, and are of too fine and subtle an essence, to fall under the discussion of pedants, commentators, or trading critics, whether they be heavy prose-drudges, or more sprightly essayers in rhyme. These beauties, in a word, are rather to be felt than described; by what precepts shall a writer be taught only to think poetically, or to trace out, among the various powers of thoughts, that particular vein or feature of it which poetry loves, and to distinguish between the good sense, which may have its weight and justness in prose, and that which is of the nature of verse? What instruction shall convey to him that flame which can alone animate a work, and give it the glow of poetry? And how, or by what industry, shall be learned, among a thousand other charms, that delicate contexture in writing by which the colours, as in the rainbow, grow out of one another, and every beauty owes its lustre to a former, and gives being to a succeeding one? Could certain methods be laid down for attaining these excellencies, every one that pleased might be a poet; as every one that pleases may be a geometrician, if he will but have due patience and attention. [pp. xvi–ix.]

SAMUEL JOHNSON, *The Rambler*, no. 156 (14 September 1751)
It is necessary, therefore, to review the systems of learning, to analyse complications into principles, and disentangle knowledge from opinion. It is not always possible, without a close and diligent inspection, to separate the genuine shoots of consequential reasoning, which grow out of some radical postulate, from the branches which art has engrafted on it. The accidental prescriptions of authority, when time has procured them veneration, are often confounded with the laws of Nature, and those rules are supposed coeval with reason, of which the first rise cannot be discovered. . . .

Among the innumerable rules which the natural desire of extending authority, or the honest ardour of promoting knowledge, has from age to age prompted men of very different abilities to prescribe to writers, all which have been received and established have not the same original right to our regard. Some are indeed to be considered as fundamental and indispensable, others only as useful and convenient; some as dictated by reason and necessity, others as enacted by despotic antiquity; some as invincibly supported by their conformity to the order of Nature and the operations of the intellect, others as formed by accident, or instituted by example, and therefore always liable to dispute and alteration.

That many rules of composition have been advanced by critics without consulting Nature or reason, we cannot but suspect, when we find it peremptorily decreed by the ancient masters, that only three speaking personages should appear at once upon the stage, a law which the variety and intricacy of modern plays has made impossible to be observed, and which, therefore, we now violate without scruple, and, as experience proves, without inconvenience.

The original of this precept was merely accidental. Tragedy was a monody or solitary song in honour of Bacchus, which was afterwards improved into a dialogue by the addition of another speaker; but remembering that the tragedy was at first pronounced only by one, they durst not for some time venture beyond two; at last when custom and impunity had made them daring, they extended their liberty to the admission of three, but restrained themselves by a critical edict from further exorbitance.

By what accident the number of acts was limited to five, I know not that any author has informed us, but certainly it is not determined by any necessity arising either from the nature of action or the propriety of exhibition. An act is only the representation of such a part of the business of the play as proceeds in an unbroken tenor without any intermediate pause. Nothing is more evident than that of every real, and, by consequence, of every dramatic action, the intervals may be more or fewer than five; and indeed the rule is upon the English stage every day broken in effect, without any other mischief than that which arises from an absurd endeavour to observe it in appearance. For whenever the scene is shifted the act ceases, since some time is necessarily supposed to elapse while the personages of the drama change their place.

With no greater right to our obedience have the critics confined the dramatic action to a certain number of hours. Probability indeed requires that the time of action should approach somewhat nearly to that of exhibition, and those plays will always be thought most happily conducted which crowd the greatest variety into the least space. But since it will frequently happen that some delusion must be admitted, I know not where the limits of imagination can be fixed; nor have I ever observed that minds not already prepossessed by criticism feel any offence from the extension of the intervals between the acts; nor can I conceive it absurd or impossible that he who can multiply three hours into twelve, or twenty-four, might imagine with equal ease a greater number. . . .

There are other rules more fixed and obligatory; it is necessary that of every play the chief action should be single, because a play represents some transaction through its regular maturation to its final event,[21] and therefore two transactions equally important must evidently constitute two plays.

[21] result, consequence.

As the design of tragedy is to instruct by moving the passions, it must always have a hero or personage apparently and incontestably superior to the rest, upon whom the attention may be fixed and the expectation suspended. Of two persons opposing each other with equal abilities and equal virtue, the auditor will indeed inevitably in time choose his favourite, but as that choice must be without any cogency of conviction, the hopes or fears which it raises will be faint and languid. Of two heroes acting in confederacy against a common enemy, the virtues or dangers will give little emotion, because each claims our concern with the same right, and the heart lies at rest between equal motives.

It ought to be the first endeavour of a writer to distinguish nature from custom, or that which is established because it is right from that which is right only because it is established; that he may neither violate essential principles by a desire of novelty, nor debar himself from the attainment of any beauties within his view by a needless fear of breaking rules which no literary dictator had authority to prescribe. [pp. 930–5.]

Regularity—Variety

The aesthetic norm may be defined as uniformity amidst variety. Regularity and order please, but allowance must be made for the diversity of nature.

JOHN DRYDEN, *An Essay of Dramatic Poesy* (1668)
I[1] shall grant Lisideius, without much dispute, a great part of what he has urged against us, for I acknowledge the French contrive their plots more regularly, observe the laws of comedy, and decorum of the stage (to speak generally), with more exactness than the English. Farther, I deny not but he has taxed us justly in some irregularities of ours which he has mentioned; yet, after all, I am of opinion that

---

[1] Neander is speaking.

neither our faults nor their virtues are considerable enough to place them above us.

For the lively imitation of nature being in the definition of a play,[2] those which best fulfil that law ought to be esteemed superior to the others. 'Tis true, those beauties of the French poesy are such as will raise perfection higher where it is, but are not sufficient to give it where it is not: they are indeed the beauties of a statue, but not of a man, because not animated with the soul of poesy, which is imitation of humour and passions; and this Lisideius himself, or any other, however biassed to their party, cannot but acknowledge, if he will either compare the humours of our comedies, or the characters of our serious plays, with theirs. . . .

And this leads me to wonder why Lisideius and many others should cry up the barrenness of the French plots above the variety and copiousness of the English. Their plots are single, they carry on one design which is pushed forward by all the actors, every scene in the play contributing and moving towards it; ours, besides the main design, have underplots or by-concernments of less considerable persons and intrigues, which are carried on with the motion of the main plot; just as they say the orb of the fixed stars, and those of the planets, though they have motions of their own, are whirled about by the motion of the *primum mobile*,[3] in which they are contained. That similitude expresses much of the English state; for if contrary motions may be found in nature to agree, if a planet can go east and west at the same time, one way by virtue of his own motion, the other by the force of the First Mover, it will not be difficult to imagine how the underplot, which is only different, not contrary to the great design, may naturally be conducted along with it.

Eugenius has already shewn us, from the confession of the French poets, that the unity of action is sufficiently preserved if all the imperfect actions of the play are conducing to the main design; but when those petty intrigues of a play are so ill ordered that they have no coherence with the other, I must grant Lisideius has reason to

[2] The definition given by Lisideius at the beginning of the *Essay* (see p. 67 above).

[3] The supposed outermost sphere revolving round the earth.

tax that want of due connexion; for co-ordination in a play is as dangerous and unnatural as in a state. In the meantime he must acknowledge our variety, if well ordered, will afford a greater pleasure to the audience. . . .

There is another part of Lisideius his discourse in which he has rather excused our neighbours than commended them; that is, for aiming only to make one person considerable in their plays. 'Tis very true what he has urged, that one character in all plays, even without the poet's care, will have advantage of all the others; and that the design of the whole drama will chiefly depend on it. But this hinders not that there may be more shining characters in the play: many persons of a second magnitude, nay, some so very near, so almost equal to the first, that greatness may be opposed to greatness, and all the persons be made considerable, not only by their quality but their action. 'Tis evident that the more the persons are, the greater will be the variety of the plot. If then the parts are managed so regularly that the beauty of the whole be kept entire, and that the variety become not a perplexed and confused mass of accidents, you will find it infinitely pleasing to be led in a labyrinth of design, where you see some of your way before you, yet discern not the end till you arrive at it. And that all this is practicable, I can produce for examples many of our English plays: as *The Maid's Tragedy*,[4] *The Alchemist*,[5] *The Silent Woman*.[5] [I, 56, 58-9, 61.]

JOHN DRYDEN, To Lord Radcliffe. Prefixed to *Examen Poeticum* (1693)

As little can I grant that the French dramatic writers excel the English. Our authors as far surpass them in genius, as our soldiers excel theirs in courage. 'Tis true, in conduct they surpass us either way; yet that proceeds not so much from the greater knowledge, as from the difference of tastes in the two nations. They content themselves with a thin design, without episodes, and managed by few persons. Our audience will not be pleased but with variety of accidents, an underplot, and many actors. They follow the ancients too servilely in the mechanic rules, and we assume too much

---

4 By Fletcher.   5 By Jonson.

license to ourselves in keeping them only in view at too great a distance. But if our audience had their tastes, our poets could more easily comply with them than the French writers could come up to the sublimity of our thoughts or to the difficult variety of our designs. [II, 794.]

ALEXANDER POPE, *An Essay on Criticism* (1711)

In wit, as nature, what affects our hearts
Is not th' exactness of peculiar parts;
245 'Tis not a *lip*, or *eye*, we beauty call,
But the joint force and full *result* of all.
Thus when we view some well-proportion'd dome,
(The *world*'s just wonder, and ev'n *thine*, O Rome!)
No single parts unequally surprise;
250 All comes *united* to th' admiring eyes;
No monstrous height, or breadth, or length appear;
The *whole* at once is *bold* and *regular*.

JOHN DENNIS, *Remarks on Prince Arthur* (1696)

The more numerous the incidents are in any narration, the more that narration delights, provided they neither corrupt the unity of the action, nor the perspicuity, the brevity and simplicity of the narration. For the mind does not care for dwelling too long upon an object, but loves to pass from one thing to another; because such a transition keeps it from languishing, and gives it more agitation. Now agitation only can give it delight. For agitation not only keeps it from mortifying reflections, which it naturally has when it is not shaken, but gives it a force which it had not before, and the consciousness of its own force delights it. Besides that every artful incident gives a fresh surprise. [I, 109.]

ANTHONY ASHLEY COOPER, THIRD EARL OF SHAFTESBURY,
The Judgment of Hercules (1713)

In short, we are to carry this remembrance still along with us, that the fewer the objects are, besides those which are absolutely necessary in a piece, the easier it is for the eye, by one simple act and in one view, to comprehend the sum or whole. The multiplication of subjects, tho' subaltern, renders the subordination more difficult to execute in the ordonnance or composition of a work. And if the subordination be not perfect, the order (which makes the beauty) remains imperfect. Now the subordination can never be perfect, except when the ordonnance is such that the eye not only runs over with ease the several parts of the design, reducing still its view each moment on the principal subject on which all turns, but when the same eye, without the least detainment in any of the particular parts, and resting, as it were, immovable in the middle or centre of the tablature, may see at once, in an agreeable and perfect correspondency, all which is there exhibited to the sight. [III, 383.]

FRANCIS HUTCHESON, *An Inquiry into the Original of our Ideas of Beauty and Virtue* (1725)

The figures that excite in us the ideas of beauty seem to be those in which there is *uniformity amidst variety*. There are many conceptions of objects that are agreeable upon other accounts, such as grandeur, novelty, sanctity, and some others, that shall be touched at afterwards. But what we call beautiful in objects, to speak in the mathematical style, seems to be in a compound ratio of uniformity and variety; so that where the uniformity of bodies is equal, the beauty is as the variety; and where the variety is equal, the beauty is as the uniformity. . . .

As to the works of art, were we to run through the various artificial contrivances or structures, we should find the foundation of the beauty which appears in them to be constantly some kind of uniformity, or unity of proportion among the parts, and of each part to the whole. As there is a vast diversity of proportions possible, and different kinds of uniformity, so there is room enough for that diversity of fancies observable in architecture, gardening, and such like arts in different nations; they all may have uniformity, though the parts in one may differ from those in another. The Chinese or Persian buildings are not like the Grecian and Roman, and yet the former has its uniformity of the various parts to each other, and to the whole, as well as the latter. In that kind of architecture which the Europeans call regular, the uniformity of parts is very obvious, the several parts are regular figures, and either equal or similar at least in the same range; the pedestals are parallelepipedons or square prisms; the pillars, cylinders nearly; the arches circular, and all those in the same row equal; there is the same proportion everywhere observed in the same range between the diameters of pillars and their heights, their capitals, the diameters of arches, the heights of the pedestals, the projections of the cornice, and all ornaments in each of our five orders. And though other countries do not follow the Grecian or Roman proportions, yet there is even among them a proportion retained, a uniformity, and resemblance of corresponding figures; and every deviation in one part from that proportion which is observed in the rest of the building is displeasing to every eye, and destroys or diminishes at least the beauty of the whole.

The same might be observed through all other works of art even to the meanest utensil, the beauty of every one of which we shall always find to have the same foundation of *uniformity amidst variety*, without which they shall appear mean, irregular and deformed. [pp. 15–16, 33–4.]

The Unities

Unity of effect is the prime requisite in any work of art. The unities of action, time and place, which critics have inferred from Aristotle's *Poetics*, conduce to that end; but they are mere mechanic rules, not fundamental laws of poetry.

JOHN DRYDEN, *An Essay of Dramatic Poesy* (1668)
Out of these two[1] have been extracted the famous rules which the French call *des trois unités*,[2] or the Three Unities, which ought to be observed in every regular play: namely, of time, place, and action.

The unity of time they comprehend in twenty-four hours, the

[1] *viz.* Aristotle's *Poetics* and Horace's *Art of Poetry*. In fact, the doctrine of the three dramatic unities originated with the Renaissance commentators on the *Poetics*.

[2] Dryden uses the title of Corneille's third *Discours* (1660): "Des trois unités". Crites is here speaking "on behalf of the ancients".

compass of a natural day, or as near as it can be contrived; and the reason of it is obvious to everyone, that the time of the feigned action, or fable of the play, should be proportioned as near as can be to the duration of that time in which it is represented; since, therefore, all plays are acted on the theatre in a space of time much within the compass of twenty-four hours, that play is to be thought the nearest imitation of nature whose plot or action is confined within that time; and, by the same rule which concludes this general proportion of time, it follows that all the parts of it are to be equally subdivided; as namely, that one act take not up the supposed time of half a day, which is out of proportion to the rest; since the other four are then to be straitened within the compass of the remaining half: for it is unnatural that one act, which being spoke or written is not longer than the rest, should be supposed longer by the audience; 'tis therefore the poet's duty to take care that no act should be imagined to exceed the time in which it is represented on the stage; and that the intervals and inequalities of time be supposed to fall out between the acts.

This rule of time, how well it has been observed by the ancients, most of their plays will witness; you see them in their tragedies (wherein to follow this rule is certainly most difficult) from the very beginning of their plays falling close into that part of the story which they intend for the action or principal object of it, leaving the former part to be delivered by narration; so that they set the audience, as it were, at the post where the race is to be concluded; and, saving them the tedious expectation of seeing the poet set out and ride the beginning of the course, you behold him not till he is in sight of the goal, and just upon you.

For the second unity, which is that of place, the ancients meant by it that the scene ought to be continued through the play, in the same place where it was laid in the beginning: for the stage on which it is represented being but one and the same place, it is unnatural to conceive it many, and those far distant from one another. I will not deny but, by the variation of painted scenes, the fancy (which in these cases will contribute to its own deceit) may sometimes imagine it several places, with some appearance of probability; yet it still carries the greater likelihood of truth if those places be supposed so near each other, as in the same town or city; which may all be comprehended under the large denomination of one place; for a greater distance will bear no proportion to the shortness of time which is allotted in the acting, to pass from one of them to another; for the observation of this, next to the ancients the French are to be most commended. They tie themselves so strictly to the unity of place that you never see in any of their plays a scene changed in the middle of an act; if an act begins in a garden, a street, or chamber, 'tis ended in the same place; and that you may know it to be the same, the stage is so supplied with persons that it is never empty all the time: he that enters the second has business with him who was on before; and before the second quits the stage, a third appears who has business with him. This Corneille calls *la liaison des scènes*, the continuity or joining of the scenes; and 'tis a good mark of a well contrived play when all the persons are known to each other, and every one of them has some affairs with all the rest.

As for the third unity, which is that of action, the ancients meant no other by it than what the logicians do by their *finis*, the end or scope of any action; that which is the first in intention, and last in execution: now the poet is to aim at one great and complete action, to the carrying on of which all things in his play, even the very obstacles, are to be subservient; and the reason of this is as evident as any of the former.

For two actions, equally laboured and driven on by the writer, would destroy the unity of the poem; it would be no longer one play, but two: not but that there may be many actions in a play, as Ben Jonson has observed in his *Discoveries*; but they must be all subservient to the great one, which our language happily expresses in the name of *under-plots*: such as in Terence's *Eunuch* is the difference and reconcilement of Thais and Phaedria, which is not the chief business of the play, but promotes the marriage of Chaerea and Chremes's sister, principally intended by the poet. There ought to be but one action, says Corneille, that is, one complete action which leaves the mind of the audience in a full repose; but this cannot be brought to pass but by many other imperfect ones which conduce to it, and hold the audience in a delightful suspense of what will be.

If by these rules (to omit many other drawn from the precepts and practice of the ancients) we should judge our modern plays, 'tis probable that few of them would endure the trial: that which should be the business of a day takes up in some of them an age; instead of one action, they are the epitomes of a man's life; and for one spot of ground (which the stage should represent) we are sometimes in more countries than the map can show us. . . .

I[3] hope I have already proved in this discourse that, though we are not altogether so punctual as the French in observing the laws of comedy, yet our errors are so few, and little, and those things wherein we excel them so considerable, that we ought of right to be preferred before them. But what will Lisideius say, if they themselves acknowledge they are too strictly tied up by those laws for breaking which he has blamed the English? I will allege Corneille's words, as I find them in the end of his "Discourse of the Three Unities": *Il est facile aux spéculatifs d'être sévères, etc.* "'Tis easy for speculative persons to judge severely; but if they would produce to public view ten or twelve pieces of this nature, they would perhaps give more latitude to the rules than I have done, when by experience they had known how much we are bound up and constrained by them, and how many beauties of the stage they banished from it." To illustrate a little what he has said, by their servile observations of the unities of time and place, and integrity of scenes, they have brought on themselves that dearth of plot, and narrowness of imagination, which may be observed in all their plays. How many beautiful accidents might naturally happen in two or three days, which cannot arrive with any probability in the compass of twenty-four hours? There is time to be allowed also for maturity of design, which, amongst great and prudent persons such as are often represented in tragedy, cannot, with any likelihood of truth, be brought to pass at so short a warning. Farther, by tying themselves strictly to the unity of place and unbroken scenes, they are forced many times to omit some beauties which cannot be shown where the act began; but might, if the scene were interrupted, and the stage cleared for the persons to enter in another place; and therefore the French poets are often forced upon absurdities: for if the act begins in a chamber, all the persons in the play must have some business or other to come thither, or else they are not to be shown that act, and

[3] This is part of Neander's reply to Lisideius, who had praised French plays.

sometimes their characters are very unfitting to appear there. As, suppose it were the King's bedchamber, yet the meanest man in the tragedy must come and dispatch his business there, rather than in the lobby or courtyard (which is fitter for him), for fear the stage should be cleared and the scenes broken. Many times they fall by it into a greater inconvenience; for they keep their scenes unbroken, and yet change the place; as in one of their newest plays,[4] where the act begins in the street. There a gentleman is to meet his friend; he sees him with his man, coming out from his father's house; they talk together, and the first goes out: the second, who is a lover, has made an appointment with his mistress; she appears at the window, and then we are to imagine the scene lies under it. This gentleman is called away, and leaves his servant with his mistress; presently her father is heard from within; the young lady is afraid the servingman should be discovered, and thrusts him in through a door which is supposed to be her closet. After this, the father enters to the daughter, and now the scene is in a house; for he is seeking from one room to another for this poor Philipin,[5] or French Diego, who is heard from within, drolling and breaking many a miserable conceit upon his sad condition. In this ridiculous manner the play goes on, the stage being never empty all the while: so that the street, the window, the two houses, and the closet, are made to walk about, and the persons to stand still. Now what, I beseech you, is more easy than to write a regular French play, or more difficult than write an irregular English one, like those of Fletcher or of Shakespeare? [I, 27–30, 63–5.]

JOHN DENNIS, *Remarks upon Cato* (1713)
We have hitherto shewn the faults that this author[6] has committed for want of observing the rules. We shall now shew the absurdities with which he abounds through a too nice observing some of them, without any manner of judgment or discretion. The unities of time and place are mechanic rules, which, if they are observed with judgment, strengthen the reasonableness of the incidents, heighten

[4] Thomas Corneille's *L'Amour à la mode* (1651).

[5] The servant is called Cliton; Philipin is a character in Quinault's *L'Amant indiscret* (1654).

[6] i.e. Joseph Addison.

the probability of the action, promote the agreeable deceit of the representation, and add cleanliness, grace, and comeliness to it. But if they are practised without discretion, they render the action more improbable, and the representation more absurd, as an unworthy performance turns an act of the highest devotion into an act of the greatest sin. . . .

But now let us lay before the reader that part of the scenary[7] of the fourth act, which may shew the absurdities which the author has run into, through the indiscreet observance of the unity of place. I do not remember that Aristotle has said anything expressly concerning the unity of place. 'Tis true, implicitly he has said enough in the rules which he has laid down for the chorus. For by making the chorus an essential part of the tragedy, and by bringing it upon the stage immediately after the opening of the scene, and retaining it there till the very catastrophe, he has so determined and fixed the place of action, that it was impossible for an author upon the Grecian stage to break through that unity. I am of opinion that, if a modern tragic poet can preserve the unity of place without destroying the probability of the incidents, 'tis always best for him to do it, because by the preservation of that unity, as we have taken notice above, he adds grace and cleanness, and comeliness to the representation. But since there are no express rules about it, and we are under no compulsion to keep it, since we have no chorus, as the Grecian poet had; if it cannot be preserved without rendering the greater part of the incidents unreasonable and absurd, and perhaps sometimes monstrous, 'tis certainly better to break it. [II, 68, 75–6.]

JOSEPH ADDISON, *The Spectator*, no. 40 (16 April 1711)
The same objections which are made to tragi-comedy may in some measure be applied to all tragedies that have a double plot in them; which are likewise more frequent upon the English stage than upon any other. For though the grief of the audience, in such performances, be not changed into another passion, as in tragi-comedies, it is diverted upon another object, which weakens their concern for the principal action, and breaks the tide of sorrow by throwing it into different channels. This inconvenience, however, may in a

[7] disposition of the scenes.

great measure be cured, if not wholly removed, by the skilful choice of an underplot, which may bear such a near relation to the principal design as to contribute towards the completion of it, and be concluded by the same catastrophe. [I, 170–1.]

HENRY HOME, LORD KAMES, *Elements of Criticism* (1762)
Upon the whole, it appears that all the facts in an historical fable ought to have a mutual connection by their common relation to the grand event or catastrophe. And this relation, in which the unity of action consists, is equally essential to epic and dramatic compositions.

How far the unities of time and of place are essential, is a question of greater intricacy. These unities were strictly observed in the Grecian and Roman theatres; and they are inculcated by the French and English critics as essential to every dramatic composition. In theory, these unities are also acknowledged by our best poets, though their practice is seldom correspondent: they are often forced to take liberties, which they pretend not to justify, against the practice of the Greeks and Romans, and against the solemn decision of their own countrymen. But in the course of this inquiry it will be made evident that the example of the ancients ought, upon this point, to have no weight with us, and that our critics are guilty of a mistake in admitting no greater latitude of place and time than was admitted in Greece and Rome. [III, 267–8.]

SAMUEL JOHNSON, Preface to *The Plays of William Shakespeare* (1765)
To the unities of time and place [Shakespeare] has shewn no regard, and perhaps a nearer view of the principles on which they stand will diminish their value, and withdraw from them the veneration which, from the time of Corneille, they have very generally received, by discovering that they have given more trouble to the poet than pleasure to the auditor.

The necessity of observing the unities of time and place arises from the supposed necessity of making the drama credible. The critics hold it impossible that an action of months or years can be possibly believed to pass in three hours; or that the spectator can suppose himself to sit in the theatre, while ambassadors go and return between distant kings, while armies are levied and towns besieged, while an exile wanders and returns, or till he whom they saw courting his mistress shall lament the untimely fall of his son. The mind revolts from evident falsehood, and fiction loses its force when it departs from the resemblance of reality.

From the narrow limitation of time necessarily arises the contraction of place. The spectator, who knows that he saw the first act at Alexandria, cannot suppose that he sees the next at Rome, at a distance to which not the dragons of Medea could, in so short a time, have transported him; he knows with certainty that he has not changed his place; and he knows that place cannot change itself; that what was a house cannot become a plain; that what was Thebes can never be Persepolis.

Such is the triumphant language with which a critic exults over the misery of an irregular poet, and exults commonly without resistance or reply. It is time therefore to tell him, by the authority of Shakespeare, that he assumes, as an unquestionable principle, a position which, while his breath is forming it into words, his understanding pronounces to be false. It is false that any representation is mistaken for reality; that any dramatic fable in its materiality was ever credible, or, for a single moment, was ever credited.

The objection arising from the impossibility of passing the first hour at Alexandria, and the next at Rome, supposes that when the play opens the spectator really imagines himself at Alexandria, and believes that his walk to the theatre has been a voyage to Egypt, and that he lives in the days of Antony and Cleopatra. Surely he that imagines this may imagine more. He that can take the stage at one time for the palace of the Ptolemies may take it in half an hour for the promontory of Actium. Delusion, if delusion be admitted, has no certain limitation; if the spectator can be once persuaded that his old acquaintance are Alexander and Caesar, that a room illuminated with candles is the plain of Pharsalia, or the bank of Granicus, he is in a state of elevation above the reach of reason, or of truth, and, from the heights of empyrean poetry, may despise the circumscriptions of terrestrial nature. There is no reason why a mind thus wandering in extasy should count the clock, or why an hour should not be a century in that calenture[8] of the brains that can make the stage a field.

[8] fever.

The truth is, that the spectators are always in their senses, and know, from the first act to the last, that the stage is only a stage, and that the players are only players. They come to hear a certain number of lines recited with just gesture and elegant modulation. The lines relate to some action, and an action must be in some place; but the different actions that complete a story may be in places very remote from each other; and where is the absurdity of allowing that space to represent first Athens, and then Sicily, which was always known to be neither Sicily nor Athens, but a modern theatre?

By supposition, as place is introduced, time may be extended; the time required by the fable elapses for the most part between the acts; for, of so much of the action as is represented, the real and poetical duration is the same. If, in the first act, preparations for war against Mithridates are represented to be made in Rome, the event of the war may, without absurdity, be represented, in the catastrophe, as happening in Pontus; we know that there is neither war, nor preparation for war; we know that we are neither in Rome nor Pontus; that neither Mithridates nor Lucullus are before us. The drama exhibits successive imitations of successive actions, and why may not the second imitation represent an action that happened years after the first, if it be so connected with it that nothing but time can be supposed to intervene? Time is, of all modes of existence, most obsequious to the imagination; a lapse of years is as easily conceived as a passage of hours. In contemplation we easily contract the time of real actions, and therefore willingly permit it to be contracted when we only see their imitation.

It will be asked, how the drama moves, if it is not credited. It is credited with all the credit due to a drama. It is credited, whenever it moves, as a just picture of a real original; as representing to the auditor what he would himself feel, if he were to do or suffer what is there feigned to be suffered or to be done. The reflection that strikes the heart is not that the evils before us are real evils, but that they are evils to which we ourselves may be exposed. If there be any fallacy, it is not that we fancy the players, but that we fancy ourselves unhappy for a moment; but we rather lament the possibility than suppose the presence of misery, as a mother weeps over her babe when she remembers that death may take it from her. The delight of tragedy proceeds from our consciousness of fiction; if we thought murders and treasons real, they would please no more.

Imitations produce pain or pleasure, not because they are mistaken for realities, but because they bring realities to mind. When the imagination is recreated by a painted landscape, the trees are not supposed capable to give us shade, or the fountains coolness; but we consider how we should be pleased with such fountains playing beside us, and such woods waving over us. We are agitated in reading the history of Henry V, yet no man takes his book for the field of Agencourt. A dramatic exhibition is a book recited with concomitants that increase or diminish its effect. Familiar comedy is often more powerful on the theatre than in the page; imperial tragedy is always less. The humour of Petruchio may be heightened by grimace; but what voice or what gesture can hope to add dignity or force to the soliloquy of Cato?

A play read affects the mind like a play acted. It is therefore evident that the action is not supposed to be real, and it follows that between the acts a longer or shorter time may be allowed to pass, and that no more account of space or duration is to be taken by the auditor of a drama than by the reader of a narrative, before whom may pass in an hour the life of a hero, or the revolutions of an empire. . . .

Yet when I speak thus slightly of dramatic rules, I cannot but recollect how much wit and learning may be produced against me; before such authorities I am afraid to stand, not that I think the present question one of those that are to be decided by mere authority, but because it is to be suspected that these precepts have not been so easily received but for better reasons than I have yet been able to find. The result of my enquiries, in which it would be ludicrous to boast of impartiality, is that the unities of time and place are not essential to a just drama; that though they may sometimes conduce to pleasure, they are always to be sacrificed to the nobler beauties of variety and instruction; and that a play, written with nice observation of critical rules, is to be contemplated as an elaborate curiosity, as the product of superfluous and ostentatious art, by which is shewn rather what is possible than what is necessary.

He that, without diminution of any other excellence, shall preserve all the unities unbroken, deserves the like applause with the architect who shall display all the orders of architecture in a citadel, without any deduction from its strength; but the principal beauty of a citadel is to exclude the enemy; and the greatest graces of a play are to copy nature and instruct life.

Perhaps, what I have here not dogmatically but deliberately written may recall the principles of the drama to a new examination. I am almost frighted at my own temerity; and when I estimate the fame and the strength of those that maintain the contrary opinion, am ready to sink down in reverential silence. . . . [pp. 117–21, 121–2.]

The Probable—the Marvellous

The fictions of the poet should be at once probable and marvellous; they must always be such as to command the reader's belief.

SIR WILLIAM DAVENANT, Preface to *Gondibert* (1650)
But to make great actions credible is the principal art of poets, who, though they avouch the utility of fictions, should not, by altering and subliming story, make use of their privilege to the detriment of the reader, whose incredulity, when things are not represented in proportion, doth much allay the relish of his pity, hope, joy, and other passions. For we may descend to compare the deceptions in poesy to those of them that profess dexterity of hand which resembles conjuring, and to such we come not with the intention of lawyers to examine the evidence of facts, but are content, if we like the carriage of their feigned motion, to pay for being well deceived. [II, 11.]

THOMAS HOBBES, Answer to Davenant's Preface to *Gondibert* (1650)
There are some that are not pleased with fiction, unless it be bold, not only to exceed the work, but also the possibility of nature; they

would have impenetrable armours, enchanted castles, invulnerable bodies, iron men, flying horses, and a thousand other such things, which are easily feigned by them that dare. Against such I defend you (without assenting to those that condemn either Homer or Virgil) by dissenting only from those that think the beauty of a poem consists in the exorbitancy of the fiction. For as truth is the bound of historical, so the resemblance of truth is the utmost limit of poetical liberty. In old time amongst the heathens such strange fictions and metamorphoses were not so remote from the articles of their faith as they are now from ours, and therefore were not so unpleasant. Beyond the actual works of nature a poet may now go; but beyond the conceived possibility of nature, never. [II, 61–2.]

JOHN DRYDEN, *An Essay of Dramatic Poesy* (1668)
I have noted one great advantage [the French] have had in the plotting of their tragedies: that is, they are always grounded upon some known history; according to that of Horace, *ex noto fictum carmen sequar*;[1] and in that they have so imitated the ancients that they have surpassed them. For the ancients, as was observed before, took for the foundation of their plays some poetical fiction such as under that consideration could move but little concernment in the audience, because they already knew the event of it. But the French goes farther:

> atque ita mentitur, sic veris falsa remiscet,
> primo ne medium, medio ne discrepet imum.[2]

He so interweaves truth with probable fiction that he puts a pleasing fallacy upon us; mends the intrigues of fate, and dispenses with the severity of history, to reward that virtue which has been rendered to us there unfortunate. Sometimes the story has left the success[3] so doubtful that the writer is free, by the privilege of a poet, to take that which of two or more relations will best suit with his design: as, for example, the death of Cyrus, whom Justin and some others report to have perished in the Scythian war, but Xenophon affirms

[1] *Ars Poetica*, 240. ("I shall ground my fiction in what is known.")
[2] *Ibid.* 151–2. ("And [Homer] feigns in such a way, mixes truth and fiction so well that there is no discrepancy between the end and the middle.")
[3] result, end.

to have died in his bed of extreme old age.[4] Nay more, when the
event is past dispute, even then we are willing to be deceived, and
the poet, if he contrives it with appearance of truth, has all the audience of his party; at least during the time his play is acting: so
naturally we are kind to virtue, when our own interest is not in
question, that we take it up as the general concernment of mankind.
On the other side, if you consider the historical plays of Shakespeare,
they are rather so many chronicles of kings, or the business many
times of thirty or forty years, cramped into a representation of two
hours and an half, which is not to imitate or paint nature, but rather
to draw her in miniature, to take her in little; to look upon her
through the wrong end of a perspective, and receive her images not
only much less, but infinitely more imperfect than the life: this,
instead of making a play delightful renders it ridiculous.

>   quodcumque ostendis mihi sic, incredulus odi.[5]

For the spirit of man cannot be satisfied but with truth, or at least
verisimility; and a poem is to contain, if not τὰ ἔτυμα, yet ἐτύμοισιν
ὁμοῖα,[6] as one of the Greek poets has expressed it. [I, 46–7.]

JOHN DRYDEN, A Defence of *An Essay of Dramatic Poesy* (1668)
Imagination in a man, or reasonable creature, is supposed to partici-
pate of reason, and when that governs, as it does in the belief of
fiction, reason is not destroyed, but misled, or blinded: that can
prescribe to the reason, during the time of the representation, somewhat like a weak belief of what it sees and hears; and reason suffers
itself to be so hoodwinked that it may better enjoy the pleasures of
the fiction: but it is never so wholly made a captive as to be drawn
headlong into a persuasion of those things which are most remote
from probability: 'tis in that case a free-born subject, not a slave; it
will contribute willingly its assent, as far as it sees convenient, but
will not be forced. Now there is a greater vicinity in nature betwixt
two rooms than betwixt two houses; betwixt two houses than

----

[4] Trogus Pompeius, *Historiae Philippicae*, abbreviated by Marcus Junianus
Justinus, I. viii, 11–13, XXXVII. iii, 2; Xenophon, *Cyropaedia*, viii. 7.

[5] *Ars Poetica*, 188. ("I cannot believe, and I dislike, anything of this kind.")

[6] Hesiod, *Theogony*, l. 27. ("the truth", "the likeness of truth".)

betwixt two cities; and so of the rest:[7] reason therefore can sooner be led by imagination to step from one room into another than to walk to two distant houses, and yet rather to go thither than to fly like a witch through the air, and be hurried from one region to another. Fancy and reason go hand in hand; the first cannot leave the last behind: and though fancy, when it sees the wide gulf, would venture over, as the nimbler, yet it is withheld by reason, which will refuse to take the leap when the distance over it appears too large. [I, 126.]

JOHN DRYDEN, Of Heroic Plays: An Essay. Prefixed to *The Conquest of Granada* (1672)

For my part, I am of opinion that neither Homer, Virgil, Statius, Ariosto, Tasso, nor our English Spenser could have formed their poems half so beautiful without those gods and spirits, and those enthusiastic parts of poetry which compose the most noble parts of all their writings. And I will ask any man who loves heroic poetry (for I will not dispute their tatses who do not), if the ghost of Polydorus in Virgil,[8] the Enchanted Wood in Tasso,[9] and the Bower of Bliss in Spenser[10] (which he borrows from that admirable Italian) could have been omitted without taking from their works some of the greatest beauties in them. And if any man object the improbabilities of a spirit appearing or of a palace raised by magic, I boldly answer him that an heroic poet is not tied to a bare representation of what is true, or exceeding probable: but that he may let himself loose to visionary objects, and to the representation of such things as, depending not on sense and therefore not to be comprehended by knowledge, may give him a freer scope for imagination. 'Tis enough that in all ages and religions the greatest part of mankind have believed the power of magic, and that there are spirits or spectres which have appeared. This, I say, is foundation enough for poetry; and I dare farther affirm that the whole doctrine

[7] Dryden is here answering Sir Robert Howard, who, in the Preface to *The Great Favourite* (1668), had attacked the unities and argued against Dryden that it is "as impossible for one stage to present two houses or two rooms truly as two countries or kingdoms, and as impossible that five hours, or four and twenty hours should be two hours and a half as that a thousand hours or years should be less than what they are."

[8] *Aeneid*, iii. 41ff.   [9] *Gerusalemme Liberata*, xiii.   [10] *Faerie Queene*, II. xii.

of separated beings, whether those spirits are incorporeal substances (which Mr. Hobbes, with some reason, thinks to imply a
contradiction), or that they are a thinner and more aerial sort of
bodies (as some of the Fathers have conjectured), may better be
explicated by poets than by philosophers or divines. For their
speculations on this subject are wholly poetical; they have only their
fancy for their guide, and that, being sharper in an excellent poet
than it is likely it should in a phlegmatic, heavy gown-man[11], will
see farther in its own empire, and produce more satisfactory notions
on those dark and doubtful problems.

   Some men think they have raised a great argument against the
use of spectres and magic in heroic poetry by saying they are
unnatural: but whether they or I believe there are such things is not
material; 'tis enough that, for aught we know, they may be in
nature; and whatever is, or may be, is not properly unnatural.
[I, 160–2.]

JOHN DENNIS, *Remarks on Prince Arthur* (1696)
Fourthly, the machines in *Prince Arthur*[12] are not delightful. By
machines, I mean the divine and infernal persons, for we have treated
of the human above. I have often, indeed, wondered why I could
never be pleased with the machines in a Christian poem. At length,
I believe I have found out the reason. Poetry pleases by an imitation
of Nature. Now the Christian machines are quite out of Nature,
and consequently cannot delight. The heathen machines are enough
out of Nature to be admirable, and enough in Nature to delight.
That which brings them nearer to Nature than the Christian machines is the distinction of sexes, human passions, and human inclinations. But, however, they are so far out of Nature that Virgil has
seldom ventured to describe any of his machines, and when he has
done it, it has been in order to move terror and not to move delight.
For he knew very well that a thing may the rather move terror for
being out of the ordinary course of Nature, but that any imitation
which excites joy must be an imitation of something in Nature.
For imitation, says Aristotle,[13] is therefore pleasing, because we are
instructed by it without pain. Now to be instructed by imitation, I

   [11] university man.
   [12] Sir Richard Blackmore's epic poem (1695).   [13] *Poetics*, iv.

must be a judge of that imitation, which I can never be if I have not
a clear and distinct idea of its object; now Virgil, knowing very well
that he had no clear and distinct idea of his gods and goddesses, saw
very well that for that reason he must not venture to paint them.
[I, 105.]

JOSEPH ADDISON, *The Spectator*, no. 315 (1 March 1712)
Aristotle observes[14] that the fable of an epic poem should abound in
circumstances that are both credible and astonishing; or, as the
French critics choose to phrase it, the fable should be filled with the
probable and the marvellous. This rule is as fine and just as any in
Aristotle's whole *Art of Poetry*.

If the fable is only probable, it differs nothing from a true history;
if it is only marvellous, it is no better than a romance. The great
secret therefore of heroic poetry is to relate such circumstances as
may produce in the reader at the same time both belief and astonishment. This is brought to pass in a well chosen fable by the account
of such things as have really happened, or at least of such things as
have happened according to the received opinions of mankind.
Milton's fable is a masterpiece of this nature; as the war in Heaven,
the condition of the fallen angels, the state of innocence, the temptation of the serpent, and the fall of man, though they are very
astonishing in themselves, are not only credible, but actual points
of faith.

The next method of reconciling miracles with credibility is by a
happy invention of the poet; as in particular, when he introduces
agents of a superior nature, who are capable of effecting what is
wonderful, and what is not to be met with in the ordinary course of
things. Ulysses' ship being turned into a rock,[15] and Aeneas' fleet
into a shoal of water nymphs,[16] though they are very surprising
accidents, are nevertheless probable, when we are told that they
were the gods who thus transformed them. It is this kind of machinery which fills the poems both of Homer and Virgil with such
circumstances as are wonderful, but not impossible, and so frequently produce in the reader the most pleasing passion that can
rise in the mind of man, which is admiration. . . . If we look into

[14] *Poetics*, xxiv.   [15] *Odyssey*, xiii. 146–83.   [16] *Aeneid*, ix. 107–22.

the fiction of Milton's fable, though we find it full of surprising
incidents, they are generally suited to our notions of the things and
persons described, and tempered with a due measure of probability.
I must only make an exception to the Limbo of Vanity,[17] with his
episode of Sin and Death,[18] and some of the imaginary persons in
his Chaos.[19] These passages are astonishing, but not credible; the
reader cannot so far impose upon himself as to see a possibility in
them, they are the description of dreams and shadows, not of things
or persons. . . .

In a word, besides the hidden meaning of an epic allegory, the plain
literal sense ought to appear probable. The story should be such as
an ordinary reader may acquiesce in, whatever natural, moral, or
political truth may be discovered in it by men of greater penetration. [III, 144–6.]

JOSEPH ADDISON, *The Spectator*, no. 419 (1 July 1712)

There is a kind of writing wherein the poet quite loses sight of
nature, and entertains his reader's imagination with the characters
and actions of such persons as have many of them no existence but
what he bestows on them. Such are fairies, witches, magicians,
demons, and departed spirits. This Mr. Dryden calls the *fairy way of
writing*,[20] which is, indeed, more difficult than any other that
depends on the poet's fancy, because he has no pattern to follow it,
and must work altogether out of his own invention.

There is a very odd turn of thought required for this sort of
writing, and it is impossible for a poet to succeed in it who has not a
particular cast of fancy, and an imagination naturally fruitful and
superstitious. Besides this, he ought to be very well versed in legends
and fables, antiquated romances, and the traditions of nurses and old
women, that he may fall in with our natural prejudices, and humour
those notions which we have imbibed in our infancy. For, otherwise,
he will be apt to make his fairies talk like people of his own species,
and not like other sets of beings, who converse with different
objects, and think in a different manner from that of mankind;

[17] *Paradise Lost*, iii. 444–97.   [18] *Paradise Lost*, ii. 648–889.

[19] *Paradise Lost*, ii. 927–1055.

[20] "that fairy kind of writing, which depends only upon the force of
imagination." Dedication of *King Arthur* (1691).

Sylvis deducti caveant, me judice, Fauni
Ne velut innati triviis ac paene forenses
Aut nimium teneris juvenentur versibus. . . .

(Horace)[21]

I do not say with Mr. Bays in the *Rehearsal*[22] that spirits must not be confined to speak sense, but it is certain their sense ought to be a little discoloured, that it may seem particular, and proper to the person and the condition of the speaker.

These descriptions raise a pleasing kind of horror[23] in the mind of the reader, and amuse[24] his imagination with the strangeness and novelty of the persons who are represented in them. They bring up into our memory the stories we have heard in our childhood, and favour those secret terrors and apprehensions to which the mind of man is naturally subject. We are pleased with surveying the different habits and behaviours of foreign countries; how much more must we be delighted and surprised when we are led, as it were, into a new creation, and see the persons and manners of another species? Men of cold fancies, and philosophical dispositions, object to this kind of poetry, that it has not probability enough to affect the imagination. But to this it may be answered that we are sure, in general, there are many intellectual beings in the world besides ourselves, and several species of spirits, who are subject to different laws and economies from those of mankind; when we see, therefore, any of these represented naturally, we cannot look upon the representation as altogether impossible; nay, many are prepossessed with such false opinions as dispose them to believe these particular delusions; at least, we have all heard so many pleasing relations in favour of them that we do not care for seeing through the falsehood, and willingly give ourselves up to so agreeable an imposture. [III, 570–72.]

JOSEPH TRAPP, *Lectures on Poetry* (1742)
The moderns seem to mistake that part of epic and tragedy which

[21] Horace, *Ars Poetica*, 244–6. ("In my opinion, fauns coming from the forests should not behave like men accustomed to streets and public places, nor should their language be refined.")

[22] *The Rehearsal* (1671), by George Villiers, Duke of Buckingham, ridiculed the extravagances of heroic plays.

[23] awe.   [24] engage the attention of.

contains the τὸ θαυμαστόν, or the *wonderful*, confounding the *wonderful* with the *improbable*, and using those two words promiscuously. If it was really so, the τὸ θαυμαστόν would always be faulty; for that is always faulty which is improbable. These poetical prodigies would be impossible, if they were represented to be performed by any human power; but the case is quite different. The Divine Power, and the agency of the gods, make all this agreeable to reason. Thus, in Homer, that the horses should speak;[25] and, in Virgil, that the myrtle roots should drop blood,[26] is wonderful, but not improbable. . . .

In such cases as these, whatsoever is possible, is probable. If you determine otherwise, poetry is deprived of one of its best ornaments, its greatest fund of surprise. And the same observation extends to some parts of the wonderful, which are not accounted for by a divine power: as in the instance of Polyphemus, and the other Cyclops, in Homer and Virgil.[27] That there were really giants, is an opinion which not only the ancients believed, but the Scriptures have confirmed. [pp. 338–9.]

SAMUEL JOHNSON, Life of Edmund Smith (1780)
Addison has, in *The Spectator*,[28] mentioned the neglect of Smith's tragedy[29] as disgraceful to the nation, and imputes it to the fondness for operas then prevailing. The authority of Addison is great; yet the voice of the people, when to please the people is the purpose, deserves regard. In this question, I cannot but think the people in the right. The fable is mythological, a story which we are accustomed to reject as false, and the manners are so distant from our own that we know them not from sympathy, but by study: the ignorant do not understand the action, the learned reject it as a schoolboy's tale; *incredulus odi*.[30] What I cannot for a moment believe, I cannot for a moment behold with interest or anxiety. [II, 16.]

[25] *Iliad*, xix. Xanthus, the horse of Achilles, foretells his master's fate.
[26] *Aeneid*, iii. 19–48.   [27] *Odyssey*, ix, and *Aeneid*, iii.
[28] No. 18, 21 March 1711.
[29] *Phaedra and Hippolitus*, produced 21 April 1707.
[30] Horace, *Ars Poetica*, 188 (paraphrased by Johnson in the following sentence).

SAMUEL JOHNSON, Life of Pope (1781)

To the praises which have been accumulated on *The Rape of the Lock* by readers of every class, from the critic to the waiting-maid, it is difficult to make any addition. Of that which is universally allowed to be the most attractive of all ludicrous compositions, let it rather be now enquired from what sources the power of pleasing is derived.

Dr. Warburton,[31] who excelled in critical perspicacity, has remarked that the preternatural agents are very happily adapted to the purposes of the poem. The heathen deities can no longer gain attention: we should have turned away from a contest between Venus and Diana. The employment of allegorical persons always excites conviction of its own absurdity: they may produce effects, but cannot conduct actions; when the phantom is put in motion, it dissolves; thus Discord may raise a mutiny,[32] but Discord cannot conduct a march, nor besiege a town. Pope brought into view a new race of beings, with powers and passions proportionate to their operation. The sylphs and gnomes act at the toilet and the tea-table what more terrific and more powerful phantoms perform on the stormy ocean or the field of battle; they give their proper help, and do their proper mischief. [III, 232-3.]

[31] In his notes to the poem.   [32] In Boileau's *Le Lutrin*.

E

Propriety

Propriety requires that in any poem the actions, characters and style should be suited to the genre. The actions and sentiments must be proper to the characters and to the circumstances in which these are presented. Propriety is to be observed, for all that is natural is not fit to be expressed.

THOMAS HOBBES, Answer to Davenant's Preface to *Gondibert* (1650)

Of the indecencies of an heroic poem the most remarkable are those that shew disproportion either between the persons and their actions, or between the manners of the poet and the poem. Of the first kind is the uncomeliness of representing in great persons the inhuman vice of cruelty or the sordid vice of lust and drunkenness. To such parts as those the ancient approved poets thought it fit to suborn,[1] not the persons of men, but of monsters and beastly giants, such as Polyphemus,[2] Cacus,[3] and the Centaurs. For it is supposed a muse, when she is invoked to sing a song of that nature, should maidenly advise the poet to set such persons to sing their own vices upon the stage, for it is not so unseemly in a tragedy. Of the same kind it is to represent scurrility or any action or language that moves much laughter. The delight of an epic poem consisteth not in mirth, but admiration. Mirth and laughter is proper to comedy and satire. Great persons that have their minds employed on great designs have not leisure enough to laugh, and are pleased with the contemplation of their own power and virtues, so as[4] they need not the infirmities and vices of other men to recommend themselves to their own favour by comparison, as all men do when they laugh. Of the second kind, where the disproportion is between the poet and the persons of his poem, one is in the dialect of the inferior sort of

[1] to introduce, to use.
[2] The Cyclops whom Ulysses blinded (*Odyssey*, ix).
[3] A monster living in a cave on the Aventine in Rome (*Aeneid*, viii).
[4] so that.

people, which is always different from the language of the court. Another is to derive the illustration of any thing from such metaphors or comparisons as cannot come into men's thoughts but by mean conversation and experience of humble or evil arts, which the person of an epic poem cannot be thought acquainted with. [II, 64.]

JOHN DRYDEN, Preface to *All for Love* (1678)

The faults my enemies have found are rather cavils concerning little, and not essential, decencies; which a master of the ceremonies may decide betwixt us. The French poets, I confess, are strict observers of these punctilios: they would not, for example, have suffered Cleopatra and Octavia to have met; or, if they had met, there must have only passed betwixt them some cold civilities, but no eagerness of repartee, for fear of offending against the greatness of their characters, and the modesty of their sex. This objection I foresaw, and at the same time contemned; for I judged it both natural and probable that Octavia, proud of her new-gained conquest, would search out Cleopatra to triumph over her; and that Cleopatra, thus attacked, was not of a spirit to shun the encounter: and 'tis not unlikely that two exasperated rivals should use such satire as I have put into their mouths; for after all, though the one were a Roman, and the other a queen, they were both women. 'Tis true, some actions, though natural, are not fit to be represented; and broad obscenities in words ought in good manners to be avoided: expressions therefore are a modest clothing of our thoughts, as breeches and petticoats are of our bodies. If I have kept myself within the bounds of modesty, all beyond it is but nicety and affectation; which is no more but modesty depraved into a vice: they betray themselves who are too quick of apprehension in such cases, and leave all reasonable men to imagine worse of them than of the poet. [I, 222–3.]

JOHN DRYDEN, A Parallel of Poetry and Painting. Preface to the Translation of C. A. du Fresnoy, *De Arte Graphica* (1695)

"In the passions," says our author,[5] "we must have a very great

---

[5] i.e. du Fresnoy.

regard to the quality of the persons who are actually possessed with them." The joy of a monarch for the news of a victory must not be expressed like the ecstasy of a harlequin on the receipt of a letter from his mistress: this is so much the same in both the arts, that it is no longer a comparison. [II, 201–2.]

THOMAS RYMER, *Tragedies of The Last Age* (1677)
Kings of tragedy are all kings by the poet's election, and if such as these[6] must be elected, certainly no Polish Diet would ever suffer poet to have a voice in choosing a king for them. Nor will it serve that Arbaces[7] is not truly a king, for he is actually such, and intended for a true and rightful king before the poet has done with him; what wants in birth the poet should make up in his merit: every one is to consent and wish him king, because the poet designs him for one; 'tis besides observed that usurpers generally take care to deserve by their conduct what is denied them by right.

We are to presume the greatest virtues where we find the highest of rewards; and though it is not necessary that heroes should be kings, yet undoubtedly all crowned heads by poetical right are heroes. This character is a flower, a prerogative, so certain, so inseparably annexed to the crown, as by no poet, no parliament of poets, ever to be invaded. . . .

And far from decorum is it that we find the king drolling and quibbling with Bessus[8] and his buffoons, and worse, that they should presume to break their little jests upon him.

This too is natural, some will say. There are in nature many things which historians are ashamed to mention, as below the dignity of an history; shall we then suffer a Tom Coriat[9] in poetry? Shall we on the most important day of a king's reign, and at court, be content with such entertainment as is not above a cobbler's shop? Might not a poet as well describe to us how the king eats and drinks, or goes to stool? for these actions are also natural. . . .

Tragedy cannot represent a woman without modesty as natural and essential to her. If a woman has got any accidental historical

---

[6] The kings in Beaumont and Fletcher's *A King and No King*.
[7] The usurper king.   [8] A captain in the same play.
[9] A buffoon at the court of James I, author of *Coryat's Crudities*.

impudence, if, documented in the school of Nanna[10] or Heloisa,[11] she is furnished with some stock of acquired impudence, she is no longer to stalk in tragedy on her high shoes, but must rub off and pack down with the carriers into the province of comedy, there to be kicked about and exposed to laughter. . . .

If I mistake not, in poetry no woman is to kill a man, except her quality gives her the advantage above him, nor is a servant to kill the master, nor a private man, much less a subject, to kill a king, nor on the contrary.

Poetical decency will not suffer death to be dealt to each other by such persons whom the laws of duel allow not to enter the lists together. [pp. 42, 44, 64, 65.]

THOMAS RYMER, *A Short View of Tragedy* (1692)
But what is most intolerable is Iago. He is no blackamoor soldier, so we may be sure he should be like other soldiers of our acquaintance; yet never in tragedy nor in comedy nor in nature was a soldier with his character. . . .

Shakespeare knew his character of Iago was inconsistent. In this very play he pronounces:

> If thou dost deliver more or less than truth,
> Thou art no soldier. . . . (II, iii, 211–12)

This he knew; but to entertain the audience with something new and surprising, against common sense and nature, he would pass upon us a close, dissembling, false, insinuating rascal, instead of an open-hearted, frank, plain-dealing soldier, a character constantly worn by them for some thousands of years in the world. [pp. 134–5.]

SAMUEL JOHNSON, *The Rambler*, no. 140 (20 July 1751)
Sentiments are proper and improper as they consist more or less with the character and circumstances of the person to whom they are attributed, with the rules of the composition in which they are found, or with the unalterable and settled nature of things. . . .

[10] Possibly the French courtesan Anne (better known as Ninon) de Lenclos (1620–1705), who was notorious for her love affairs and her sceptical principles.

[11] The lover of Abelard.

Milton has, by his learning, which acquainted him with the manners of the ancient Eastern nations, and by his invention, which required no assistance from the common cant of poetry, been preserved from frequent outrages of local or chronological propriety. Yet he has mentioned Chalybean steel,[12] of which it is not very likely that his chorus should have heard, and has made *Alp* the general name of a mountain, in a region where the Alps could not be known. . . .[13]

He has taught Samson the tales of Circe and the sirens, at which he apparently hints in his colloquy with Dalilah. . . .[14]

But the grossest error of this kind is the solemn introduction of the phoenix in the last scene, which is faulty, not only as it is incongruous to the personage to whom it is ascribed, but as it is so evidently contrary to reason and nature that it ought never to be mentioned but as a fable in any serious poem. . . .

Another species of impropriety is the unsuitableness of thoughts to the general character of the poem. The seriousness and solemnity of tragedy necessarily rejects all pointed or epigrammatical expressions, all remote conceits and opposition of ideas. Samson's complaint is therefore too elaborate to be natural. . . .[15]

All allusions to low and trivial objects with which contempt is usually associated are doubtless unsuitable to a species of composition which ought to be always awful though not always magnificent. The remark therefore of the chorus on good and bad news seems to want elevation:

> *Manoah.* A little stay will bring some notice hither.
> *Chor.* Of good or bad so great, of bad the sooner;
>   For evil news *rides post*, while good news *baits*.[16]

But of all meanness, that has least to plead which is produced by mere verbal conceits, which depending, only upon sounds, lose their existence by the change of a word. Of this kind is the following dialogue:

[12] *Samson Agonistes*, 133.   [13] *Samson Agonistes*, 627–8.
[14] *Samson Agonistes*, 932–5.   [15] *Samson Agonistes*, 99–105.
[16] *Samson Agonistes*, 1536–8. Johnson probably objected to the proverbial saying.

Chor. But had we best retire? I see a storm.
Sam. Fair days have oft contracted wind and rain.
Chor. But this another kind of tempest brings.
Sam. Be less abstruse, my riddling days are past.
Chor. Look now for no enchanting voice, nor fear
   The bait of honied words; a rougher tongue
   Draws hitherward, I know him by his stride,
   The giant Harapha. . . .[17] [pp. 833–5.]

[17] *Samson Agonistes*, 1061–8.

II THE GENRES

Tragedy

Tragedy deals with the actions of great persons and moves pity and terror in order to rectify or purge our passions. Each character must be moved by a dominant inclination or passion. These must be suitable to each kind of person and be constant throughout the play. When staging characters known through history, the poet must conform to received opinion. (Dryden)

Tragedy represents the disorders of the great. (Shaftesbury)

Barbarous actions are too frequent on the English stage, but to report all such actions, as the French do, leads to absurdities. (Addison)

Tragedy improves our virtuous sensibility. (Blair)

JOHN DRYDEN, The Grounds of Criticism in Tragedy. Prefixed to *Troilus and Cressida* (1679)

Tragedy is thus defined by Aristotle[1] (omitting what I thought unnecessary in his definition). 'Tis an imitation of one entire, great, and probable action; not told, but represented; which, by moving in us fear and pity, is conducive to the purging of those two passions in our minds. More largely thus: tragedy describes or paints an action, which action must have all the properties above named. First, it must be one or single; that is, it must not be a history of one man's life, suppose of Alexander the Great, or Julius Caesar, but one single action of theirs. This condemns all Shakespeare's historical plays, which are rather chronicles represented than tragedies, and all double action of plays. As to[2] avoid a satire upon others, I will make bold with my own *Marriage-à-la-Mode*, where there are manifestly two actions, not depending on one another: but in *Oedipus*[3] there cannot properly be said to be two actions, because the love of Adrastus and Eurydice has a necessary dependence on the principal design into which it is woven. The

[1] *Poetics*, vi.   [2] in order to.   [3] Dryden's play (1679).

natural reason of this rule is plain; for two different independent actions distract the attention and concernment of the audience, and consequently destroy the intention of the poet: if his business be to move terror and pity, and one of his actions be comical, the other tragical, the former will divert the people, and utterly make void his greater purpose. Therefore, as in perspective, so in tragedy, there must be a point of sight in which all the lines terminate; otherwise the eye wanders, and the work is false. This was the practice of the Grecian stage. But Terence made an innovation in the Roman: all his plays have double actions; for it was his custom to translate two Greek comedies, and to weave them into one of his, yet so that both the actions were comical, and one was principal, the other but secondary or subservient. And this has obtained on the English stage to give us the pleasure of variety.

As the action ought to be one, it ought, as such, to have order in it; that is, to have a natural beginning, a middle, and an end. A natural beginning, says Aristotle,[4] is that which could not necessarily have been placed after another thing, and so of the rest. This consideration will arraign all plays after the new model of Spanish plots, where accident is heaped upon accident, and that which is first might as reasonably be last: an inconvenience not to be remedied but by making one accident naturally produce another, otherwise 'tis a farce and not a play. Of this nature is the *Slighted Maid*,[5] where there is no scene in the first act which might not by as good reason be in the fifth. And if the action ought to be one, the tragedy ought likewise to conclude with the action of it. Thus in *Mustapha*,[6] the play should naturally have ended with the death of Zanger, and not have given us the grace-cup after dinner of Solyman's divorce from Roxolana.

The following properties of the action are so easy that they need not my explaining. It ought to be great, and to consist of great persons, to distinguish it from comedy, where the action is trivial, and the persons of inferior rank. The last quality of the action is that it ought to be probable, as well as admirable and great. 'Tis not necessary that there should be historical truth in it; but always necessary that there should be a likeness of truth, something that is

[4] *Poetics*, vii.   [5] By Sir Robert Stapylton (1663).
[6] By the Earl of Orrery (1665).

more than barely possible, *probable* being that which succeeds or happens oftener than it misses. To invent therefore a probability, and to make it wonderful, is the most difficult undertaking in the art of poetry; for that which is not wonderful is not great; and that which is not probable will not delight a reasonable audience. This action, thus described, must be represented and not told, to distinguish dramatic poetry from epic: but I hasten to the end or scope of tragedy, which is, to rectify or purge our passions, fear and pity.[7]

To instruct delightfully is the general end of all poetry. Philosophy instructs, but it performs its work by precept; which is not delightful, or not so delightful as example. To purge the passions by example is therefore the particular instruction which belongs to tragedy. Rapin, a judicious critic, has observed from Aristotle that pride and want of commiseration are the most predominant vices in mankind;[8] therefore, to cure us of these two, the inventors of tragedy have chosen to work upon two other passions, which are fear and pity. We are wrought to fear by their setting before our eyes some terrible example of misfortune which happened to persons of the highest quality; for such an action demonstrates to us that no condition is privileged from the turns of fortune; this must of necessity cause terror in us, and consequently abate our pride. But when we see that the most virtuous, as well as the greatest, are not exempt from such misfortunes, that consideration moves pity in us, and insensibly works us to be helpful to, and tender over, the distressed; which is the noblest and most god-like of moral virtues. Here 'tis observable that it is absolutely necessary to make a man virtuous, if we desire he should be pitied: we lament not, but detest, a wicked man; we are glad when we behold his crimes are punished, and that poetical justice is done upon him. . . .

But as the manners are useful in this art, they may be all comprised under these general heads: first, they must be apparent; that is, in every character of the play, some inclinations of the person must appear; and these are shown in the actions and discourse. Secondly, the manners must be suitable, or agreeing to the persons; that is, to the age, sex, dignity, and the other general heads of

---

[7] *Poetics*, xiii.   [8] *Réflexions sur la Poétique d'Aristote*, II. xvii.

manners: thus, when a poet has given the dignity of a king to one of his persons, in all his actions and speeches that person must discover majesty, magnanimity, and jealousy of power, because these are suitable to the general manners of a king. The third property of manners is resemblance; and this is founded upon the particular characters of men, as we have them delivered to us by relation or history; that is, when a poet has the known character of this or that man before him he is bound to represent him such, at least not contrary to that which fame has reported him to have been. Thus, it is not a poet's choice to make Ulysses choleric, or Achilles patient, because Homer has described 'em quite otherwise. Yet this is a rock on which ignorant writers daily split; and the absurdity is as monstrous as if a painter should draw a coward running from a battle, and tell us it was the picture of Alexander the Great.

The last property of manners is that they be constant and equal; that is, maintained the same through the whole design: thus, when Virgil had once given the name of *pious* to Aeneas,[9] he was bound to show him such, in all his words and actions, through the whole poem. [I, 243–5, 249.]

ANTHONY ASHLEY COOPER, THIRD EARL OF SHAFTESBURY,
Advice to an Author (1710)

The genius of this poetry consists in the lively representation of the disorders and misery of the great; to the end that the people and those of a lower condition may be taught the better to content themselves with privacy, enjoy their safer state, and prize the equality and justice of their guardian laws. If this be found agreeable to the just tragic model which the ancients have delivered to us, 'twill easily be conceived how little such a model is proportioned to the capacity or taste of those[10] who in a long series of degrees, from the lowest peasant to the high slave of royal blood, are taught to idolize the next in power above them, and think nothing so adorable as that unlimited greatness, and tyrannic power, which is raised at their own expense, and exercised over themselves. [I, 218–19.]

9 *Aeneid*, i. 379 ("Sum pius Aeneas").   10 i.e. the French.

JOSEPH ADDISON, *The Spectator*, no. 44 (20 April 1711)

But among all our methods of moving pity or terror, there is none so absurd and barbarous, and what more exposes us to the contempt and ridicule of our neighbours, than that dreadful butchering of one another which is so very frequent upon the English stage. To delight in seeing men stabbed, poisoned, racked, or impaled, is certainly the sign of a cruel temper: and as this is often practised before the British audience, several French critics,[11] who think these are grateful spectacles to us, take occasion from them to represent us as a people that delight in blood. It is indeed very odd to see our stage strowed with carcasses in the last scene of a tragedy; and to observe in the wardrobe of the playhouse several daggers, poniards, wheels, bowls for poison, and many other instruments of death. Murders and executions are always transacted behind the scenes in the French theatre; which in general is very agreeable to the manners of a polite and civilised people. But as there are no exceptions to this rule on the French stage, it leads them into absurdities almost as ridiculous as that which falls under our present censure. [I, 187–8.]

HUGH BLAIR, *Lectures on Rhetoric and Belles-Lettres* (1783)

The account which Aristotle gives of the design of tragedy is that it is intended to purge our passions by means of pity and terror. This is somewhat obscure. Various senses have been put upon his words, and much altercation has followed among his commentators. Without entering into any controversy upon this head, the intention of tragedy may, I think, be more shortly and clearly defined, to improve our virtuous sensibility. If an author interests us in behalf of virtue, forms us to compassion for the distressed, inspires us with proper sentiments on beholding the vicissitudes of life, and, by means of the concern which he raises for the misfortunes of others, leads us to guard against errors in our own conduct, he accomplishes all the moral purposes of tragedy. [II, 479–80.]

[11] e.g. Rapin, *Réflexions*, II. xx, xxiii.

Poetic Justice

In order to instruct delightfully the tragic poet should administer justice by punishing vice and rewarding virtue. (Rymer, Dennis, Johnson)

An impartial execution of poetic justice defeats the purpose of tragedy, which is to move terror and pity. (Addison)

Since tragedy is an image of life, it may sometimes dispense with poetic justice. (Johnson)

THOMAS RYMER, *Tragedies of the Last Age* (1677)
[Socrates] instructed in a pleasant facetious manner, by witty questions, allusions and parables.

[Sophocles and Euripides] were for teaching by examples, in a graver way, yet extremely pleasant and delightful. And, finding in history the same end happen to the righteous and to the unjust, virtue often oppressed, and wickedness on the throne, they saw these particular yesterday truths were imperfect and unproper to illustrate the universal and eternal truths by them intended. Finding also that this unequal distribution of rewards and punishments did perplex the wisest, and by the atheist was made a scandal to the Divine Providence, they concluded that a poet must of necessity see justice exactly administered, if he intended to please. For, said they, if the world can scarce be satisfied with God Almighty, whose holy will and purposes are not to be comprehended, a poet in these matters shall never be pardoned, who, they are sure, is not incomprehensible, whose ways and walks may, without impiety, be penetrated and examined. [p. 22.]

JOHN DENNIS, *Remarks upon Cato* (1713)
'Tis certainly the duty of every tragic poet, by an exact distribution of a poetical justice, to imitate the divine dispensation, and to inculcate a particular Providence. 'Tis true, indeed, upon the stage of the world the wicked sometimes prosper, and the guiltless suffer.

But that is permitted by the Governor of the world, to shew from the attribute of his infinite justice that there is a compensation in futurity, to prove the immortality of the human soul, and the certainty of future rewards and punishments. But the poetical persons in tragedy exist no longer than the reading or the representation; the whole extent of their entity is circumscribed by those; and therefore during that reading or representation, according to their merits or demerits, they must be punished or rewarded. If this is not done, there is no impartial distribution of poetical justice, no instructive lecture of a particular Providence, and no imitation of the divine dispensation. And yet the author of this tragedy[1] does not only run counter to this in the fate of his principal character, but everywhere throughout it makes virtue suffer, and vice triumph; for not only Cato is vanquished by Caesar, but the treachery and perfidiousness of Syphax prevails over the honest simplicity and the credulity of Juba, and the sly subtlety and dissimulation of Portius over the generous frankness and open-heartedness of Marcus. [II, 49.]

SAMUEL JOHNSON, Preface to *The Plays of William Shakespeare*
(1765)
[Shakespeare's] first defect is that to which may be imputed most of the evil in books or in men. He sacrifices virtue to convenience, and is so much more careful to please than to instruct that he seems to write without any moral purpose. From his writings indeed a system of social duty may be selected, for he that thinks reasonably must think morally; but his precepts and axioms drop casually from him; he makes no just distribution of good or evil, nor is always careful to shew in the virtuous a disapprobation of the wicked; he carries his persons indifferently through right and wrong, and at the close dismisses them without further care, and leaves their examples to operate by chance. This fault the barbarity of his age cannot extenuate; for it is always a writer's duty to make the world better, and justice is a virtue independent on time or place. [p. 114.]

JOSEPH ADDISON, *The Spectator*, no. 40 (16 April 1711)
The English writers of tragedy are possessed with a notion that,

[1] Addison's *Cato*.

when they represent a virtuous or innocent person in distress, they ought not to leave him till they have delivered him out of his troubles, and made him triumph over his enemies. This error they have been led into by a ridiculous doctrine in modern criticism, that they are obliged to an equal distribution of rewards and punishments, and an impartial execution of poetical justice. Who were the first that established this rule I know not; but I am sure it has no foundation in nature, in reason, or in the practice of the ancients. We find that good and evil happen alike to all men on this side of the grave; and as the principal design of tragedy is to raise commiseration and terror in the minds of the audience, we shall defeat this great end if we always make virtue and innocence happy and successful. Whatever crosses and disappointments a good man suffers in the body of the tragedy, they will make but small impression on our minds when we know that in the last act he is to arrive at the end of his wishes and desires. When we see him engaged in the depth of his afflictions, we are apt to comfort ourselves, because we are sure he will find his way out of them; and that his grief, how great soever it may be at present, will soon terminate in gladness. For this reason the ancient writers of tragedy treated men in their plays as they are dealt with in the world, by making virtue sometimes happy and sometimes miserable, as they found it in the fable which they made choice of, or as it might affect their audience in the most agreeable manner. Aristotle[2] considers the tragedies that were written in either of these kinds, and observes that those which ended unhappily had always pleased the people, and carried away the prize in the public disputes of the stage from those that ended happily. Terror and commiseration leave a pleasing anguish in the mind, and fix the audience in such a serious composure of thought, as is much more lasting and delightful than any little transient starts of joy and satisfaction. Accordingly we find that more of our English tragedies have succeeded in which the favourites of the audience sink under their calamities, than those in which they recover themselves out of them. The best plays of this kind are the *Orphan*,[3] *Venice Preserved*,[3] *Alexander the Great*,[4] *Theodosius*,[5] *All for*

[2] *Poetics*, xiii.   [3] By Otway.
[4] *The Rival Queens, or The Death of Alexander the Great*, by Lee.
[5] By Lee.

Love,[6] *Oedipus*,[7] *Oroonoko*,[8] *Othello*, etc. *King Lear* is an admirable tragedy of the same kind, as Shakespeare wrote it; but as it is reformed according to the chimerical notion of poetical justice,[9] in my humble opinion it has lost half its beauty. At the same time I must allow that there are very noble tragedies which have been framed upon the other plan, and have ended happily; as indeed most of the good tragedies which have been written since the starting of the above mentioned criticism have taken this turn: as the *Mourning Bride*,[10] *Tamerlane*,[11] *Ulysses*,[12] *Phaedra and Hippolitus*,[13] with most of Mr. Dryden's. I must also allow that many of Shakespeare's, and several of the celebrated tragedies of antiquity, are cast in the same form. I do not therefore dispute against this way of writing tragedies, but against the criticism that would establish this as the only method; and by that means would very much cramp the English tragedy, and perhaps give a wrong bent to the genius of our writers. [I, 168–70.]

SAMUEL JOHNSON, Life of Addison (1780)
Whatever pleasure there may be in seeing crimes punished and virtue rewarded, yet, since wickedness often prospers in real life, the poet is certainly at liberty to give it prosperity on the stage. For if poetry is an imitation of reality, how are its laws broken by exhibiting the world in its true form? The stage may sometimes gratify our wishes; but, if it be truly the *mirror of life*, it ought to shew us sometimes what we are to expect. [II, 135.]

[6] By Dryden.   [7] By Dryden and Lee.
[8] By Southerne.   [9] Tate's adaptation, with a happy ending.
[10] By Congreve.   [11] By Rowe.
[12] By Rowe.   [13] By Edmund Smith.

Heroic Tragedy

Heroic tragedy, like the heroic poem, moves admiration; its proper subject is love and valour. (Dryden)

JOHN DRYDEN, *Of* Heroic Plays: An Essay, Prefixed to *The Conquest of Granada* (1672)

For heroic plays (in which only I have used [rhyme] without the mixture of prose), the first light we had of them on the English theatre was from the late Sir William Davenant. It being forbidden him in the rebellious times to act tragedies and comedies, because they contained some matter of scandal to those good people who could more easily dispossess their lawful sovereign than endure a wanton jest, he was forced to turn his thoughts another way, and to introduce the examples of moral virtue writ in verse, and performed in recitative music. The original of this music, and of the scenes which adorned his work, he had from the Italian operas; but he heightened his characters (as I may probably imagine) from the example of Corneille and some French poets. In this condition did this part of poetry remain at His Majesty's return; when, growing bolder, as being now owned by a public authority, he reviewed his *Siege of Rhodes*,[1] and caused it be acted as a just drama. But as few men have the happiness to begin and finish any new project, so neither did he live to make his design perfect: there wanted the fulness of a plot, and the variety of characters to form it as it ought; and, perhaps, something might have been added to the beauty of the style. All which he would have performed with more exactness, had he pleased to have given us another work of the same nature. For myself and others, who come after him, we are bound with all veneration to his memory to acknowledge what advantage we received from that excellent groundwork which he laid; and, since it is an easy thing to add to what already is invented, we ought

[1] Acted June 1661.

all of us, without envy to him, or partiality to ourselves, to yield him the precedence in it.

Having done him this justice, as my guide, I may do myself so much as to give an account of what I have performed after him. I observed then, as I said, what was wanting to the perfection of his *Siege of Rhodes*; which was design, and variety of characters. And in the midst of this consideration, by mere accident, I opened the next book that lay by me, which was an Ariosto in Italian; and the very first two lines of that poem gave me light to all I could desire:

> Le donne, i cavalier, l'arme, gli amori,
> Le cortesie, l'audaci imprese io canto, etc.[2]

For the very next reflection which I made was this, that an heroic play ought to be an imitation, in little, of an heroic poem; and, consequently, that love and valour ought to be the subject of it. Both these Sir William Davenant had begun to shadow; but it was so, as first discoverers draw their maps, with headlands, and promontories, and some few outlines of somewhat taken at a distance, and which the designer saw not clearly. The common drama obliged him to a plot well formed and pleasant, or, as the ancients called it, one entire and great action. But this he afforded not himself in a story which he neither filled with persons, nor beautified with characters, nor varied with accidents. The laws of an heroic poem did not dispense with those of the other, but raised them to a greater height, and indulged him a farther liberty of fancy, and of drawing all things as far above the ordinary proportion of the stage as that is beyond the common words and actions of human life; and therefore, in the scanting of his images and design, he complied not enough with the greatness and majesty of an heroic poem. [I, 157–9.]

[2] *Orlando Furioso* ("Of ladies, knights, arms, love, courtesy, and high attempts I sing").

Tragi-comedy

The mixture of comic and tragic elements affords relief, and the contraries set each other off. (Dryden)

Tragi-comedy is an unnatural mingle. (Dryden, Addison)

The mixture of comic and tragic elements in drama reflects the real course of the world; besides, all pleasure consists in variety. (Johnson)

JOHN DRYDEN, *An Essay of Dramatic Poesy* (1668)
I[1] grant the French have performed what was possible on the groundwork of the Spanish plays; what was pleasant before, they have made regular; but there is not above one good play to be writ upon all those plots; they are too much alike to please often, which we need not the experience of our own stage to justify. As for their new way of mingling mirth with serious plot, I do not with Lisideius condemn the thing, though I cannot approve their manner of doing it. He tells us we cannot so speedily recollect ourselves after a scene of great passion and concernment as to pass to another of mirth and humour, and to enjoy it with any relish: but why should he imagine the soul of man more heavy than his senses? Does not the eye pass from an unpleasant object to a pleasant in a much shorter time than is required to this? and does not the unpleasantness of the first commend the beauty of the latter? The old rule of logic[2] might have convinced him that contraries, when placed near, set off each other. A continued gravity keeps the spirit too much bent; we must refresh it sometimes, as we bait[3] upon a journey, that we may go on with greater ease. A scene of mirth mixed with tragedy has the same effect upon us which our music has betwixt the acts; and that we find a relief to us from the plots and language

[1] Neander is putting the case for English plays.
[2] See, for instance, Burgersdijck's *Institutionum logicarum libri duo* (1626), which went through several editions in England in the seventeenth century.
[3] rest.

of the stage, if the discourses have been long. I must therefore have stronger arguments ere I am convinced that compassion and mirth in the same subject destroy each other; and in the meantime cannot but conclude, to the honour of our nation, that we have invented, increased, and perfected a more pleasant way of writing for the stage than was ever known to the ancients or moderns of any nation, which is tragi-comedy. [I, 58.]

JOHN DRYDEN, A Parallel of Poetry and Painting. Preface to the Translation of C. A. du Fresnoy, *De Arte Graphica* (1695)

Our English tragi-comedy must be confessed to be wholly Gothic, notwithstanding the success which it has found upon our theatre, and in the *Pastor Fido* of Guarini, even though Corisca and the Satyr contribute somewhat to the main action. Neither can I defend my *Spanish Friar*, as fond as otherwise I am of it, from this imputation: for though the comical parts are diverting, and the serious moving, yet they are of an unnatural mingle: for mirth and gravity destroy each other, and are no more to be allowed for decent than a gay widow laughing in a mourning habit. [II, 202.]

JOSEPH ADDISON, *The Spectator*, no. 40 (16 April 1711)

The tragi-comedy, which is the product of the English theatre, is one of the most monstrous inventions that ever entered into a poet's thoughts. An author might as well think of weaving the adventures of Aeneas and Hudibras into one poem, as of writing such a motley piece of mirth and sorrow. But the absurdity of these performances is so very visible that I shall not insist upon it. [I, 170.]

SAMUEL JOHNSON, Preface to *The Plays of William Shakespeare* (1765)

Shakespeare's plays are not in the rigorous and critical sense either tragedies or comedies, but compositions of a distinct kind; exhibiting the real state of sublunary nature, which partakes of good and evil, joy and sorrow, mingled with endless variety of proportion and innumerable modes of combination; and expressing the course of the world, in which the loss of one is the gain of another; in which, at the same time, the reveller is hasting to his wine, and the

mourner burying his friend; in which the malignity of one is sometimes defeated by the frolic of another; and many mischiefs and
many benefits are done and hindered without design. . . .

Shakespeare has united the powers of exciting laughter and
sorrow not only in one mind, but in one composition. Almost all
his plays are divided between serious and ludicrous characters, and,
in the successive evolutions of the design, sometimes produce
seriousness and sorrow, and sometimes levity and laughter.

That this is a practice contrary to the rules of criticism will be
readily allowed; but there is always an appeal open from criticism to
nature. The end of writing is to instruct; the end of poetry is to
instruct by pleasing. That the mingled drama may convey all the
instruction of tragedy or comedy cannot be denied, because it
includes both in its alternations of exhibition, and approaches
nearer than either to the appearance of life, by shewing how great
machinations and slender designs may promote or obviate[4] one
another, and the high and low co-operate in the general system by
unavoidable concatenation.

It is objected, that by this change of scenes the passions are
interrupted in their progression, and that the principal event, being
not advanced by a due gradation of preparatory incidents, wants
at last the power to move, which constitutes the perfection of
dramatic poetry. This reasoning is so specious[5] that it is received as
true even by those who in daily experience feel it to be false. The
interchanges of mingled scenes seldom fail to produce the intended
vicissitudes of passion. Fiction cannot move so much but that the
attention may be easily transferred; and though it must be allowed
that pleasing melancholy be sometimes interrupted by unwelcome
levity, yet let it be considered likewise that melancholy is often not
pleasing, and that the disturbance of one man may be the relief of
another; that different auditors have different habitudes; and that,
upon the whole, all pleasure consists in variety. [pp. 109–11.]

4 oppose.   5 plausible.

Comedy

Comedy delights through the ornaments of wit; it is not bound to administer justice. (Dryden)

Comedy deals with low persons and reprehends vices and follies by making them ridiculous. (Shadwell)

English comedy excels the ancient because it presents a greater variety of humours. (Temple)

Comedy does not set patterns for imitation, it corrects the follies of men by ridiculing men. (Dennis)

JOHN DRYDEN, Preface to *An Evening's Love* (1671)
Comedy consists, though of low persons, yet of natural actions and characters; I mean such humours, adventures, and designs as are to be found and met with in the world. Farce, on the other side, consists of forced humours and unnatural events. Comedy presents us with the imperfections of human nature: farce entertains us with what is monstrous and chimerical. The one causes laughter in those who can judge of men and manners, by the lively representation of their folly or corruption; the other produces the same effect in those who can judge of neither, and that only by its extravagances. The first works on the judgment and fancy; the latter on the fancy only: there is more of satisfaction in the former kind of laughter, and in the latter more of scorn. . . .

I will not deny but that I approve most the mixed way of comedy; that which is neither all wit, nor all humour, but the result of both. Neither so little of humour as Fletcher shows, nor so little of love and wit as Jonson; neither all cheat, with which the best plays of the one are fulfilled, nor all adventure, which is the common practice of the other. I would have the characters well chosen, and kept distant from interfering with each other; which is more than Fletcher or Shakespeare did: but I would have more of the *urbana, venusta,*

salsa, faceta, and the rest which Quintilian reckons up as the ornaments of wit;[1] and these are extremely wanting in Ben Jonson. As
for repartee in particular, as it is the very soul of conversation, so it
is the greatest grace of comedy, where it is proper to the characters. . . .

Thus tragedy fulfils one great part of its institution: which is, by
example, to instruct. But in comedy it is not so; for the chief end of
it is divertisement and delight: and that so much, that it is disputed, I
think, by Heinsius,[2] before Horace his *Art of Poetry,* whether
instruction be any part of its employment. At least I am sure it can
be but its secondary end; for the business of the poet is to make you
laugh: when he writes humour, he makes folly ridiculous; when wit,
he moves you, if not always to laughter, yet to a pleasure that is
more noble. And if he works a cure on folly, and the small imperfections in mankind, by exposing them to public view, that cure is
not performed by an immediate operation. For it works first on the
ill-nature of the audience; they are moved to laugh by the representation of deformity; and the shame of that laughter teaches us to
amend what is ridiculous in our manners. This being then established, that the first end of comedy is delight, and instruction only
the second, it may reasonably be inferred that comedy is not so much
obliged to the punishment of faults which it represents, as tragedy.
For the persons in comedy are of a lower quality, the action is little,
and the faults and vices are but the sallies of youth, and the
frailties of human nature, and not premeditated crimes; such to
which all men are obnoxious,[3] not such as are attempted only by
few, and those abandoned to all sense of virtue; such as move pity
and commiseration, not detestation and horror; such, in short, as
may be forgiven, not such as must of necessity be punished. [I, 146,
148–9, 151–2.]

THOMAS SHADWELL, Preface to *The Humourists* (1671)
My design was in [*The Humourists*] to reprehend some of the vices
and follies of the age, which I take to be the most proper and most

---

[1] *Institutio Oratoria,* VI. iii. 17–20. ("urbane, graceful, witty, facetious".)
[2] Daniel Heinsius, who edited Horace's *Ars Poetica* (1610); contrary to
what Dryden states, Heinsius said that comedy both teaches and delights.
[3] prone.

useful way of writing comedy. If I do not perform this well enough, let not my endeavours be blamed.

Here I must take leave to dissent from those[4] who seem to insinuate that the ultimate end of a poet is to delight, without correction or instruction. Methinks a poet should never acknowledge this, for it makes him of as little use to mankind as a fiddler or dancing-master, who delights the fancy only, without improving the judgment. [p. 153.]

SIR WILLIAM TEMPLE, Of Poetry (1690)

Yet I am deceived if our English [dramatic poetry] has not in some kind excelled both the modern and the ancient, which has been by force of a vein natural perhaps to our country, and which with us is called humour, a word peculiar to our language too, and hard to be expressed in any other; nor is it (that I know of) found in any foreign writers, unless it be Molière, and yet his itself has too much of the farce to pass for the same with ours. Shakespeare was the first that opened this vein upon our stage, which has run so freely and so pleasantly ever since that I have often wondered to find it appear so little upon any others, being a subject so proper for them; since humour is but a picture of particular life, as comedy is of general; and though it represents dispositions and customs less common, yet they are not less natural than those that are more frequent among men; for if humour itself be forced, it loses all the grace, which has been indeed the fault of some of our poets most celebrated in this kind.

It may seem a defect in the ancient stage that the characters introduced were so few, and those so common: as a covetous old man, an amorous young, a witty wench, a crafty slave, a bragging soldier; the spectators met nothing upon the stage but what they met in the streets, and at every turn. All the variety is drawn only from different and uncommon events; whereas, if the characters are so too, the diversity and the pleasure must needs be the more. But as of most general customs in a country there is usually some ground from the nature of the people or the climate, so there may be

[4] Shadwell is replying to Dryden's Preface to *An Evening's Love* (1671); Dryden only argued that the *chief* end of comedy is divertisement and delight (see preceding extract).

amongst us for this vein of our stage and a greater variety of humour in the picture, because there is a greater variety in the life. This may proceed from the native plenty of our soil, the unequalness of our climate, as well as the ease of our government and the liberty of professing opinions and factions, which perhaps our neighbours may have about them, but are forced to disguise, and thereby they may come in time to be extinguished. Plenty begets wantonness and pride; wantonness is apt to invent, and pride scorns to imitate; liberty begets stomach or heart, and stomach will not be constrained. Thus we come to have more originals, and more that appear what they are; we have more humour, because every man follows his own, and takes a pleasure, perhaps a pride, to shew it.[5] [pp. 198–9.]

JOHN DENNIS, *A Defence of Sir Fopling Flutter* (1722)
How little do they know of the nature of true comedy who believe that its proper business is to set us patterns for imitation;[6] for all such patterns are serious things, and laughter is the life and the very soul of comedy. 'Tis its proper business to expose persons to our view whose views we may shun, and whose follies we may despise; and by shewing us what is done upon the comic stage, to shew us what ought never to be done upon the stage of the world. [II, 245.]

Opera

Operas admit of more marvellous elements than other plays. (Dryden)

JOHN DRYDEN, Preface to *Albion and Albanius* (1685)
An opera is a poetical tale or fiction, represented by vocal and instrumental music, adorned with scenes, machines, and dancing.

[5] The view that humour was an English characteristic and that the variety of humours was due to the greater freedom of manners became a commonplace.

[6] Dennis is glancing at Steele's conception of comedy; his pamphlet appeared a few days before Steele's *The Conscious Lovers* was acted.

The supposed persons of this musical drama are generally super-natural, as gods, and goddesses, and heroes, which at least are descended from them, and are in due time to be adopted into their number. The subject therefore being extended beyond the limits of human nature, admits of that sort of marvellous and surprising conduct which is rejected in other plays. Human impossibilities are to be received as they are in faith; because, where gods are intro-duced, a supreme power is to be understood, and second causes are out of doors. Yet propriety is to be observed even here. The gods are all to manage their peculiar provinces; and what was attributed by the heathens to one power ought not to be performed by any other. Phoebus must foretell, Mercury must charm with his caduceus, and Juno must reconcile the quarrels of the marriage-bed. To conclude, they must all act according to their distinct and pecu-liar characters. If the persons represented were to speak upon the stage, it would follow of necessity that the expressions should be lofty, figurative, and majestical: but the nature of an opera denies the frequent use of those poetical ornaments; for vocal music, though it often admits a loftiness of sound, yet always exacts an harmonious sweetness; or, to distinguish yet more justly, the recita-tive part of the opera requires a more masculine beauty of expres-sion and sound; the other, which (for want of a proper English word) I must call the *songish part*, must abound in the softness and variety of numbers; its principal intention being to please the hearing rather than to gratify the understanding.[1] [II, 35.]

[1] For a satirical account of opera, see Addison, *The Spectator*, no. 18 (21 March 1711).

The Epic Poem

Epic poetry is the highest genre. (Dryden)

The end of epic poetry is to form the mind to heroic virtue by example. The action, characters and style must be sublime. (Dryden)

The fable or moral, the action, the characters. The fable is the soul of the epic poem. (Dennis)

How to make an epic poem. (Pope)

JOHN DRYDEN, Heroic Poetry and Poetic Licence. Prefixed to *The State of Innocence* (1677)

Heroic poetry, which [little critics] contemn, has ever been esteemed, and ever will be, the greatest work of human nature: in that rank has Aristotle placed it;[1] and Longinus is so full of the like expressions that he abundantly confirms the other's testimony. Horace as plainly delivers his opinion, and particularly praises Homer in these verses:

> Trojani Belli scriptorem, Maxime Lolli,
> dum tu declamas Romae, Praeneste relegi:
> qui quid sit pulchrum, quid turpe, quid utile, quid non,
> planius ac melius Chrysippo et Crantore dicit.[2]

And in another place, modestly excluding himself from the number of poets, because he only writ odes and satires, he tells you a poet is such an one,

> cui mens divinior, atque os
> magna sonaturum.[3]

[1] Aristotle argued (*Poetics*, xxvi) that tragedy is a higher form of art than the epic, but most Renaissance and seventeenth-century commentators held the opposite view. In "A Discourse Concerning Satire" Dryden states Aristotle's view correctly (*ed. cit.*, II, 620).

[2] *Epistles*, I. ii. 1–4. ("My dear Lollius Maximus, while you are studying eloquence in Rome, at Praeneste I have read again the poet of the Trojan war, who shows better and more fully than Chrysippus and Crantor have done what is noble and what is base, what is useful and what is not.")

[3] *Satires*, I. iv. 43–4. ("whose soul is more divine, and whose mouth is able to express sublime things".)

Quotations are superfluous in an established truth: otherwise I could reckon up, amongst the moderns, all the Italian commentators on Aristotle's book of poetry; and, amongst the French, the greatest of this age, Boileau[4] and Rapin;[5] the latter of which is alone sufficient, were all other critics lost, to teach anew the rules of writing. Any man who will seriously consider the nature of an epic poem, how it agrees with that of poetry in general, which is to instruct and to delight, what actions it describes, and what persons they are chiefly whom it informs, will find it a work which indeed is full of difficulty in the attempt, but admirable when 'tis well performed. [I, 198–9.]

JOHN DRYDEN, Dedication of the *Aeneid* (1697)

A heroic poem, truly such, is undoubtedly the greatest work which the soul of man is capable to perform. The design of it is to form the mind to heroic virtue by example; 'tis conveyed in verse, that it may delight while it instructs. The action of it is always one, entire, and great. The least and most trivial episodes, or under-actions, which are interwoven in it, are parts either necessary, or convenient to carry on the main design: either so necessary that without them the poem must be imperfect, or so convenient that no others can be imagined more suitable to the place in which they are. There is nothing to be left void in a firm building; even the cavities ought not to be filled with rubbish, which is of a perishable kind, destructive to the strength, but with brick or stone, though of less pieces, yet of the same nature, and fitted to the crannies. Even the least portions of them must be of the epic kind; all things must be grave, majestical, and sublime: nothing of a foreign nature, like the trifling novels[6] which Ariosto and others have inserted in their poems, by which the reader is misled into another sort of pleasure, opposite to that which is designed in an epic poem. One raises the soul and hardens it to virtue, the other softens it again and unbends it into vice. One conduces to the poet's aim, the completing of his work, which he is driving on, labouring and hastening in every line: the other slackens his pace, diverts him from his way, and

4 See *Art Poétique* (1674), iii. 160 ff.
5 *Réflexions sur la poétique d'Aristote* (1674), II. ii–xvi.
6 tales, usually of love.

locks him up like a knight-errant in an enchanted castle, when he should be pursuing his first adventure. [III, 1003.]

JOHN DENNIS, *Remarks on Prince Arthur* (1696)
I think myself obliged to give the reader an account of the method which I propounded to use in the following remarks. In the first part I intended to shew that Mr. Blackmore's action has neither unity, nor integrity, nor morality, nor universality, and consequently that he can have no fable and no heroic poem. In the second part I designed to come to the narration; and to shew that it is neither probable, delightful, nor wonderful. I propounded to shew that there are three things that make a narration delightful: the persons introduced, the things related, and the manner of relating them. I resolved to consider the first of these, and to prove that the poetical persons ought to have manners, and that those manners ought to have the following qualifications: that they ought to be good, convenient, resembling, and equal, and that besides there ought to be an unity of character in the principal person; and that that unity of character, like an universal soul, was to run through the whole poem. Next, I determined to make it appear that Mr. Blackmore's characters have none of the forementioned qualifications. Then I pretended[7] to convince the reader that the things contained in Mr. Blackmore's narration are neither in their own natures delightful, nor numerous enough, nor various enough, nor rightly disposed, nor surprising, nor pathetic. [I, 46.]

JOHN DENNIS, *On the Moral of an Epic Poem* (1721)
You[8] say that an epic poet is not obliged to have the moral first in his mind: for, say you, no author can form the narration of any great and memorable action but some moral will arise from it, whether the writer intends it or not. Suppose this were true, a poet is to instruct by his art and not by chance. But the very contrary of this is true: a poet may form the narration of a hundred great and memorable actions, if these actions are particular and historical, and not one moral shall arise from them all; as the battle of Pharsalia, the

[7] intended, designed.

[8] i.e. Sir Richard Blackmore, in his "Essay upon Epic Poetry" published in *Essays upon Several Subjects* (1716).

death of Brutus and Cassius, the death of Cato, the death of King Lear, the death of Hamlet, the death of Harry the Fourth. And I defy any poet to form a general action, and general characters, but he must form them upon a moral, and consequently that moral must be first in his head. Can any one believe that Aesop first told a story of a cock and a bull, and afterwards made a moral to it? Or is it reasonable to believe that he made his moral first, and afterwards, to prove it, contrived his fable? Now I know no difference that there is between one of Aesop's Fables and the fable of an epic poem, as to their natures, though there be many and great ones as to their circumstances. 'Tis impossible for a poet to form any fable unless the moral be first in his head. [II, 110.]

ALEXANDER POPE, The Art of Sinking in Poetry (1728)

A RECEIPT TO MAKE AN EPIC POEM[9]

An epic poem, the critics agree, is the greatest work human nature is capable of. They have already laid down many mechanical rules for compositions of this sort, but at the same time they cut off almost all undertakers from the possibility of ever performing them; for the first qualification they unanimously require in a poet is a genius. I shall here endeavour (for the benefit of my countrymen) to make it manifest that epic poems may be made *without a genius*, nay, without learning or much reading. This must necessarily be of great use to all those who confess they never *read*, and of whom the world is convinced they never *learn*. What Molière observes[10] of making a dinner, that any man can do it *with money*, and if a professed cook cannot do it *without* he has his art for nothing; the same may be said of making a poem, 'tis easily brought about by him that *has* a genius, but the skill lies in doing it without one. In pursuance of this end, I shall present the reader with a plain and

---

[9] Pope here satirises the little wits' pretence—particularly Blackmore's—to writing epic poetry. His advice is to be inverted all through. This chapter of "The Art of Sinking in Poetry" first appeared in *The Guardian*, no. 78, 10 June 1713.

[10] *L'Avare*, III. i.

certain *recipe*, by which any author in the *bathos*[11] may be qualified for this grand performance.

FOR THE FABLE

Take out of any old poem, history-book, romance, or legend, (for instance *Geoffrey of Monmouth* or *Don Belianis of Greece*[12]) those parts of story which afford most scope for *long descriptions*. Put these pieces together, and throw all the adventures you fancy into *one* tale. Then take a hero, whom you may choose for the sound of his name, and put him into the midst of these adventures. There let him *work* for twelve books; at the end of which you may take him out, ready prepared to *conquer* or to *marry*; it being necessary that the conclusion of an epic poem be *fortunate*.

TO MAKE AN EPISODE

Take any remaining adventure of your former collection in which you could no way involve your hero; or any unfortunate accident that was too good to be thrown away; and it will be of use, applied to any other person, who may be lost and *evaporate* in the course of the work, without the least damage to the composition.

FOR THE MORAL AND ALLEGORY

These you may extract out of the fable afterwards, at your leisure: be sure you *strain* them sufficiently.

FOR THE MANNERS

For those of the hero, take all the best qualities you can find in the most celebrated heroes of antiquity; if they will not be reduced to a *consistency*, lay 'em *all on a heap* upon him. But be sure they are qualities which your *patron* would be thought to have; and to

[11] Pope is making fun of the false sublime and therefore writing upon *bathos* in mock imitation of Longinus' treatise on *hupsos*, i.e. on the sublime.

[12] Francis Kirkman, *The Famous and Delectable History of Don Bellianis of Greece* (1673), founded on the romance originally written in Spanish by Geronimo Fernandez (1587).

prevent any mistake which the world may be subject to, select from the alphabet those capital letters that compose his name, and set them at the head of a dedication before your poem. However, do not absolutely observe the exact quantity of these virtues, it not being determined whether or no it be necessary for the hero of a poem to be an honest man. For the *under-characters*, gather them from Homer and Virgil, and change the names as occasion serves.

FOR THE MACHINES

Take of *deities*, male and female, as many as you can use. Separate them into two equal parts, and keep Jupiter in the middle. Let Juno put him in a ferment, and Venus mollify him. Remember on all occasions to make use of volatile Mercury. If you have need of devils, draw them out of Milton's *Paradise*, and extract your *spirits* from Tasso. The use of these machines is evident; for since no epic poem can possibly subsist without them, the wisest way is to reserve them for your greatest necessities. When you cannot extricate your hero by any human means, or yourself by your own wit, seek relief from Heaven, and the gods will do your business very readily. This is according to the direct prescription of Horace in his *Art of Poetry*:

> Nec deus intersit, nisi dignus vindice nodus
> Inciderit.[13]

That is to say, a poet should never call upon the gods for their assistance but when he is in great perplexity.

FOR THE DESCRIPTIONS

For a *tempest*. Take Eurus,[14] Zephyr,[15] Auster[16] and Boreas,[17] and cast them together in one verse. Add to these of rain, lightning and of thunder (the loudest you can) *quantum sufficit*.[18] Mix your

---

[13] *Ars Poetica*, 191–2. ("Let no god interfere unless the dénouement requires divine intervention.") Note Pope's deliberate mistranslation.

[14] east or south-east wind.   [15] west wind.

[16] south wind.   [17] north wind.

[18] as much as is necessary.

F

clouds and billows well together till they foam, and thicken your description here and there with a quicksand. Brew your tempest well in your head, before you set it a blowing.

For a *battle*. Pick a large quantity of images and descriptions from Homer's *Iliads*, with a spice or two of Virgil, and if there remain any overplus, you may lay them by for a *skirmish*. Season it well with *similes*, and it will make an *excellent battle*.

For a *burning town*. If such a description be necessary (because it is certain there is one in Virgil), old Troy is ready burnt to your hands. But if you fear that would be thought borrowed, a chapter or two of the *Theory of the Conflagration*,[19] well circumstanced, and done into verse, will be a good succedaneum.

As for *similes* and *metaphors*, they may be found all over the creation; the most ignorant may *gather* them, but the danger is in *applying* them. For this advise with your *bookseller*. [pp. 80–5.]

The Pastoral

The pastoral is an image of the golden age. Its chief qualities are simplicity, brevity and delicacy. (Pope)

ALEXANDER POPE, A Discourse on Pastoral Poetry (1717)
A pastoral is an imitation of the action of a shepherd, or one considered under that character.[1] The form of this imitation is dramatic, or narrative, or mixed of both; the fable simple, the manners not too polite nor too rustic. The thoughts are plain, yet admit a little quickness and passion, but that short and flowing; the expression humble, yet as pure as the language will afford; neat, but not florid; easy, and yet lively. In short, the fable, manners, thoughts, and expressions are full of the greatest simplicity in nature.

The complete character of this poem consists in simplicity,

[19] Thomas Burnet's *Telluris Theoria Sacra* (1681).
[1] Pope follows Rapin's *Dissertatio de Carmine Pastorali* (1659) fairly closely.

brevity, and delicacy; the two first of which render an eclogue natural, and the last delightful.

If we would copy Nature, it may be useful to take this idea along with us, that pastoral is an image of what they call the golden age. So that we are not to describe our shepherds as shepherds at this day really are, but as they may be conceived then to have been, when the best of men followed the employment. To carry this resemblance yet farther, it would not be amiss to give these shepherds some skill in astronomy, as far as it may be useful to that sort of life. And an air of piety to the gods should shine through the poem, which so visibly appears in all the works of antiquity. And it ought to preserve some relish of the old way of writing; the connections should be loose, the narrations and descriptions short, and the periods concise. Yet it is not sufficient that the sentences only be brief, the whole eclogue should be so too. For we cannot suppose poetry in those days to have been the business of men, but their recreation at vacant hours.

But with a respect to the present age, nothing more conduces to make these composures natural than when some knowledge in rural affairs is discovered. This may be made to appear rather done by chance than on design, and sometimes is best shewn by inference; lest by too much study to seem natural we destroy that easy simplicity from whence arises the delight. For what is inviting in this sort of poetry proceeds not so much from the idea of that business as of the tranquillity of a country life.[2]

We must therefore use some illusion to render a pastoral delightful; and this consists in exposing the best side only of a shepherd's life, and in concealing its miseries. [I, 24-7.]

[2] This was Fontenelle's premiss in his *Discours sur la nature de l'églogue* (1688). Pope thus blends the principles derived from imitation of the ancients (Rapin) with those based on a rational explanation of the kind of pleasure given by pastorals (Fontenelle).

The Ode

The ode has the majesty of the epic poem, but is bolder and more vehement. (Dennis)

The Pindaric ode is not irregular, as has been generally assumed. The structure of Pindar's odes should be imitated. (Congreve)

JOHN DENNIS, Preface to *The Court of Death* (1695)
Thus far goes Rapin;[1] and we may conclude from the words of that famous critic, that the ode ought to have as much boldness, elevation and majesty as epic poetry itself; but then it is certain that it ought to have more vehemence, more transport and more enthusiasm. The reason is evident, for the design of the ode (I mean upon great occasions) is, like that of heroic poetry, to move the reader, and cause in him admiration. Now, by heroic poetry the reader's mind is exalted gradually, with a more sedate and composed majesty; but the ode, by reason of the shortness of its compass, is obliged to fly into transport at first, and to make use immediately of all its fury, and its most violent efforts, or else it would want time to work its effect. [I, 42.]

WILLIAM CONGREVE, A Discourse on the Pindarique Ode. Prefixed to *A Pindarique Ode* (1706)
The character of these late Pindarics is a bundle of rambling incoherent thoughts, expressed in a like parcel of irregular stanzas, which also consist of such another complication of disproportioned, uncertain and perplexed verses and rhymes. And I appeal to any reader, if this is not the condition in which these titular odes appear.
    On the contrary, there is nothing more regular than the odes of Pindar, both as to the exact observation of the measures and numbers of his stanzas and verses, and the perpetual coherence of his thoughts.

[1] Dennis has quoted Rapin's remarks on the ode (*Réflexions*, II. xxx).

For though his digressions are frequent, and his transitions sudden, yet is there ever some secret connexion, which, though not always appearing to the eye, never fails to communicate itself to the understanding of the reader.

The liberty which he took in his numbers, and which has been so misunderstood and misapplied by his pretended imitators, was only in varying the stanzas in different odes; but in each particular ode they are ever correspondent one to another in their turns, and according to the order of the ode. . . .

The method observed in the composition of these odes was therefore as follows. The poet, having made choice of a certain number of verses to constitute his *strophe* or first stanza, was obliged to observe the same in his *antistrophe* or second stanza; . . . which accordingly perpetually agreed whenever repeated, both in number of verses and quantity of feet. He was then again at liberty to make a new choice for his third stanza, or *epode*; where, accordingly, he diversified his numbers as his ear or fancy led him, composing that stanza of more or fewer verses than the former, and those verses of different measures and quantities, for the greater variety of harmony, and entertainment of the ear.

But then this *epode* being thus formed, he was strictly obliged to the same measure, as often as he should repeat it in the order of his ode, so that every *epode* in the same ode is eternally the same in measure and quantity, in respect to itself; as is also every *strophe* and *antistrophe*, in respect to each other. . . .

However, though there be no necessity that our triumphal odes should consist of the three afore-mentioned stanzas; yet if the reader can observe that the great variation of the numbers in the third stanza (call it *epode*, or what you please) has a pleasing effect in the ode, and makes him return to the first and second stanzas with more appetite than he could do if always cloyed with the same quantities and measures, I cannot see why some use may not be made of Pindar's example, to the great improvement of the English ode. There is certainly a pleasure in beholding anything that has art and difficulty in the contrivance; especially if it appears so carefully executed that the difficulty does not shew itself, till it is sought for; and that the seeming easiness of the work first sets us upon the enquiry. Nothing can be called beautiful without proportion.

When symmetry and harmony are wanting, neither the eye nor the ear can be pleased. Therefore certainly poetry, which includes painting and music, should not be destitute of them; and of all poetry especially the ode, whose end and essence is harmony. [sig. A, Av, Az.]

Satire

Personal satire is justified when it is the only means of revenge, or when it makes examples of vicious men. A satire should caution against one particular vice or folly. (Dryden)

The satirist can shame men whom the law cannot touch. (Pope)

The finest kind of satire is mock-epic, which laughs folly out of countenance. The verse best suited to it is the heroic couplet. (Dryden)

JOHN DRYDEN, A Discourse Concerning the Original and Progress
                of Satire. Prefixed to *The Satires of Juvenal and
                Persius* (1693)

That former sort of satire, which is known in England by the name of lampoon, is a dangerous sort of weapon, and for the most part unlawful. We have no moral right on the reputation of other men. 'Tis taking from them what we cannot restore to them. There are only two reasons for which we may be permitted to write lampoons; and I will not promise that they can always justify us. The first is revenge, when we have been affronted in the same nature, or have been any ways notoriously abused, and can make ourselves no other reparation. . . . The second reason which may justify a poet when he writes against a particular person . . . is when he is become a public nuisance. All those whom Horace in his Satires, and Persius and Juvenal have mentioned in theirs with a brand of infamy, are wholly such. 'Tis an action of virtue to make examples of vicious men. They may and ought to be upbraided with their crimes and follies: both for their own amendment, if they are not yet incorrigible, and for the terror of others, to hinder them from falling into those enormities which they see are so severely punished in the persons of others. . . .

Will Your Lordship be pleased to prolong my audience only so far, till I tell you my own trivial thoughts how a modern satire should be made? I will not deviate in the least from the precepts and examples of the ancients, who were always our best masters. I will only illustrate them, and discover some of the hidden beauties in their designs, that we thereby may form our own in imitation of them. Will you please but to observe that Persius, the least in dignity of all the three,[1] has, notwithstanding, been the first who has discovered to us this important secret in the designing of a perfect satire; that it ought only to treat of one subject; to be confined to one particular theme; or, at least, to one principally. If other vices occur in the management of the chief, they should only be transiently lashed, and not be insisted on so as to make the design double. . . .

Under this unity of theme, or subject, is comprehended another rule for perfecting the design of true satire. The poet is bound, and that *ex officio*, to give his reader some one precept of moral virtue, and to caution him against some one particular vice or folly. Other virtues, subordinate to the first, may be recommended under that chief head; and other vices or follies may be scourged, besides that which he principally intends. But he is chiefly to inculcate one virtue, and insist on that. [II, 645-6, 661-2.]

ALEXANDER POPE, *Epilogue to the Satires*, Dialogue II (1738)

> Ask you what provocation I have had?
> The strong antipathy of good to bad.
> When truth or virtue an affront endures,
> 200 Th 'affront is mine, my friend, and should be yours.

[1] Horace, Juvenal, Persius.

Mine, as a foe professed to false pretence,
Who think a coxcomb's honour like his sense;
Mine, as a friend to ev'ry worthy mind;
And mine as man, who feel for all mankind.
   Fr.[2] You're strangely proud.
205   *P.*[3] So proud, I am no slave:
So impudent, I own myself no knave:
So odd, my country's ruin makes me grave.
Yes, I am proud; I must be proud to see
Men not afraid of God, afraid of me:
210 Safe from the bar, the pulpit, and the throne,
Yet touched and shamed by *ridicule* alone.
   O sacred weapon! left for truth's defence,
Sole dread of folly, vice, and insolence!
To all but Heav'n-directed hands denied,
215 The Muse may give thee, but the Gods must guide.
Rev'rent I touch thee! but with honest zeal;
To rouse the watchmen of the public weal,
To virtue's work provoke the tardy Hall,[4]
And goad the prelate slumb'ring in his stall.

JOHN DRYDEN, A Discourse Concerning the Original and Progress of Satire. Prefixed to *The Satires of Juvenal and Persius* (1693)

Of the best and finest manner of satire I have said enough in the comparison betwixt Juvenal and Horace: 'tis that sharp, well-mannered way of laughing a folly out of countenance, of which your Lordship[5] is the best master in this age. I will proceed to the versification, which is most proper for it, and add somewhat to what I have said already on that subject. The sort of verse which is called burlesque, consisting of eight syllables, or four feet, is that which our excellent Hudibras[6] has chosen.... His satire is of the Varronian kind,[7] though unmixed with prose. The choice of his numbers is suitable enough to his design, as he has managed it.

[2] Friend.   [3] Pope.
[4] Westminster Hall, the seat of the High Court of Justice.
[5] The Earl of Dorset.   [6] Samuel Butler.
[7] parody or mock-epic.

But in any other hand, the shortness of his verse, and the quick returns of rhyme, had debased the dignity of style. And besides, the double rhyme (a necessary companion of burlesque writing) is not so proper for manly satire, for it turns earnest too much to jest, and gives us a boyish kind of pleasure. It tickles awkwardly with a kind of pain, to the best sort of readers; we are pleased ungratefully, and, if I may say so, against our liking. . . . 'Tis, indeed, below so great a master to make use of such a little instrument. But his good sense is perpetually shining through all he writes; it affords us not the time of finding faults: we pass through the levity of his rhyme, and are immediately carried into some admirable useful thought. . . .

The quickness of your imagination, my Lord, has already prevented[8] me; and you know beforehand that I would prefer the verse of ten syllables, which we call the English heroic, to that of eight. This is truly my opinion. For this sort of number is more roomy; the thought can turn itself with greater ease in a larger compass. When the rhyme comes too thick upon us, it straitens the expression; we are thinking of the close, when we should be employed in adorning the thought. It makes a poet giddy with turning in a space too narrow for his imagination; he loses many beauties without gaining one advantage. For a burlesque rhyme I have already concluded to be none; or if it were, 'tis more easily purchased in ten syllables than in eight: in both occasions 'tis as in a tennis-court, when the strokes of greater force are given when we strike out and play at length. Tassoni and Boileau have left us the best examples of this way in the *Secchia Rapita* and the *Lutrin*, and next them Merlin Coccaius in his *Baldus*.[9] I will speak only of the two former, because the last is written in Latin verse. The *Secchia Rapita* is an Italian poem, a satire of the Varronian kind. 'Tis written in the stanza of eight,[10] which is their measure for heroic verse. The words are stately, the numbers smooth, the turn both of thoughts and words is happy. The first six lines of the stanza seem majestical and severe: but the two last turn them all into a

[8] forestalled.

[9] Alessandro Tassoni, *La Secchia Rapita* (1622); Boileau, *Le Lutrin* (1674, 1683); Merlinus Coccaius, *Poema macaronicum de gestis Baldi* (1517).

[10] i.e. ottava rima.

pleasant ridicule. Boileau, if I am not much deceived, has modelled from hence his famous *Lutrin*. He had read the burlesque poetry of Scarron[11] with some kind of indignation, as witty as it was, and found nothing in France that was worthy of his imitation. But he copied the Italian so well, that his own may pass for an original. He writes it in the French heroic verse, and calls it an heroic poem: his subject is trivial, but his verse is noble. I doubt not but he had Virgil in his eye, for we find many admirable imitations of him, and some parodies. . . .

This,[12] I think, my Lord, to be the most beautiful, and most noble kind of satire. Here is the majesty of the heroic finely mixed with the venom of the other; and raising the delight which otherwise would be flat and vulgar, by the sublimity of the expression. [II, 663–5.]

Translation

Three methods: literal translation, paraphrase and imitation. It is best to steer a middle course between literal translation and paraphrase. The aim is to make the ancient author speak as he would have done if he had lived in the present age. (Dryden)

The main difficulty in translating is to keep the same level of style as in the original. (Pope)

JOHN DRYDEN, Preface to *Ovid's Epistles* (1680)
All translation I suppose may be reduced to these three heads.

First, that of metaphrase, or turning an author word by word, and line by line, from one language into another. Thus, or near this manner, was Horace his *Art of Poetry* translated by Ben Jonson. The second way is that of paraphrase, or translation with latitude, where

[11] *Virgile Travesti* (1648–59).
[12] i.e. mock-epic, as exemplified by Boileau's *Lutrin*.

the author is kept in view by the translator so as never to be lost, but his words are not so strictly followed as his sense, and that too is admitted to be amplified, but not altered. Such is Mr. Waller's translation of Virgil's fourth *Aeneid*.[1] The third way is that of imitation, where the translator (if now he has not lost that name) assumes the liberty not only to vary from the words and sense, but to forsake them both as he sees occasion; and, taking only some general hints from the original, to run division on the groundwork,[2] as he pleases. Such is Mr. Cowley's practice in turning two odes of Pindar and one of Horace into English.[3] [I, 182.]

JOHN DRYDEN, Dedication of the *Aeneis* (1697)
On the whole matter, I thought fit to steer betwixt the two extremes of paraphrase and literal translation: to keep as near my author as I could without losing all his graces, the most eminent of which are in the beauty of his words. And those words, I must add, are always figurative. Such of these as would retain their elegance in our tongue, I have endeavoured to graff on it; but most of them are of necessity to be lost, because they will not shine in any but their own.[4] Virgil has sometimes two of them in a line; but the scantiness of our heroic verse is not capable of receiving more than one, and that too must expiate for many others which have none. Such is the difference of the languages, or such my want of skill in choosing words. Yet I may presume to say, and I hope with as much reason as the French translator,[5] that taking all the materials of this divine author, I have endeavoured to make Virgil speak such English as he would himself have spoken, if he had been born in England, and in this present age. [III, 1055.]

ALEXANDER POPE, Preface to *The Iliad* (1715)
It should then be considered what methods may afford some equivalent in our language for the graces of these in the Greek. It is certain no literal translation can be just to an excellent original

---

[1] *The Passion of Dido* (1658), by Edmund Waller and Sidney Godolphin.
[2] to produce variations on a theme.
[3] In Cowley's *Poems* (1656).
[4] See extract p. 181 below (from Dryden's Dedication of the *Aeneis*).
[5] J. R. de Segrais, *Enéide* (1668).

in a superior language: but it is a great mistake to imagine (as many have done) that a rash paraphrase can make amends for this general defect; which is no less in danger to lose the spirit of an ancient by deviating into the modern manners of expression. If there be sometimes a *darkness*, there is often a *light* in antiquity, which nothing better preserves than a version almost literal. I know no liberties one ought to take but those which are necessary for transfusing the spirit of the original, and supporting the poetical style of the translation: and I will venture to say, there have not been more men misled in former times by a servile dull adherence to the letter, than have been deluded in ours by a chimerical insolent hope of raising and improving their author. It is not to be doubted that the *fire* of the poem is what a translator should principally regard, as it is most likely to expire in his managing. However, it is his safest way to be content with preserving this to his utmost in the whole, without endeavouring to be more than he finds his author is in any particular place. 'Tis a great secret in writing to know when to be plain, and when poetical and figurative; and it is what Homer will teach us if we will but follow modestly in his footsteps. Where his diction is bold and lofty, let us raise ours as high as we can; but where his is plain and humble, we ought not to be deterred from imitating him by the fear of incurring the censure of a mere English critic. Nothing that belongs to Homer seems to have been more commonly mistaken than the just pitch of his style: some of his translators having swelled into fustian in a proud confidence of the *sublime*; others sunk into flatness in a cold and timorous notion of *simplicity*. . . . There is a *graceful* and *dignified* simplicity, as well as a *bald* and *sordid* one, which differ as much from each other as the air of a *plain* man from that of a *sloven*: 'tis one thing to be tricked up, and another not to be dressed at all. Simplicity is the mean between ostentation and rusticity. [VII, 17–18.]

III STYLE

Style

Figurative language condemned. (Sheffield)

Similitudes v. metaphors. (Dryden)

Different genres require different styles. (Dryden, Pope)

General requirements for style: propriety, perspicuity, elegance and cadence. (Hughes)

In epic poetry the language should be both perspicuous and sublime. Metaphors contribute to sublimity. (Addison)

Poetic diction. (Johnson)

JOHN SHEFFIELD, EARL OF MULGRAVE, *An Essay upon Poetry*
(1682)

> Figures of speech, which poets think so fine,[1]
> Art's needless varnish to make nature shine,
> Are all but paint upon a beauteous face,
> And in descriptions only claim a place. [II, 291.]

JOHN DRYDEN, Dedication of the *Aeneis* (1697)
Similitudes, as I have said, are not for tragedy, which is all violent, and where the passions are in a perpetual ferment; for there they deaden where they should animate; they are not of the nature of dialogue, unless in comedy. A metaphor is almost all the stage can suffer, which is a kind of similitude comprehended in a word. But this figure has a contrary effect in heroic poetry: there 'tis employed to raise the admiration, which is its proper business. And admiration is not of so violent a nature as fear or hope, compassion or horror, or any concernment we can have for such or such a person on the stage. Not but I confess, that similitudes

[1] Cf. extract p. 180 below (from Dryden's Preface to *Troilus and Cressida*).

and descriptions, when drawn into an unreasonable length, must needs nauseate the reader. [III, 1036–7.]

JOHN DRYDEN, Preface to *Religio Laici* (1682)
If anyone be so lamentable a critic as to require the smoothness, the numbers and the turn of heroic poetry in this poem, I must tell him that if he has not read Horace, I have studied him, and hope the style of his Epistles is not ill imitated here. The expressions of a poem designed purely for instruction ought to be plain and natural, and yet majestic: for here the poet is presumed to be a kind of law-giver, and those three qualities which I have named are proper to the legislative style. The florid, elevated and figurative way is for the passions; for love and hatred, fear and anger, are begotten in the soul by shewing their objects out of their true proportion; either greater than the life, or less; but instruction is to be given by shewing them what they naturally are. A man is to be cheated into passion, but to be reasoned into truth. [I, 311.]

ALEXANDER POPE, Postscript to *The Odyssey* (1726)
From the nature of the poem we shall form an idea of the *style*. The diction is to follow the images, and to take its colour from the complexion of the thoughts. Accordingly the *Odyssey* is not always clothed in the majesty of verse proper to tragedy, but sometimes descends into the plainer narrative, and sometimes even to that familiar dialogue essential to comedy. However, where it cannot support a sublimity, it always preserves a dignity, or at least a propriety. . . .

The question is, how far a poet, in pursuing the description or image of an action, can attach himself to *little circumstances*, without vulgarity or trifling? what particulars are proper, and enliven the image; or what are impertinent, and clog it? In this matter painting is to be consulted, and the whole regard had to those circumstances which contribute to form a full, and yet not a confused, idea of the thing.

Epithets are of vast service to this effect, and the right use of these is often the only expedient to render the narration poetical.

The great point of judgment is to distinguish when to speak simply, and when figuratively: but whenever the poet is obliged by the nature of his subject to descend to the lower manner of writing, an elevated style would be affected, and therefore ridiculous; and the more he was forced upon figures and metaphors to avoid that lowness, the more the image would be broken, and consequently obscure.

One may add that the use of the grand style on little subjects is not only ludicrous, but a sort of transgression against the rules of proportion and mechanics: 'tis using a vast force to lift a *feather*.

I believe, now I am upon this head, it will be found a just observation that the *low actions of life* cannot be put into a figurative style without being ridiculous, but *things natural* can. Metaphors raise the latter into dignity, as we see in the *Georgics*; but throw the former into ridicule, as in the *Lutrin*. I think this may very well be accounted for: laughter implies censure; inanimate and irrational beings are not objects of censure, therefore these may be elevated as much as you please, and no ridicule follows: but when rational beings are represented above their real character, it becomes ridiculous in art, because it is vicious in morality. The bees in Virgil,[2] were they rational beings, would be ridiculous by having their actions and manners represented on a level with creatures so superior as men; since it would imply folly or pride, which are the proper objects of ridicule.

The use of pompous expression for low actions or thoughts is the *true sublime* of *Don Quixote*. How far unfit it is for epic poetry appears in its being the perfection of the mock-epic. It is so far from being the sublime of *tragedy*, that it is the cause of all *bombast*, when poets instead of being (as they imagine) constantly lofty, only preserve throughout a painful equality of fustian. That continued swell of language (which runs indiscriminately even through their lowest characters, and rattles like some mightiness of meaning in the most indifferent subjects) is of a piece with that perpetual elevation of tone which the players have learned from it; and which is not *speaking*, but *vociferating*.

There is still more reason for a variation of style in *epic* poetry than in *tragic*, to distinguish between that *language of the gods* proper to the muse who sings, and is inspired; and that of *men* who

[2] *Georgics*, iv. 67 ff.

are introduced speaking only according to nature. Farther, there ought to be a difference of style observed in the speeches of human persons and those of deities; and again, in those which may be called set harangues or orations, and those which are only conversation or dialogue. Homer has more of the latter than any other poet: what Virgil does by two or three words of narration, Homer still performs by speeches; not only replies, but even rejoinders are frequent in him, a practice almost unknown to Virgil. This renders his poems more animated, but less grave and majestic; and consequently necessitates the frequent use of a lower style. . . .

The *sublime* style is more easily counterfeited than the *natural*; something that passes for it, or sounds like it, is common in all false writers. But nature, purity, perspicuity and simplicity, never walk in the clouds; they are obvious to all capacities; and where they are not evident, they do not exist. . . .

Whoever expects here the same pomp of verse and the same ornaments of diction as in the *Iliad*, he will, and he ought to be disappointed. Were the original otherwise, it had been an offence against nature; and were the translation so, it were an offence against Homer, which is the same thing. [X, 386–9.]

JOHN HUGHES, Of Style (1698)

All the qualifications of a good style, I think, may be reduced under these four heads: propriety, perspicuity, elegance, and cadence; and each of these, except the last, has some relation to the thoughts, as well as to the words.

Propriety of thoughts is two-fold: the first is when the thoughts are proper in themselves, and so it is opposed to nonsense; and the other when they are proper to the occasion, and so it is opposed to impertinence.

Propriety of words, the first qualification of a good style, is when the words do justly and exactly represent, or signify, the thoughts which they stand for. . . .

There is another particular which I shall mention here, because I think it differs but little from propriety, and that is purity, which I take more particularly to respect the language, as it is now spoken or written. The rule of this is modern use, according to that of Horace:

Multa renascentur quae iam cecidere, cadentque
Quae nunc sunt in honore vocabula, si volet usus,
Quem penes arbitrium est, et ius et norma loquendi.[3]

By this rule, all obsolete words are to be avoided. But to a man of long practice and reputation in the language, the privilege may be allowed sometimes of reviving old, or bringing in new words, where the common ones are deficient. For this reason, we dare not censure so great a man as Milton for his antiquated words, which he took from Spenser. . . .

Little need be said of the second qualification, *viz*. perspicuity. If your thoughts be not clear, 'tis impossible your words should, and consequently you can't be understood. The chief secret here is to express yourself in such a manner as to transfer your ideas into the reader's mind, and to set the thing before him in the very same light in which it appears to yourself. Here an extreme is to be shunned, lest, while you aim to make your meaning fully understood, you become verbose. So that the art lies in expressing your thought clearly in as few words as possible. . . .

Elegance of thought is what we commonly call wit; which adds to propriety, beauty, and pleases our fancy, while propriety entertains our judgment. This depends so much on genius, that 'tis impossible to teach it by rules. To the elegance of words, or style, belong all the figures of rhetoric, and to use these to advantage requires a judgment well formed by observation. In this therefore, as in learning the graces upon an instrument of music, good examples are the best instruction. . . .

The last qualification I mentioned is cadence, in poetry called the numbers. It consists in a disposing of the words in such order, and with such variation of periods, as may strike the ear with a sort of musical delight, which is a considerable part of eloquence. This is chiefly that which makes a style smooth, and not merely the avoiding of harsh words. The best way to attain it is to prepare yourself, before you begin to write, by reading in some

---

[3] *Ars Poetica*, 70–2. ("Many words will revive which today have become obsolete, and many will disappear which are now current, if usage so decides, which is the arbiter and norm of language.") Cf. extract p. 181 below from Dryden's Dedication of the *Aeneis*.

harmonious style, that so you may get your ear well in tune. [pp. 248–52].

JOSEPH ADDISON, *The Spectator*, no. 285 (26 January 1712)

If clearness and perspicuity were only to be consulted, the poet would have nothing else to do but to clothe his thoughts in the most plain and natural expressions. But, since it often happens that the most obvious phrases, and those which are used in ordinary conversation, become too familiar to the ear, and contract a kind of meanness by passing through the mouths of the vulgar, a poet should take particular care to guard himself against idiomatic[4] ways of speaking. Ovid and Lucan have many poornesses of expression upon this account, as taking up with the first phrases that offered, without putting themselves to the trouble of looking after such as would not only be natural, but also elevated and sublime. Milton has but a few failings in this kind. . . .

The great masters in composition know very well that many an elegant phrase becomes improper for a poet or an orator, when it has been debased by common use. For this reason the works of ancient authors, which are written in dead languages, have a great advantage over those which are written in languages that are now spoken. Were there any mean phrases or idioms in Virgil and Homer, they would not shock the ear of the most delicate modern reader so much as they would have done that of an old Greek or Roman, because we never hear them pronounced in our streets, or in ordinary conversation.

It is not therefore sufficient that the language of an epic poem be perspicuous, unless it be also sublime. To this end it ought to deviate from the common forms and ordinary phrases of speech. The judgment of a poet very much discovers itself in shunning the common roads of expression without falling into such ways of speech as may seem stiff and unnatural; he must not swell into a false sublime, by endeavouring to avoid the other extreme. Among the Greeks, Aeschylus, and sometimes Sophocles, were guilty of this fault; among the Latins, Claudian and Statius; and among our own countrymen, Shakespeare and Lee. In these authors the affectation of greatness often hurts the perspicuity of the style, as in many others the endeavour after perspicuity prejudices its greatness.

[4] colloquial.

Aristotle has observed, that the idiomatic style may be avoided, and the sublime formed, by the following methods. First, by the use of metaphors; such are those in Milton:

> *Imparadis'd* in one another's arms,
> . . . And in his hand a reed
> Stood waving *tipt* with fire; . . .
> The grassy clods now *calved*. . . .
> *Spangled* with eyes. . . .[5]

In these and innumerable other instances the metaphors are very bold but just; I must however observe that the metaphors are not thick sown in Milton, which always savours too much of wit; that they never clash with one another, which, as Aristotle observes,[6] turns a sentence into a kind of an enigma or riddle; and that he seldom has recourse to them where the proper and natural words will do as well. [III, 10–12.]

SAMUEL JOHNSON, Life of Dryden (1779)
There was therefore before the time of Dryden no poetical diction; no system of words at once refined from the grossness of domestic use and free from the harshness of terms appropriated to particular arts. Words too familiar or too remote defeat the purpose of a poet. From those sounds which we hear on small or on coarse occasions we do not easily receive strong impressions or delightful images; and words to which we are nearly strangers, whenever they occur, draw that attention on themselves which they should transmit to things. [I, 420.]

[5] *Paradise Lost*, iv. 506; vi. 579–80; vii. 463; xi. 130.
[6] *Poetics*, xxii.

The English Language

The English language has improved since the last age. (Dryden)

English is still barbarous, it has neither a tolerable dictionary nor a grammar. The language may be refined through borrowing from ancient authors. (Dryden)

It is necessary to fix the language once it has attained a certain standard of perfection. (Swift)

No language can be secured from corruption and decay. (Johnson)

JOHN DRYDEN, Preface to *Troilus and Cressida* (1679)
In the age of [Aeschylus] the Greek tongue was arrived to its full perfection; they had then amongst them an exact standard of writing and of speaking. The English language is not capable of such a certainty; and we are at present so far from it that we are wanting in the very foundation of it, a perfect grammar. Yet it must be allowed to the present age that the tongue in general is so much refined since Shakespeare's time that many of his words, and more of his phrases, are scarce intelligible. And of those which we understand, some are ungrammatical, others coarse; and his whole style is so pestered with figurative expressions that it is as affected as it is obscure. [I, 239.]

JOHN DRYDEN, A Discourse Concerning The Original and Progress of Satire. Prefixed to *The Satires of Juvenal and Persius* (1693)
I might descend also to the mechanic beauties of heroic verse; but we have yet no English *prosodia*, not so much as a tolerable dictionary, or a grammar; so that our language is in a manner barbarous; and what government will encourage any one, or more, who are capable of refining it, I know not. But nothing under a public expense can go through with it. And I rather fear a declination of the language than hope an advancement of it in the present age. [II, 667.]

JOHN DRYDEN, Dedication of the *Aeneis* (1697)
Poetry requires ornament and that is not to be had from our old
Teuton monosyllables; therefore if I find any elegant word in a
classic author, I propose it to be naturalised by using it myself;
and if the public approves of it, the Bill passes. But every man cannot
distinguish betwixt pedantry and poetry: every man therefore is not
fit to innovate. Upon the whole matter, a poet must first be certain
that the word he would introduce is beautiful in the Latin; and is to
consider, in the next place, whether it will agree with the English
idiom. After this, he ought to take the opinion of judicious friends,
such as are learned in both languages. And lastly, since no man is
infallible, let him use this license very sparingly; for if too many
foreign words are poured in upon us, it looks as if they were designed
not to assist the natives, but to conquer them. [III, 1059–60.]

JONATHAN SWIFT, *A Proposal for Correcting, Improving and Ascertaining the English Tongue*. In a Letter to
Robert, Earl of Oxford (1712)
The Roman language arrived at great perfection before it began to
decay: the French, for these last fifty years, has been polishing as
much as it will bear; and appears to be declining by the natural
inconstancy of that people, as well as the affectation of some late
authors, to introduce and multiply cant words, which is the most
ruinous corruption in any language. La Bruyère, a late celebrated
writer among them, makes use of many new terms which are not
to be found in any of the common dictionaries before his time. But
the English tongue is not arrived to such a degree of perfection as,
upon that account, to make us apprehend any thoughts of its decay;
and if it were once refined to a certain standard, perhaps there might
be ways to fix it for ever, or at least till we are invaded, and made a
conquest by some other state. And even then, our best writings
might probably be preserved with care, and grow into esteem,
and the authors have a chance for immortality. [pp. 8–9.]

SAMUEL JOHNSON, *A Dictionary of the English Language* (1755)
Of the event[1] of this work,[2] for which, having laboured it with
so much application, I cannot but have some degree of parental
        [1] possible effect.   [2] His *Dictionary*.

fondness, it is natural to form conjectures. Those who have been persuaded to think well of my design require that it should fix our language, and put a stop to those alterations which time and chance have hitherto been suffered to make in it without opposition. With this consequence I will confess that I flattered myself for a while; but now begin to fear that I have indulged expectation which neither reason nor experience can justify. When we see men grow old and die at a certain time one after another, from century to century, we laugh at the elixir that promises to prolong life to a thousand years; and with equal justice may the lexicographer be derided, who being able to produce no example of a nation that has preserved their words and phrases from mutability, shall imagine that his dictionary can embalm his language, and secure it from corruption and decay, that it is in his power to change sublunary nature, or clear the world at once from folly, vanity, and affectation. [sig. C2.]

Prosody

The development of the closed couplet. (Dryden)

Syllabic prosody. (Bysshe)

Rhyme v. blank verse in drama. (Dryden, Howard, Addison)

JOHN DRYDEN, To Roger, Earl of Orrery. Prefixed to *The Rival Ladies* (1664)

But the excellence and dignity of [rhyme] were never fully known till Mr. Waller taught it; he first made writing easily an art; first showed us to conclude the sense most commonly in distichs, which, in the verse of those before him, runs on for so many lines together that the reader is out of breath to overtake it. This sweetness of Mr. Waller's lyric poesy was afterwards followed in the epic by Sir John Denham, in his *Cooper's Hill*, a poem which, your Lordship knows, for the majesty of the style is, and ever will be, the exact standard of good writing. But if we owe the invention of it to Mr. Waller, we are acknowledging for the noblest use of it to Sir William Davenant, who at once brought it upon the stage and made it perfect, in the *Siege of Rhodes*. [I, 7.]

EDWARD BYSSHE, *The Art of English Poetry* (1708)
The structure of our verses, whether blank or in rhyme, consists in a certain number of syllables; not in feet composed of long and short syllables, as the verses of the Greeks and Romans. And though some ingenious persons[1] formerly puzzled themselves in prescribing rules for the quantity of English syllables, and, in imitation of the Latins, composed verses by the measure of spondees, dactyls, etc., yet the success of their undertaking has fully evinced the vainness of their attempt, and given ground to suspect they had not throughly weighed what the genius of our language would bear; nor reflected that each tongue has its peculiar beauties, and what is agreeable and natural to one is very often disagreeable, nay, inconsistent with another. But that design being now wholly exploded, it is sufficient to have mentioned it.

Our verses then consist in a certain number of syllables; but the verses of double rhyme require a syllable more than those of single rhyme. Thus in a poem whose verses consist of ten syllables, those of the same poem that are accented on the last save one, which we call verses of double rhyme, must have eleven. [pp. 1–2.]

JOHN DRYDEN, To Roger, Earl of Orrery. Prefixed to *The Rival Ladies* (1664)
But that benefit which I consider most in [rhyme], because I have not seldom found it, is that it bounds and circumscribes the fancy. For imagination in a poet is a faculty so wild and lawless that, like an high-ranging spaniel, it must have clogs tied to it, lest it outrun the judgment. The great easiness of blank verse renders the poet too luxuriant; he is tempted to say many things which might better be omitted, or at least shut up in fewer words; but when the difficulty of artful rhyming is interposed, where the poet commonly confines his sense to his couplet, and must contrive that sense into such

[1] Sidney, Spenser, and Gabriel Harvey.

words that the rhyme shall naturally follow them, not they the rhyme; the fancy then gives leisure to the judgment to come in, which, seeing so heavy a tax imposed, is ready to cut off all unnecessary expenses. This last consideration has already answered an objection which some have made, that rhyme is only an embroidery of sense, to make that which is ordinary in itself pass for excellent with less examination. But certainly that which most regulates the fancy, and gives the judgment its busiest employment, is like to bring forth the richest and clearest thoughts. [I, 8–9.]

SIR ROBERT HOWARD, Preface to *The Great Favourite* (1668)
I cannot therefore but beg leave of the reader to take a little notice of the great pains the author of an *Essay of Dramatic Poesy* has taken to prove rhyme as natural in a serious play, and more effectual than blank verse: thus he states the question, but pursues that which he calls natural in a wrong application; for 'tis not the question whether rhyme or not rhyme be best or most natural for a grave and serious subject, but what is nearest the nature of that which it presents. Now, after all the endeavours of that ingenious person, a play will still be supposed to be a composition of several persons speaking *ex tempore*, and 'tis as certain that good verses are the hardest things that can be imagined to be so spoken; so that if any will be pleased to impose the rule of measuring things to be the best by being nearest nature, it is granted, by consequence, that which is most remote from the thing supposed must needs be most improper. [p. 107.]

JOHN DRYDEN, Of Heroic Plays: An Essay. Prefixed to
The Conquest of Granada (1672)
Whether heroic verse ought to be admitted into serious plays is not now to be disputed: 'tis already in possession of the stage, and I dare confidently affirm that very few tragedies, in this age, shall be received without it. All the arguments which are formed against it can amount to no more than this, that it is not so near conversation as prose, and therefore not so natural. But it is very clear to all who understand poetry that serious plays ought not to imitate conversation too nearly. If nothing were to be raised above that level, the foundation of poetry would be destroyed. And, if you once admit of a latitude, that thoughts may be exalted and that

images and actions may be raised above the life, and described in measure without rhyme, that leads you insensibly from your own principles to mine: you are already so far onward of your way that you have forsaken the imitation of ordinary converse. You are gone beyond it; and to continue where you are, is to lodge in the open fields betwixt two inns. You have lost that which you call natural, and have not acquired the last perfection of art. [I, 156–7.]

JOSEPH ADDISON, *The Spectator*, no. 39 (14 April 1711)
Aristotle observes[2] that the iambic verse in the Greek tongue was the most proper for tragedy; because at the same time that it lifted up the discourse from prose, it was that which approached nearer to it than any other kind of verse. For, says he, we may observe that men in ordinary discourse very often speak iambics without taking notice of it. We may make the same observation of our English blank verse, which often enters into our common discourse though we do not attend to it, and is such a due medium between rhyme and prose that it seems wonderfully adapted to tragedy. I am therefore very much offended when I see a play in rhyme, which is as absurd in English as a tragedy in hexameters would have been in Greek or Latin. [I, 164.]

[2] *Poetics*, iv.

IV NATIVE LITERATURE
THE HISTORICAL SENSE

Native Literature

Shakespeare and Fletcher praised. (Sheffield)

Praise of Shakespeare in spite of the mistakes he made through ignorance of art. (Dennis, Pope)

Milton's invention and sublimity of thought. (Addison)

The Fairie Queene, though not a true epic poem, praised. (Hughes)

JOHN SHEFFIELD, EARL OF MULGRAVE, *An Essay upon Poetry*
(1682)
  Shakespeare and Fletcher are the wonders now;
  Consider them, and read them o're and o're,
  Go see them played, then read them as before.
  For though in many things they grossly fail,
  Over our passions still they so prevail,
  That our own grief by theirs is rocked asleep,
  The dull are forced to feel, the wise to weep.
  Their beauties imitate, avoid their faults. . . . [II, 292.]

JOHN DENNIS, *Essay on the Genius and Writings of Shakespeare* (1712)
Shakespeare was one of the greatest geniuses that the world e'er saw for the tragic stage. Though he lay under greater disadvantages than any of his successors, yet had he greater and more genuine beauties than the best and greatest of them. And what makes the brightest glory of his character, those beauties were entirely his own, and owing to the force of his own nature; whereas his faults were owing to his education, and to the age that he lived in. One may say of him as they did of Homer, that he had none to imitate, and is himself inimitable. His imaginations were often as just as they were bold and strong. He had a natural discretion which never could have

been taught him, and his judgment was strong and penetrating. He seems to have wanted nothing but time and leisure for thought, to have found out those rules of which he appears so ignorant. His characters are always drawn justly, exactly, graphically, except where he failed by not knowing history or the poetical art. He has for the most part more fairly distinguished them than any of his successors have done, who have falsified them, or confounded them, by making love the predominant quality in all. He had so fine a talent for touching the passions, and they are so lively in him, and so truly in nature, that they often touch us more without their due preparations than those of other tragic poets who have all the beauty of design and all the advantage of incidents.[1] His master-passion was terror, which he has often moved so powerfully and so wonderfully that we may justly conclude that, if he had had the advantage of art and learning, he would have surpassed the very best and strongest of the ancients. His paintings are often so beautiful and so lively, so graceful and so powerful, especially where he uses them in order to move terror, that there is nothing perhaps more accomplished in our English poetry. His sentiments for the most part in his best tragedies are noble, generous, easy and natural, and adapted to the persons who use them. His expression is in many places good and pure after a hundred years; simple though elevated, graceful though bold, and easy though strong. . . .

If Shakespeare had these great qualities by nature, what would he not have been if he had joined to so happy a genius learning and the poetical art? For want of the latter, our author has sometimes made gross mistakes in the characters which he has drawn from history, against the equality and conveniency of manners of his dramatical persons. [II, 4–5.]

ALEXANDER POPE, Preface to *The Works of Shakespeare* (1725)
I will conclude by saying of Shakespeare that, with all his faults, and with all the irregularity of his drama, one may look upon his works, in comparison of those that are more finished and regular,

[1] Dennis's remark implies that there are other ways of attaining the end of tragedy besides Aristotle's requirements for design and conduct of incidents; Shakespeare's tragedies succeed through fine characterisation and moving scenes.

as upon an ancient majestic piece of Gothic architecture,[2] compared with a neat modern building: the latter is more elegant and glaring, but the former is more strong and more solemn. It must be allowed that in one of these there are materials enough to make many of the other. It has much the greater variety, and much the nobler apartments, though we are often conducted to them by dark, odd, and uncouth passages. Nor does the whole fail to strike us with greater reverence, though many of the parts are childish, ill-placed, and unequal to its grandeur. [p. 58.]

JOSEPH ADDISON, *The Spectator*, no. 279 (19 January 1712)

Virgil has excelled all others in the propriety of his sentiments.[3] Milton shines likewise very much in this particular. Nor must we omit one consideration which adds to his honour and reputation: Homer and Virgil introduced persons whose characters are commonly known among men, and such as are to be met with either in history or in ordinary conversation. Milton's characters, most of them, lie out of nature, and were to be formed purely by his own invention. It shews a greater genius in Shakespeare to have drawn his Caliban than his Hotspur or Julius Caesar: the one was to be supplied out of his own imagination, whereas the other might have been formed upon tradition, history and observation. It was much easier therefore for Homer to find proper sentiments for an assembly of Grecian generals, than for Milton to diversify his infernal council with proper characters, and inspire them with a variety of sentiments. The loves of Dido and Aeneas are only copies of what has passed between other persons. Adam and Eve, before the Fall, are a different species from that of mankind, who are descended from them; and none but a poet of the most unbounded invention, and the most exquisite judgment, could have filled their conversation and behaviour with so many apt circumstances during their state of innocence. . . .

[2] For a similar comparison, see John Hughes and Richard Hurd on *The Faerie Queene*, pp. 190–191, 195–6 below.

[3] That Virgil excelled in propriety and Homer in sublimity is a commonplace of neo-classical criticism. The first parallel comparison of Virgil and Homer appeared in J. C. Scaliger's *Poetices libri septem* (1651), which extolled Virgil above Homer.

Milton's chief talent, and indeed his distinguishing excellence, lies in the sublimity of his thoughts. There are others of the moderns who rival him in every other part of poetry; but in the greatness of his sentiments he triumphs over all the poets both modern and ancient, Homer only excepted. It is impossible for the imagination of man to distend itself with greater ideas than those which he has laid together in his first, second and sixth Books. The seventh, which describes the creation of the world, is likewise wonderfully sublime, though not so apt to stir up emotion in the mind of the reader, nor consequently so perfect in the epic way of writing, because it is filled with less action. Let the judicious reader compare what Longinus has observed on several passages in Homer,[4] and he will find parallels for most of them in the *Paradise Lost*. [II, 586-8.]

JOHN HUGHES, Remarks on *The Fairy Queen* (1715)
That which seems the most liable to exception in this work is the model of it, and the choice the author has made of so romantic a story. The several books appear rather like so many several poems than one entire fable. Each of them has its peculiar knight, and is independent of the rest; and though some of the persons make their appearance in different books, yet this has very little effect in connecting them. Prince Arthur is indeed the principal person, and has therefore a share given him in every legend; but his part is not considerable enough in any one of them; he appears and vanishes again like a spirit, and we lose sight of him too soon to consider him as the hero of the poem.

These are the most obvious defects in the fable of the *Fairy Queen*. The want of unity in the story makes it difficult for the reader to carry it in his mind, and distracts too much his attention to the several parts of it; and indeed the whole frame of it would appear monstrous if it were to be examined by the rules of epic poetry, as they have been drawn from the practice of Homer and Virgil. But as it is plain the author never designed it by those rules, I think it ought rather to be considered as a poem of a particular kind, describing in a series of allegorical adventures or episodes the most noted virtues and vices: to compare it therefore with the models of antiquity, would be like drawing a parallel between the

4 *On the Sublime*, ix.

Roman and the Gothic architecture. In the first there is doubtless a more natural grandeur and simplicity: in the latter, we find great mixtures of beauty and barbarism, yet assisted by the invention of a variety of inferior ornaments; and though the former is more majestic in the whole, the latter may be very surprising and agreeable in its parts. [I, lix–lxi.]

The Historical Sense

The faults of Elizabethan dramatists are due to the age in which they lived. (Dryden, Gildon, Rowe, Johnson)
What pleased the Athenians may not please the English. (Dennis)
Gothic v. classical structure. (Hurd)

JOHN DRYDEN, Epilogue to the Second Part of *The Conquest of Granada* (1672)

> They who have best succeeded on the stage,
> Have still conformed their genius to their age.
> Thus Jonson did mechanic humour show,
> When men were dull, and conversation low.
> Then, comedy was faultless, but 'twas coarse:
> Cobb's[1] tankard was a jest, and Otter's horse.[2]
> And, as their comedy, their love was mean:
> Except, by chance, in some one laboured scene,
> Which must atone for an ill-written play:
> They rose, but at their height could seldom stay.
> Fame then was cheap, and the first comer sped;
> And they have kept it since, by being dead.
> But, were they now to write, when critics weigh
> Each line, and ev'ry word, throughout a play,
> None of 'em, no, not Jonson in his height,
> Could pass without allowing grains for weight.

[1] The water-carrier in Jonson's *Every Man in His Humour*.
[2] A captain in Jonson's *Epicoene*, whose favourite tankard is called "Horse".

Think it not envy that these truths are told,
Our poet's not malicious, though he's bold.
'Tis not to brand 'em that their faults are shown,
But, by their errors, to excuse his own.
If love and honour now are higher raised,
'Tis not the poet but the age is praised.
Wit's now arrived to a more high degree;
Our native language more refined and free.
Our ladies and our men now speak more wit
In conversation than those poets writ.
Then one of these is, consequently, true:
That what this poet writes comes short of you,
And imitates you ill (which most he fears),
Or else his writing is not worse than theirs. [I, 134–5.]

JOHN DRYDEN, Defence of the Epilogue to the Second Part of
The Conquest of Granada (1672)
But the times were ignorant in which [Shakespeare and Fletcher]
lived. Poetry was then, if not in its infancy among us, at least not
arrived to its vigour and maturity: witness the lameness of their
plots; many of which, especially those which they writ first (for
even that age refined itself in some measure), were made up of some
ridiculous, incoherent story, which in one play many times took
up the business of an age. I suppose I need not name *Pericles, Prince
of Tyre*, nor the historical plays of Shakespeare; besides many of the
rest, as the *Winter's Tale, Love's Labour Lost, Measure for Measure*,
which were either grounded on impossibilities, or at least so meanly
written that the comedy neither caused your mirth, nor the serious
part your concernment. If I would expatiate on this subject, I could
easily demonstrate that our admired Fletcher, who writ after him,
neither understood correct plotting, nor that which they call
the decorum of the stage. [I, 172.]

CHARLES GILDON, *Miscellaneous Letters and Essays* (1694)
Had our critic[3] entertained but common justice for the heroes of
his own country, he would have set Shakespeare's faults in their

[3] Gildon's essay is an answer to Rymer's *A Short View of Tragedy* (1693).

true light, and distinguished betwixt his, and the vices of the age; for as Rapin (a much juster and more candid critic) observes,[4] the poet often falls into vices by complying with the palate of the age he lives in; and to this may we truly and justly refer a great many of these faults Shakespeare is guilty of. For, he not having that advantage the Greek poets had, of a proper subsistence, or to be provided for at the public charge, what fruit he was to expect of his labours was from the applause of the audience; so that his chief aim was to please them, who, not being so skilful in criticism as Mr. Rymer, would not be pleased without some extravagances mingled in (though contrary to) the characters such and such a player was to act. This is the reason that most of his tragedies have a mixture of something comical; the Dalilah[5] of the age must be brought in, the clown, and the valet jesting with their betters, if he resolved not to disoblige the auditors. [p. 88.]

NICHOLAS ROWE, Some Account of the Life of Mr. William
Shakespeare (1709)

If one undertook to examine the greatest part of [Shakespeare's tragedies] by those rules which are established by Aristotle, and taken from the model of the Grecian stage, it would be no very hard task to find a great many faults. But as Shakespeare lived under a kind of mere light of nature,[6] and had never been made acquainted with the regularity of those written precepts, so it would be hard to judge him by a law he knew nothing of. We are to consider him as a man that lived in a state of almost universal license and ignorance: there was no established judge, but everyone took the liberty to write according to the dictates of his own fancy. When one considers that there is not one play before him of a reputation good enough to entitle it to an appearance on the present stage, it cannot but be a matter of great wonder that he should advance dramatic poetry so far as he did. [p. 15.]

[4] In his *Comparison of Homer and Virgil*, viii.

[5] Cf. Dryden's censure, in the Dedication of *The Spanish Friar* (1681), of some of his verses in *Tyrannic Love* (1670) and *The Conquest of Granada* (1672): "I draw a stroke over all those Dalilahs of the theatre."

[6] The comparison is with natural religion, which must be supplemented by Revelation.

SAMUEL JOHNSON, Preface to *The Plays of William Shakespeare* (1765)

Those whom my arguments[7] cannot persuade to give their approbation to the judgment of Shakespeare, will easily, if they consider the condition of his life, make some allowance for his ignorance.

Every man's performances, to be rightly estimated, must be compared with the state of the age in which he lived, and with his own particular opportunities;[8] and though to the reader a book be not worse or better for the circumstances of the author, yet as there is always a silent reference of human works to human abilities, and as the enquiry, how far man may extend his designs, or how high he may rate his native force, is of far greater dignity than in what rank we shall place any particular performance, curiosity is always busy to discover the instruments as well as to survey the workmanship, to know how much is to be ascribed to original powers, and how much to casual and adventitious help. The palaces of Peru or Mexico were certainly mean and incommodious habitations, if compared to the houses of European monarchs; yet who could forbear to view them with astonishment, who remembered that they were built without the use of iron? [p. 122.]

JOHN DENNIS, *The Impartial Critick* (1693)

I now beg leave, Sir, to give a particular instance of something that must needs have been very moving with the Athenians, which yet would have been but ill received amongst us:[9] and that is a passage in the *Antigone* of Sophocles. That story, as it is managed by that admirable poet, is one of the most moving that ever was; and there

[7] Against the mechanic rules.

[8] Cf. Pope, *An Essay on Criticism*, 119–23:

> Know well each ancient's proper character
> His fable, subject, scope in ev'ry page,
> Religion, country, genius of his age:
> Without all these at once before your eyes,
> Cavil you may, but never criticize.

[9] *The Impartial Critic* was a reply to Rymer's *Short View of Tragedy* (1693). Dennis argues that English dramatists cannot imitate ancient practice in all respects, for instance in the use of a chorus, which Rymer had advocated.

is no part of it that touches me more than the complaints of Antigone upon her condemnation by Creon. But there is one thing peculiar in it which must needs have excited compassion in the Athenians in an extraordinary manner; for otherwise Sophocles, who perfectly understood his audience, would never have made her repeat it at least four times in the same act: for when she was condemned to the severest punishment, which was to be buried alive, the thing that lay most heavy upon her heart was that she was to go to Hell with her maiden-head. I think, Sir, I need not take pains to demonstrate that this passage would have been laughed at with us. Now what reason can be given why that should appear so contemptible to us which moved the Athenians so much? The only reason that can be assigned is the difference of climate and customs. The Athenians, by using their women as the modern Italians do theirs, plainly declared their opinion of them; which was, that passion was predominant over reason in them; and that they were perpetually thinking how they might make some improvement of the talent which Nature had given their sex. The Athenians therefore having these thoughts of their women, the complaint that Antigone made could not appear peculiar and surprising to them. Now it is evident that everything which is ridiculous must be both particular and surprising; for nothing which is general and expected can excite a sensible man to laughter. But we having quite contrary thoughts of our women, which is plain by the confidence which we so generously repose in them, a maid who had said what Antigone did, upon our stage, would have said something that would have appeared a frailty particular and surprising, and would have been ridiculous. . . .

By what I have said, Sir, it may be easily guessed that it is in vain to think of setting up a chorus upon the English stage because it succeeded at Athens; or to think of expelling love from our theatre because it was rarely in Grecian tragedies.[10] [I, 12, 13.]

RICHARD HURD, *Letters on Chivalry and Romance* (1762)
When an architect examines a Gothic structure by Grecian rules, he finds nothing but deformity. But the Gothic architecture has its own rules, by which when it comes to be examined, it is seen to

[10] Rymer had argued that love is not a proper subject for tragedy.

have its merit, as well as the Grecian. The question is not, which of the two is conducted in the simplest or truest taste: but whether there be not sense and design in both, when scrutinized by the laws on which each is projected.

The same observation holds of the two sorts of poetry. Judge of the *Faery Queen* by the classic models, and you are shocked with its disorder: consider it with an eye to its Gothic original, and you find it regular. The unity and simplicity of the former are more complete; but the latter has that sort of unity and simplicity which results from its nature.

The *Faery Queen*, then, as a Gothic poem, derives its method, as well as the other characters of its composition, from the established modes and ideas of chivalry. . . .

If you ask, then, what is this unity of Spenser's poem? I say, it consists in the relation of its several adventures to one common original, the appointment of the *Faery Queen*; and to one common end, the completion of the Faery Queen's injunctions. The knights issued forth on their adventures on the breaking up of this annual feast; and the next annual feast, we are to suppose, is to bring them together again from the achievement of their several charges.

This, it is true, is not the classic unity, which consists in the representation of one entire action; but it is an unity of another sort, an unity resulting from the respect which a number of related actions have to one common purpose. In other words, it is an unity of design, and not of action. [pp. 61–2, 66–7.]

V THE BUSINESS OF CRITICISM
TASTE

The Business of Criticism

The task of the critic is to point out excellences. (Dryden, Addison)

Dryden and Rymer compared. (Johnson)

JOHN DRYDEN, Heroic Poetry and Poetic Licence. Prefixed to
The State of Innocence (1677)

In the first place, I must take leave to tell them that they wholly
mistake the nature of criticism who think its business is principally
to find fault. Criticism, as it was first instituted by Aristotle, was
meant a standard of judging well; the chiefest part of which is to
observe those excellencies which should delight a reasonable reader.
If the design, the conduct, the thoughts, and the expressions of a
poem be generally such as proceed from a true genius of poetry, the
critic ought to pass his judgment in favour of the author. 'Tis
malicious and unmanly to snarl at the little lapses of a pen, from
which Virgil himself stands not exempted. Horace acknowledges
that honest Homer nods sometimes,[1] he is not equally awake in
every line; but he leaves it also as a standing measure for our
judgments,

> non, ubi plura nitent in carmine, paucis
> offendar maculis, quas aut incuria fudit,
> aut humana parum cavit natura.[2]

And Longinus, who was undoubtedly, after Aristotle, the greatest
critic amongst the Greeks, in his twenty-seventh chapter *ΠΕΡΙ
'ΥΨΟΥΣ*,[3] has judiciously preferred the sublime genius that sometimes errs to the middling or indifferent one which makes few faults,

[1] *Ars Poetica*, 359.

[2] *Ars Poetica*, 351-3. ("Verum ubi plura nitent in carmine, non ego
paucis/Offendar etc." "If beauties abound in a poem, I shall not find
fault with a few blemishes due to negligence or human frailty.")

[3] *On the Sublime.*

but seldom or never rises to any excellence. He compares the first to a man of large possessions who has not leisure to consider of every slight expense, will not debase himself to the management of every trifle: particular sums are not laid out or spared to the greatest advantage in his economy, but are sometimes suffered to run to waste, while he is only careful of the main. On the other side, he likens the mediocrity of wit to one of a mean fortune, who manages his store with extreme frugality, or rather parsimony; but who, with fear of running into profuseness, never arrives to the magnificence of living. This kind of genius writes indeed correctly. A wary man he is in grammar, very nice as to solecism or barbarism, judges to a hair of little decencies, knows better than any man what is not to be written, and never hazards himself so far as to fall, but plods on deliberately, and, as a grave man ought, is sure to put his staff before him; in short, he sets his heart upon it, and with wonderful care makes his business sure; that is, in plain English, neither to be blamed nor praised. I could, says my author,[4] find out some blemishes in Homer; and am, perhaps, as naturally inclined to be disgusted at[5] a fault as another man; but after all, to speak impartially, his failings are such as are only marks of human frailty: they are little mistakes, or rather negligences, which have escaped his pen in the fervour of his writing; the sublimity of his spirit carries it with me against his carelessness; and though Apollonius his *Argonauts*[6] and Theocritus his *Eidullia*[7] are more free from errors, there is not any man of so false a judgment who would choose rather to have been Apollonius or Theocritus than Homer.

'Tis worth our consideration a little to examine how much these hypercritics of English poetry differ from the opinion of the Greek and Latin judges of antiquity; from the Italians and French who have succeeded them; and, indeed, from the general taste and approbation of all ages. [I, 196–8.]

JOSEPH ADDISON, *The Spectator*, no. 291 (2 February 1712)
A true critic ought to dwell rather upon excellencies than imperfec-

---

[4] *On the Sublime*, xxxiii.   [5] to dislike.
[6] Apollonius Rhodius (*c.* 295–215 B.C.) wrote a Greek epic on the story of Jason and the Argonauts.   [7] The *Idylls*.

tions, to discover the concealed beauties of a writer, and communicate to the world such things as are worth their observation. The most exquisite words and finest strokes of an author are those which very often appear the most doubtful and exceptionable to a man who wants a relish for polite learning;[8] and they are these which a sour undistinguishing critic generally attacks with the greatest violence. Tully observes[9] that it is very easy to brand or fix a mark upon what he calls *verbum ardens*, or, as it may be rendered into English, *a glowing bold expression*, and to turn it into ridicule by a cold ill-natured criticism. A little wit is equally capable of exposing a beauty and of aggravating a fault; and though such a treatment of an author naturally produces indignation in the mind of an understanding reader, it has however its effect among the generality of those whose hands it falls into, the rabble of mankind being very apt to think that everything which is laughed at with any mixture of wit is ridiculous in itself. [III, 36–7.]

SAMUEL JOHNSON, Life of Dryden (1779)
In this, and in all his other essays on the same subject, the criticism of Dryden is the criticism of a poet; not a dull collection of theorems, nor a rude detection of faults, which perhaps the censor was not able to have committed; but a gay and vigorous dissertation, where delight is mingled with instruction, and where the author proves his right of judgment by his power of performance.

The different manner and effect with which critical knowledge may be conveyed was perhaps never more clearly exemplified than in the performances of Rymer and Dryden. It was said of a dispute between two mathematicians, "malim cum Scaligero errare, quam cum Clavio recte sapere";[10] that "it was more eligible to go wrong with one than right with the other." A tendency of the same kind every mind must feel at the perusal of Dryden's prefaces and Rymer's discourses. With Dryden we are wandering in quest of

[8] Usually taken to refer to Dennis.

[9] Cicero, *Ad Marcum Brutum Orator*, viii. 27.

[10] Clavius, who by order of Pope Gregory XIII corrected the calendar, was attacked by Joseph Scaliger. The saying applied to him derives from Cicero's "Errare malo cum Platone quam cum istis vera sentire" (*Tusc.* I. xvii. 39).

Truth, whom we find, if we find her at all, dressed in the graces of elegance; and if we miss her, the labour of the pursuit rewards itself: we are led only through fragrance and flowers. Rymer, without taking a nearer, takes a rougher way; every step is to be made through thorns and brambles, and Truth, if we meet her, appears repulsive by her mien and ungraceful by her habit. Dryden's criticism has the majesty of a queen; Rymer's has the ferocity of a tyrant. [I, 412–13.]

Taste

There is a good taste and a bad taste. Few are qualified to judge of the greater poetry, but works which please the best judges will ultimately please all. (Dennis)

Simplicity pleases the most refined as well as the most ordinary reader. (Addison)

A natural talent is not enough to form a true taste; art and learning must be joined to it. (Steele)

Taste must be educated through use, practice and culture. (Shaftesbury)

The general principles of taste are uniform in human nature. (Hume)

There is a common standard of taste. (Kames)

The standard of taste is fixed in the nature of things. (Reynolds)

JOHN DENNIS, *Remarks on Prince Arthur* (1696)
But before we come to examine whether Mr. Blackmore's narration be or be not delightful, it will be convenient to answer an objection. For, says one, to make short of the matter, the narration of *Prince Arthur* pleases me, and pleases ten thousand more, and therefore it is delightful. I can bring a gentleman who will use the same argument in the behalf of Quarles,[1] that he pleases him and

[1] Francis Quarles (1592–1644), whose *Emblems* (1635) were considered by all neo-classicists as fit only for the uneducated.

ten thousand more, and therefore he is delightful. I do not say this to make any comparison between Mr. Blackmore and Quarles. I know very well there is none. I only say this to put the reader in mind that there is a good taste, and that there is a bad, and that the latter very often prevails. I am perfectly persuaded that Bavius and Maevius² had a formidable party in ancient Rome, a party who thought them by much superior both to Horace and Virgil. For I cannot believe that those two great men would have made it their business to fix an eternal brand upon them, if they had not been coxcombs in more than ordinary credit. But some will tell me that men of good sense are pleased with Mr. Blackmore's poem: 'tis granted. But that which is commonly called good sense is not sufficient to form a good taste in poetry, though the good sense should be joined with an inclination for poetry, and with a tolerable share of experience in it. For if this were sufficient, it would undeniably follow that all who have this experience, this inclination, and this good sense, would have the same taste: whereas it is manifest that they who are not without these qualities differ very considerably in their opinions and in their taste of verses and poems. Nay, men differ very much from themselves. A man of sense is a man of sense at five and twenty; and yet at that age he has often a quite different taste from what he has at five and thirty. I think I need not be troubled to prove that in each of the nations of Western Europe there are a great many men of good sense who have an inclination for poetry, and who are not without some experience in it. This will be easily granted, nor can that which follows be easily denied: that there are some of our neighbouring nations in which a good taste is very rarely or not at all to be found. From whence I conclude that good sense and experience, joined with an inclination for poetry, are all insufficient to the forming a good taste. I will venture to affirm yet further, that there are several persons who are not without a taste for the little poetry, and who can judge exactly of elegies, and songs, and amorous and bacchanalian odes; who can tell whether they have a poetical spirit in them, and whether nature be not too much beholden to art. I say, there are several of these who, besides that their judgments are often

² Poetasters who criticized Virgil and Horace (see Virgil's 3rd Eclogue and Horace's 10th Epode).

perverted by affection or interest, which frequently debauch the very understanding, as well as they corrupt the will, have not the least knowledge of the rules or the least notion of that which the French and we call genius; and consequently cannot be rightly qualified to judge of the greater poetry. But here it will be convenient to obviate³ an objection. For, says one, if a true taste for epic poetry were confined to so small a number, and consequently so few were capable of receiving the true delight from it, it would follow from hence that its instructions, which it conveys to the reader by pleasure, would not only be restrained to a very few, but to those who want it least; whereas a general instruction being designed by it, the pleasure must be general too. To this I answer: first, that by pleasing the best judges, it will infallibly please the rest, and please them more than it could have done if the others had not been satisfied; secondly, that if the best judges and those who have a true taste are disgusted, the rest will quickly be cloyed. For time will be sure to propagate truth, when it is once discovered. Pebbles may, by their false glittering, be imposed on the ignorant for diamonds, but they cannot be long in an error. The first artist that sees the stones will soon discover their want of solidity, and others then will find out their want of beauty. 'Tis in poems as it is in stones, time will easily make the discovery, whether they are solid or no, and the more solid they are found, the more and the longer will they be seen to shine, for their full and their lasting lustre depends on their perfect solidity. But now if any one shall tell me that persons every way qualified for judges commend Mr. Blackmore's poem; to that I answer that there are several things in it which may stand before the strictest judges. But that the greater part of the narration neither is nor can be delightful to men of the best taste, is what I shall now endeavour to prove. [I, 70-1.]

JOHN DENNIS, *A Large Account of Taste* (1702)
To conclude that a play is good because Mr. Granville is pleased by it is but a reasonable way of arguing. But to say that it is good because it pleases the generality of an audience is a very absurd one. For every man has, and will have his different pleasure. Wise men will be sure to be pleased with things that are wise, and fools

³ meet, dispose of.

will be inclined to be pleased with things that are foolish. Montaigne was pleased with playing with his cat;[4] but at the same time he does her and himself the justice to believe she thought him an ass for it. Would to Heaven that some part of our audiences were but as just as the Frenchman, and some part of our authors but as reasonable as the beast. Before a play can be concluded to be good because it pleases, we ought to consider who are pleased by it, they who understand, or they who do not. They who understand? Alas, they are but few, and are seldom pleased there of late. They who do not? That methinks is odd. Suppose a man should tell an author he never so much as heard of his play, and should the very moment following tell him he liked it. Would he be satisfied with this approbation? Would he not be really mortified at it? Now every one who talks like an ass tells the world, though against his will, that he does not understand one word of a play; and is not he who never heard a word of a cause as justly qualified to determine it, as he who never understood a word of it?

'Tis for this reason, Sir,[5] that whenever I write I make it my business to please such men as you are, as very well knowing that whatever is writ has its immediate success from fortune, but its lasting one from art and nature; that the people are always uncertain and fluctuating, and guided by opinion, and not by judgment, that the surest way to arrive at reputation is to please the knowing few, for that they at last must draw in the multitude, but are never to be drawn in by them.

I have been already tedious, or it would be an easy matter to shew that they who in all ages have appeared at once good poets and good critics have writ to a few persons, I mean to a few at present. For he who writes to the many at present writes only to them, and his works are sure never to survive their admirers; but he who writes to the knowing few at present writes to the race of mankind in all succeeding ages. But I am glad that this is addressed to a gentleman who needs only be put in mind of this, who is perfectly well acquainted with Horace and Boileau, and who has often read the *Satires* and the *Epistles* of both; and who consequently is able to inform others that those two celebrated poets directed their writings

4 "Apologie de Raymond de Sebond", *Essais*, II. xii.
5 George Granville, Lord Lansdowne.

to the knowing few, and were neither exalted by the approbation, nor
dejected by the censure of the rest, and that by such a proceeding they
came to please universally; that some of the most agreeable parts of
those *Satires* and those *Epistles* are those in which they laugh at the
taste of the vulgar,[6] and that among the vulgar they reckoned not only
a great many who were distinguished by their rank from others, but
several whom the world called wits and poets; and that they had a
greater contempt for those wits and poets than they had for any sort
of people whatever, unless for those who admired them. [I, 287-8.]

JOSEPH ADDISON, *The Spectator*, no. 70 (21 May 1711)
I know nothing which more shews the essential and inherent perfection of simplicity of thought above that which I call the Gothic
manner in writing, than this, that the first pleases all kinds of palates,
and the latter only such as have formed to themselves a wrong
artificial taste upon little fanciful authors and writers of epigram.
Homer, Virgil, or Milton, so far as the language of their poems is
understood, will please a reader of plain common sense who would
neither relish nor comprehend an epigram of Martial or a poem of
Cowley. So, on the contrary, an ordinary song or ballad that is the
delight of the common people cannot fail to please all such readers
as are not unqualified for the entertainment by their affectation or
ignorance; and the reason is plain, because the same paintings of
nature which recommend it to the most ordinary reader will appear
beautiful to the most refined.[7] [I, 297-8.]

SIR RICHARD STEELE, *The Englishman*. no. 7 (20 October 1713)
A man who trusts entirely to his natural talents is often governed
by caprices, and can give no reason why he is pleased. Thus a fanciful
fellow who amuses himself with the woods and mountains which
he discovers in the clouds is angry if his friends are not charmed
with the airy landscape. On the contrary, a critic who tastes just
according to law[8] deceives his own heart, and talks of beauties celebrated by others which he cannot see himself; like good-natured
travellers, who own they perceive objects at a distance out of pure
complaisance to the master of the company. But a true judge of

6 the multitude.   7 This introduces Addison's praise of old ballads.
8 who merely judges by rules.

writing is like a painter or a statuary who doth not content himself with shewing fine images of nature, unless he likewise informs the spectator wherein the beauties consist; whence arises the propriety of colouring, and justness of symmetry.

To a good natural discernment art must therefore be joined to finish a critic. Without a natural talent, all the acquirements of learning are vain; but nature, unassisted, will go no great lengths. The soul of man indeed loves truth alone; but is easily led to mistake appearances for realities, if judgment, which is built upon experience, does not direct penetration. Life, being short, will not give us time to gather a necessary stock of experience ourselves; for which reason we must borrow from our ancestors, as they borrowed from those who went before them. By their writings we can trace the several arts back to their originals, and learn in an hour what by tedious and gradual deductions was the work perhaps of several ages. A *natural* critic will readily own that he formed his judgment by degrees, that he grew wiser and wiser by experience. One who joins art to nature doth the same thing, but doth it more effectually: he throws himself back into ancient time, lives a thousand years of criticism in a month, and without stirring out of his closet, is a Greek, a Roman, a Frenchman, and a Briton. . . .

A nice and subtle judgment in poetry hath in all polite nations, ancient and modern, been happily compared to the delicacy of taste. Now a taste cannot be fine if it only distinguishes things sweet from bitter, or pleasant from nauseous. No gentleman that drinks his bottle pretends to a tolerable palate unless he can distinguish the wines of France from those of Portugal; and if he is perfectly nice, he will tell you, with his eyes shut, what province, what mountain supplied the liquor. Every man born healthful is indeed naturally capable of distinguishing one juice from another: but if he hath debauched himself with sophisticated mixtures, it is odds that he will prefer the bad to the good; that he will swallow, with transport, what was squeezed from the sloe, and make faces at the Burgundian grape. [pp. 31-3.]

ANTHONY ASHLEY COOPER, THIRD EARL OF SHAFTESBURY,
Miscellaneous Reflections (1711)
Our joint endeavour, therefore, must appear this, to shew: That

nothing which is found charming or delightful in the polite world, nothing which is adopted as pleasure, or entertainment, of whatever kind, can any way be accounted for, supported, or established, without the pre-establishment or supposition of a certain taste. Now a taste or judgment, 'tis supposed, can hardly come ready formed with us into the world. Whatever principles or materials of this kind we may possibly bring with us; whatever good faculties, senses, or anticipating sensations, and imaginations may be of nature's growth, and arise properly of themselves, without our art, promotion, or assistance; the general idea which is formed of all this management, and the clear notion we attain of what is preferable and principal in all these subjects of choice and estimation, will not, as I imagine, by any person, be taken for *innate*. Use, practice and culture must precede the understanding and wit of such an advanced size and growth as this. A legitimate and just taste can neither be begotten, made, conceived or produced, without the antecedent labour and pains of criticism.

For this reason we presume not only to defend the cause of critics; but to declare open war against those indolent supine authors, performers, readers, auditors, actors or spectators, who, making their humour alone the rule of what is beautiful and agreeable, and having no account to give of such their humour or odd fancy, reject the criticizing or examining art, by which alone they are able to discover the true beauty and worth of every object. According to that affected ridicule which these insipid remarkers pretend to throw upon just critics, the enjoyment of all real arts or natural beauties would be entirely lost. Even in behaviour and manners we should at this rate become in time as barbarous as in our pleasures and diversions. I would presume it, however, of these critic-haters, that they are not yet so uncivilized, or void of all social sense, as to maintain that the most barbarous life, or brutish pleasure, is as desirable as the most polished or refined. [III, 164–5.]

DAVID HUME, Of the Standard of Taste (1757)
It is very natural for us to seek a *standard of taste*; a rule by which the various sentiments of men may be reconciled; or at least, a decision afforded, confirming one sentiment, and condemning another.

There is a species of philosophy which cuts off all hopes of success in such an attempt, and represents the impossibility of ever attaining any standard of taste. The difference, it is said, is very wide between judgment and sentiment. All sentiment is right, because sentiment has a reference to nothing beyond itself, and is always real, wherever a man is conscious of it. But all determinations of the understanding are not right; because they have a reference to something beyond themselves, to wit, real matter of fact; and are not always conformable to that standard. Among a thousand different opinions which different men may entertain of the same subject, there is one, and but one, that is just and true; and the only difficulty is to fix and ascertain it. On the contrary, a thousand different sentiments excited by the same object are all right, because no sentiment represents what is really in the object. It only marks a certain conformity or relation betwixt the object and the organs or faculties of the mind; and if that conformity did not really exist, the sentiment could never possibly have a being. Beauty is no quality in things themselves: it exists merely in the mind which contemplates them; and each mind perceives a different beauty. One person may even perceive deformity where another is sensible of beauty; and every individual ought to acquiesce in his own sentiment, without pretending to regulate those of others. To seek the real beauty, or real deformity, is as fruitless an enquiry as to pretend to ascertain the real sweet or real bitter. According to the disposition of the organs, the same object may be both sweet and bitter; and the proverb[9] has justly determined it to be fruitless to dispute concerning tastes. It is very natural, and even quite necessary, to extend this axiom to mental, as well as bodily taste; and thus common sense, which is so often at variance with philosophy, especially with the sceptical kind, is found, in one instance at least, to agree in pronouncing the same decision.

But though this axiom, by passing into a proverb, seems to have attained the sanction of common sense; there is certainly a species of common sense which opposes it, or at least serves to modify and restrain it. Whoever would assert an equality of genius and elegance betwixt Ogilby[10] and Milton, or Bunyan and Addison, would be thought to defend no less an extravagance than if he had maintained

[9] *De gustibus non disputandum est*, there is no disputing about tastes.
[10] John Ogilby (1600–76), who translated Virgil and Homer.

a molehill to be as high as Teneriffe, or a pond as extensive as the ocean. Though there may be found persons who give the preference to the former authors, no one pays attention to such a taste; and we pronounce without scruple the sentiment of these pretended critics to be absurd and ridiculous. The principle of the natural equality of tastes is then totally forgot; and while we admit of it on some occasions, where the objects seem near an equality, it appears an extravagant paradox, or rather a palpable absurdity, where objects so disproportioned are compared together.

It is evident that none of the rules of composition are fixed by reasonings *a priori*, or can be esteemed abstract conclusions of the understanding, from comparing those habitudes and relations of ideas which are eternal and immutable. Their foundation is the same with that of all the practical sciences, experience; nor are they anything but general observations concerning what has been universally found to please in all countries and in all ages. Many of the beauties of poetry and even of eloquence are founded on falsehood and fiction, on hyperboles, metaphors, and an abuse or perversion of expressions from their natural meaning. To check the sallies of the imagination, and to reduce every expression to geometrical truth and exactness, would be the most contrary to the laws of criticism; because it would produce a work which, by universal experience, has been found the most insipid and disagreeable. But though poetry can never submit to exact truth, it must be confined by rules of art, discovered to the author either by genius or observation. If some negligent or irregular writers have pleased, they have not pleased by their transgressions of rule or order, but in spite of these transgressions: they have possessed other beauties, which were conformable to just criticism; and the force of these beauties has been able to overpower censure, and give the mind a satisfaction superior to the disgust arising from the blemishes. Ariosto pleases; but not by his monstrous and improbable fictions, by his bizarre mixture of the serious and comic styles, by the want of coherence in his stories, or by the continual interruption of his narrations. He charms by the force and clearness of his expression, by the readiness and variety of his inventions, and by his natural pictures of the passions, especially those of the gay and amorous kind: and however his faults may diminish our satisfaction, they are not able entirely to destroy it. Did our pleasure really arise from those parts of his poem which we denominate faults, this would be no objection to criticism in general: it would only be an objection to those particular rules of criticism which would establish such circumstances to be faults, and would represent them as universally blameable. If they are found to please, they cannot be faults; let the pleasure which they produce be ever so unexpected and unaccountable.

But though all the general rules of art are founded only on experience and on the observation of the common sentiments of human nature, we must not imagine that, on every occasion, the feelings of men will be conformable to these rules. Those finer emotions of the mind are of a very tender and delicate nature, and require the concurrence of many favourable circumstances to make them play with facility and exactness, according to their general and established principles. The least exterior hindrance to such small springs, or the least internal disorder, disturbs their motion, and confounds the operation of the whole machine. When we would make an experiment of this nature, and would try the force of any beauty or deformity, we must choose with care a proper time and place, and bring the fancy to a suitable situation and disposition. A perfect serenity of mind, a recollection of thought, a due attention to the object—if any of these circumstances be wanting our experiment will be fallacious, and we shall be unable to judge of the catholic and universal beauty. The relation which nature has placed betwixt the form and the sentiment will at least be more obscure; and it will require greater accuracy to trace and discern it. We shall be able to ascertain its influence not so much from the operation of each particular beauty, as from the durable admiration which attends those works that have survived all the caprices of mode and fashion, all the mistakes of ignorance and envy.

The same Homer who pleased at Athens and Rome two thousand years ago is still admired at Paris and at London. All the changes of climate, government, religion, and language have not been able to obscure his glory. Authority or prejudice may give a temporary vogue to a bad poet or orator; but his reputation will never be durable or general. When his compositions are examined by posterity or by foreigners, the enchantment is dissipated, and his faults appear in their true colours. On the contrary, a real genius, the longer his works endure, and the more wide they are spread, the more sincere is the admiration which he meets with. Envy and jealousy have too much place in a narrow circle; and even familiar acquaintance with his person may diminish the applause due to his performances: but when these obstructions are removed, the beauties, which are naturally fitted to excite agreeable sentiments, immediately display their energy; and while the world endures, they maintain their authority over the minds of men.

It appears, then, that amidst all the variety and caprices of taste there are certain general principles of approbation or blame, whose influence a careful eye may trace in all operations of the mind. Some particular forms or qualities, from the original structure of the internal fabric, are calculated to please, and others to displease; and if they fail of their effect, in any particular instance, it is from some apparent defect or imperfection in the organ. A man in a fever would not insist on his palate as able to decide concerning flavours; nor would one affected with the jaundice pretend to give a verdict with regard to colours. In each creature there is a sound and a defective state; and the former alone can be supposed to afford us a true standard of taste and sentiment. If, in the sound state of the organs, there be an entire or a considerable uniformity of sentiment among men, we may thence derive an idea of the perfect and universal beauty, in like manner as the appearance of objects in daylight to the eye of a man in health is denominated their true and real colour, even while colour is allowed to be merely a phantasm of the senses. . . .

But notwithstanding all our endeavours to fix a standard of taste, and reconcile the various apprehensions of men, there still remain two sources of variation, which, though they be not sufficient to confound all the boundaries of beauty and deformity, will often serve to vary the degrees of our approbation or blame. The one is the different humours of particular men; the other, the particular manners and opinions of our age and country. The general principles of taste are uniform in human nature: where men vary in their judgments, some defect or perversion in the faculties may commonly be remarked, proceeding either from prejudice, from want of practice, or want of delicacy; and there is just reason for approving one taste and condemning another. But where there is such a diversity in the internal frame or external situation as is entirely blameless on both sides, and leaves no room to give one the preference above the other; in that case a certain diversity of judgment is unavoidable, and we seek in vain for a standard, by which we can reconcile the contrary sentiments. [pp. 207–15, 232–3.]

HENRY HOME, LORD KAMES, *Elements of Criticism* (1762)
This conviction of a common nature or standard, and of its perfection, is the foundation of morality, and accounts clearly for that remarkable conception we have of a right and a wrong taste in morals. It accounts not less clearly for the conception we have of a right and a wrong taste in the fine arts. A person who rejects objects generally agreeable, and delights in objects generally disagreeable, is condemned as a monster: we disapprove his taste as bad or wrong, and we have a clear conception that he deviates from the common standard. If man were so framed as not to have any notion of a common standard, the proverb[11] mentioned in the beginning would hold universally, not only in the fine arts but in morals: upon that supposition, the taste of every man, with respect to both, would to himself be an ultimate standard. But the conviction of a common standard being made a part of our nature, we intuitively conceive a taste to be right or good if conformable to the common standard, and wrong or bad if disconformable.

No particular concerning human nature is more universal than the uneasiness a man feels when in matters of importance his opinions are rejected by others. Why should difference in opinion create uneasiness more than difference in stature, in countenance, or in dress? The sense of a common standard is the only principle that can explain this mystery. Every man, generally speaking, taking it for granted that his opinions agree with the common sense of mankind, is therefore disgusted with those of a contrary opinion, not as differing from him, but as differing from the common standard. Hence in all disputes, we find the parties, each of them equally, appealing constantly to the common sense of mankind as the ultimate rule or standard. [II, 358–9.]

[11] See n. 9 above.

SIR JOSHUA REYNOLDS, Discourse 7 (1776)

The internal fabric of our minds, as well as the external form of our bodies, being nearly uniform, it seems then to follow of course that as the imagination is incapable of producing anything originally of itself, and can only vary and combine those ideas with which it is furnished by means of the senses, there will be necessarily an agreement in the imaginations, as in the senses of men. There being this agreement, it follows that in all cases, in our lightest amusements, as well as in our most serious actions and engagements of life, we must regulate our affections[12] of every kind by that of others. The well-disciplined mind acknowledges this authority, and submits its own opinion to the public voice. It is from knowing what are the general feelings and passions of mankind that we acquire a true idea of what imagination is; though it appears as if we had nothing to do but to consult our own particular sensations, and these were sufficient to ensure us from all error and mistake.

A knowledge of the disposition and character of the human mind can be acquired only by experience; a great deal will be learned, I admit, by a habit of examining what passes in our bosoms, what are our own motives of action, and of what kind of sentiments we are conscious on any occasion. We may suppose an uniformity, and conclude that the same effect will be produced by the same cause in the minds of others. This examination will contribute to suggest to us matters of inquiry; but we can never be sure that our own sentiments are true and right till they are confirmed by more extensive observation. One man opposing another determines nothing; but a general union of minds, like a general combination of the forces of all mankind, makes a strength that is irresistible. In fact, as he who does not know himself, does not know others, so it may be said with equal truth that he who does not know others, knows himself but very imperfectly.

A man who thinks he is guarding himself against prejudices by resisting the authority of others leaves open every avenue to singularity, vanity, self-conceit, obstinacy, and many other vices, all tending to warp the judgment, and prevent the natural operation of his faculties. This submission to others is a deference which we owe, and, indeed, are forced involuntarily to pay. In fact, we never

[12] emotions.

are satisfied with our opinions, whatever we may pretend, till they are ratified and confirmed by the suffrages of the rest of mankind. We dispute and wrangle for ever; we endeavour to get men to come to us, when we do not go to them.

He, therefore, who is acquainted with the works which have pleased different ages and different countries, and has formed his opinion on them, has more materials, and more means of knowing what is analogous to the mind of man, than he who is conversant only with the works of his own age or country. What has pleased, and continues to please, is likely to please again: hence are derived the rules of art, and on this immovable foundation they must ever stand. . . .

We may therefore conclude that the real substance, as it may be called, of what goes under the name of taste, is fixed and established in the nature of things; that there are certain and regular causes by which the imagination and passions of men are affected; and that the knowledge of these causes is acquired by a laborious and diligent investigation of nature, and by the same slow progress as wisdom or knowledge of every kind, however instantaneous its operations may appear when thus acquired. . . .

It has been the main scope and principal end of this discourse to demonstrate the reality of a standard in taste, as well as in corporeal beauty; that a false or depraved taste is a thing as well known, as easily discovered, as anything that is deformed, misshapen, or wrong in our form or outward make, and that this knowledge is derived from the uniformity of sentiments among mankind, from whence proceeds the knowledge of what are the general habits of nature; the result of which is an idea of perfect beauty.

If what has been advanced be true—that beside this beauty or truth, which is formed on the uniform, eternal, and immutable laws of nature, and which of necessity can be but *one*; that beside this one immutable verity there are likewise what we have called apparent or secondary truths, proceeding from local and temporary prejudices, fancies, fashions or accidental connexion of ideas; if it appears that these last have still their foundation, however slender, in the original fabric of our minds; it follows that all these truths or beauties deserve and require the attention of the artist, in proportion to their stability or duration, or as their influence is more or less extensive. And let me add that, as they ought not to pass their just bounds, so neither do they, in a well-regulated taste, at all prevent or weaken the influence of those general principles, which alone can give to art its true and permanent dignity.

To form this just taste is undoubtedly in your own power, but it is to reason and philosophy that you must have recourse; from them you must borrow the balance by which is to be weighed and estimated the value of every pretension that intrudes itself on your notice. [pp. 132-3, 134, 141-2.]

Editions Used

The texts of extracts printed in this book are taken from the following editions:

ADDISON, Joseph, *The Spectator*, ed. D. F. Bond, Oxford, 1965, 5 vols. Reprinted by courtesy of the Clarendon Press.

BEATTIE, James, "Of Imagination", in *Dissertations Moral and Critical*, London and Edinburgh, 1783.

BLAIR, Hugh, *Lectures on Rhetoric and Belles Lettres* (1783), ed. H. F. Harding, Carbondale and Edwardsville, 1965.

BYSSHE, Edward, *The Art of English Poetry* (1708), Augustan Reprint Society, Publication No. 40, Los Angeles, 1953.

CONGREVE, William, "A Discourse on the Pindarique Ode". Prefixed to *A Pindarique Ode*, London, 1706.

DAVENANT, Sir William, Preface to *Gondibert* (1650), in *Critical Essays of the Seventeenth Century*, ed. J. E. Spingarn, Oxford, 1957, vol. II. Reprinted by courtesy of the Clarendon Press.

DENNIS, John, *Critical Works*, ed. E. N. Hooker. Baltimore, 2nd edition 1964, 2 vols. Reprinted by courtesy of the Johns Hopkins University Press.

DILLON, Wentworth, Earl of Roscommon, *An Essay on Translated Verse* (1684), in *Critical Essays of the Seventeenth Century*, ed. J. E. Spingarn, Oxford, 1957, vol. II.

DRYDEN, John, *Poems*, ed. James Kinsley, Oxford, 1958. 4 vols. (for prefaces to poems). Reprinted by courtesy of the Clarendon Press.

Of Dramatic Poesy and Other Critical Essays, ed. G. Watson, London, 1962, 2 vols. Reprinted by courtesy of J. M. Dent & Sons Limited.

FARQUHAR, George, *A Discourse upon Comedy* (1702), in *Works*, London, 2nd edition 1711, vol. II.

GERARD, Alexander, *An Essay on Taste* (1759), Edinburgh, 1764.

GILDON, Charles, *Miscellaneous Letters and Essays*, London, 1694.

The Complete Art of Poetry, London, 1718.

GLANVILL, Joseph, *An Essay Concerning Preaching*, London, 1678.

HOBBES, Thomas, Answer to Davenant's Preface to *Gondibert* (1650), in *Critical Essays of the Seventeenth Century*, ed. J. E. Spingarn, Oxford, 1957, vol. II. Reprinted by courtesy of the Clarendon Press.

　　Leviathan, ed. M. Oakeshott, Oxford, 1955. Reprinted by courtesy of Basil Blackwell & Mott Limited.

　　Preface to *Homer's Odyssey* (1671), in *Critical Essays of the Seventeenth Century*, ed. J. E. Spingarn, Oxford, 1957, vol. II. Reprinted by courtesy of the Clarendon Press.

HOME, Henry, Lord Kames, *Elements of Criticism*, London and Edinburgh, 1762, 3 vols.

HOWARD, Sir Robert, Preface to *The Great Favourite* (1668), in *Critical Essays of the Seventeenth Century*, ed. J. E. Spingarn, Oxford, 1957, vol. II.

HUGHES, John, "Of Style", in *Poems on Several Occasions. With Some Select Essays in Prose*. London, 1735.

　　"Remarks on *The Fairy Queen*", in *The Works of Mr. Edmund Spenser*. London, 1715, 6 vols.

HUME, David, "Of the Standard of Taste", in *Four Dissertations*. London, 1757.

HURD, Richard, "Dissertation on the Idea of Universal Poetry" (1766), in *Works*, London, 1811, vol. II.

　　Letters on Chivalry and Romance, London, 1762.

HUTCHESON, Francis, *An Inquiry into the Original of our Ideas of Beauty and Virtue*, London, 1725.

JOHNSON, Samuel, *The Rambler*, London, 1751.

　　A Dictionary of the English Language, London, 1755, vol. I.

　　History of Rasselas, Prince of Abyssinia, ed. G. Birkbeck Hill, Oxford, 1927. Reprinted by courtesy of the Clarendon Press.

　　Preface to *The Plays of William Shakespeare*, in *Eighteenth Century Essays on Shakespeare*, ed. D. Nichol Smith, Oxford, 2nd edition 1963. Reprinted by courtesy of the Clarendon Press.

　　Lives of the English Poets, ed. G. Birkbeck Hill, Oxford, 1905, 3 vols.

LOWTH, Robert, *Lectures on the Sacred Poetry of the Hebrews*, London, 1787.

[PARNELL, Thomas], *An Essay on the Different Stiles of Poetry*, London, 1713.

POPE, Alexander, *Pastoral Poetry and An Essay on Criticism*, ed. E. Audra and Aubrey Williams, Twickenham ed., vol. I, London, 1961. Reprinted by courtesy of Methuen & Company Limited.

The Iliad, ed. Maynard Mack. Twickenham ed., vols. VII and VIII, London, 1967. Reprinted by courtesy of Methuen & Company Limited.

The Odyssey, ed. Maynard Mack. Twickenham ed., vols. IX and X, London, 1967. Reprinted by courtesy of Methuen & Company Limited.

Preface to *The Works of Shakespeare* (1725), in *Eighteenth Century Essays on Shakespeare*, ed. D. Nichol Smith, Oxford, 2nd edition, 1963. Reprinted by courtesy of the Clarendon Press.

ΠΕΡΙ ΒΑΘΟΥΣ, or Martinus Scriblerus his Treatise of The Art of Sinking in Poetry (1728), ed. E. L. Steeves, New York, 1952. Reprinted by courtesy of Crown Publishers, Incorporated.

Epilogue to the Satires. Dialogue II, in *Imitations of Horace*, ed. John Butt. Twickenham ed., vol. IV, London, 1953. Reprinted by courtesy of Methuen & Company Limited.

REYNOLDS, Sir Joshua, *Discourses*, ed. R. S. Wark, San Marino, 1959. Reprinted by courtesy of The Huntington Library.

ROWE, Nicholas, "Some Account of the Life of Mr. William Shakespeare", in *Eighteenth Century Prefaces to Shakespeare*, ed. D. Nichol Smith, Oxford, 2nd edition 1963.

RYMER, Thomas, *Critical Works*, ed. C. A. Zimansky, New Haven, 1956. Reprinted by courtesy of Yale University Press.

SHADWELL, Thomas, Preface to *The Humourists* (1671), in *Critical Essays of the Seventeenth Century*, ed. J. E. Spingarn. Oxford, 1957, vol. II.

SHAFTESBURY, Anthony Ashley Cooper, Third Earl of, *Characteristics of Men, Manners, and Opinions*, London, 2nd edition 1714, 3 vols.

SHEFFIELD, John, Earl of Mulgrave, Duke of Buckinghamshire, *An Essay upon Poetry* (1682), in *Critical Essays of the Seventeenth Century*, ed. J. E. Spingarn. Oxford, 1957, vol. II.

STEELE, Sir Richard, *The Englishman*, ed. Rae Blanchard, Oxford, 1955, Reprinted by courtesy of the Clarendon Press.

SWIFT, Jonathan, *The Battle of the Books*, in *Prose Writings*, ed. Herbert Davis, vol. I, Oxford, 1957. Reprinted by courtesy of Basil Blackwell & Mott, Ltd.

A Proposal for Correcting, Improving and Ascertaining the English Tongue, in *Prose Writings*, ed. Herbert Davis, vol. IV, Oxford, 1957.

TEMPLE, Sir William, *Five Miscellaneous Essays*, ed. S. H. Monk, Ann Arbor, 1963. Reprinted by courtesy of the University of Michigan Press.

TRAPP, Joseph, *Lectures on Poetry*. Translated from the Latin, London, 1742.

WARTON, Joseph, *An Essay on the Writings and Genius of Pope*. London, 1756, 1782, 2 vols.

WELSTED, Leonard, "A Dissertation Concerning the Perfection of the English Language, the State of Poetry, etc.", in *Epistles, Odes, etc.*, London, 1724.

WOTTON, William, *Reflections upon Ancient and Modern Learning*, London, 1694.

YOUNG, Edward, *Conjectures on Original Composition*, London, 1749.

INDEX

2. CRITICAL CONCEPTS

See also titles and headings to sub-chapters